Computer Security: Principles and Practice

Computer Security: Principles and Practice

Dariel Wyatt

WILLFORD PRESS

www.willfordpress.com

Published by Willford Press,
118-35 Queens Blvd., Suite 400,
Forest Hills, NY 11375, USA

ISBN: 978-1-68285-745-8

Cataloging-in-Publication Data

Computer security : principles and practice / Dariel Wyatt.
p. cm.
Includes bibliographical references and index.
ISBN 978-1-68285-745-8
1. Computer security. 2. Computer networks--Security measures.
3. Data protection. I. Wyatt, Dariel.
QA76.9.A25 C66 2019
005.8--dc23

For information on all Willford Press publications
visit our website at www.willfordpress.com

Contents

Preface VII

Chapter 1 **Introduction to Computer Security**...1
    i.   Computer Security... 1
    ii. Asset.. 2
    iii. Attack.. 2
    iv. Passive Attack... 11
    v. Active Attack.. 22

Chapter 2 **Computer Security: Access Control Principles**.......................................53
    i.   Computer Access Control... 53
    ii. Attribute-based Access Control.. 60
    iii. Discretionary Access Control..64
    iv. Identity-based Security..66
    v. Mandatory Access Control...66
    vi. Organisation-based Access Control......................................71
    vii. Role-based Access Control..72

Chapter 3 **Fundamental Steps in Computer Security**..77
    i.   Security by Design... 77
    ii. Vulnerability Management...101
    iii. Reducing Vulnerabilities...105
    iv. Hardware Protection Mechanisms......................................115
    v. Secure Coding..133

Chapter 4 **Network and Internet Security**...137
    i.   Network Security..137
    ii. Firewall...138
    iii. Intrusion Detection System...141
    iv. Honeypot...149
    v. Internet Security...153
    vi. Browser Security..159
    vii. Trust No One...164
    viii. IP Fragmentation Attack..165

ix.   VoIP Vulnerabilities..172

x.   Transport Layer Security 173

Chapter 5   **Malicious Software: Computer Threats**.. 205

i.   Malware...205

ii.   Computer Virus...214

iii.   Computer Worm.. 225

iv.   Trojan Horse.. 228

v.   Ransomware 230

vi.   Spyware.. 237

vii.   Adware.. 249

viii.   Scareware 251

Chapter 6   **Computer Security Software**.. 255

i.   Antivirus Software.. 255

ii.   Anti-keylogger...264

iii.   Anti-Subversion Software.. 266

iv.   Anti-tamper Software... 267

v.   Encryption Software...268

Permissions

Index

Preface

Computer security refers to the protection of computers from any theft or damage to their software, hardware and data. It is also concerned with safeguarding computer systems from any disruption or misdirection of the services that they provide. Some of the threats to computer security can be classified as backdoor, denial-of-service attacks, phishing, spoofing and direct-access attacks, among many others. Computer security is becoming increasingly important due to the increased reliance on computer technology, Internet, wireless networks and smart devices. The countermeasures that can be employed for the management of such attacks are security by design, secure coding, security architecture, hardware protection mechanisms, etc. This book aims to shed light on some of the unexplored aspects of computer security. Most of the topics introduced herein cover new techniques and applications of computer security. This textbook is an essential guide for students who wish to develop a comprehensive understanding of this field.

A foreword of all Chapters of the book is provided below:

Chapter 1 - The protection of computer systems, including hardware, software and data, from theft or damage is under the domain of computer security. It is crucial for protection of sensitive and personal information. This is an introductory chapter, which will introduce briefly the importance of computer security and all the significant aspects related to it; **Chapter 2** - Access control involves authentication, identification, audit and authorization in computer security. This chapter explores different access control modes such as attribute-based, identity-based and role-based access control, among others. The chapter closely examines the key concepts of access control to provide an extensive understanding of computer security; **Chapter 3** - A device can be protected from an attack, threat or vulnerability by adopting some countermeasures. This chapter is a compilation of topics that discuss different countermeasures such as security by design, vulnerability management, hardware protection mechanisms, etc. This chapter discusses in detail the theories and methodologies related to computer protection measures; **Chapter 4** - Network and internet security are important aspects of computer security. In order to completely understand computer security, it is necessary to understand the processes related to network and internet security. The following chapter elucidates the varied processes and mechanisms associated with these areas of study; **Chapter 5** - Malware is the software that is designed to damage a computer, server or a computer network. This chapter discusses about some common malicious software such as virus, worm, Trojan horses, adware and spyware besides many others. This chapter has been carefully written to provide an easy understanding of the varied kinds of malicious software; **Chapter 6** - Computer security software is designed to enhance information security and defence against any intrusion and unauthorized access. This chapter elaborates the different kinds of security software and their applications to provide a holistic understanding of computer security.

I would like to thank the entire editorial team who made sincere efforts for this book and my family who supported me in my efforts of working on this book. I take this opportunity to thank all those who have been a guiding force throughout my life.

Dariel Wyatt

Introduction to Computer Security

The protection of computer systems, including hardware, software and data, from theft or damage is under the domain of computer security. It is crucial for protection of sensitive and personal information. This is an introductory chapter, which will introduce briefly the importance of computer security and all the significant aspects related to it.

Computer Security

Computer security is a branch of information technology known as information security which is intended to protect computers. Computer security has three main goals:

- Confidentiality: Making sure people cannot acquire information they should not (*keeping secrets*).

- Integrity: Making sure people cannot change information they should not (*protecting data*).

- Availability: Making sure people cannot stop the computer from doing its job.

Computer security involves telling computers what they are *not to do*. This makes computer security unique because most programming makes computers *do* things. Security takes much of a computers power.

Basic computer security methods (in approximate order of strength) can be:

- Limit access to computers to "safe" users.

- Peripherals which block any "unsafe" activity.

- Firewall and antivirus software.

An example of complexity and pervasiveness of the issue is vending machines.

Asset

In information security, computer security and network security, an asset is any data, device, or other component of the environment that supports information-related activities. Assets generally include hardware (e.g. servers and switches), software (e.g. mission critical applications and support systems) and confidential information. Assets should be protected from illicit access, use, disclosure, alteration, destruction, and/or theft, resulting in loss to the organization.

The CIA Triad

The goal of Information Security is to ensure the Confidentiality, Integrity and Availability of assets from various threats. For example, a hacker might attack a system in order to steal credit card numbers by exploiting a vulnerability. Information Security experts must assess the likely impact of an attack and employ appropriate countermeasures. In this case they might put up a firewall and encrypt their credit card numbers.

Risk Analysis

When performing risk analysis it is important to weigh how much to spend protecting each asset against the cost of losing the asset. It is also important to take into account the chance of each loss occurring. Intangible costs must also be factored in. If a hacker makes a copy of all a company's credit card numbers it does not cost them anything directly but the loss in fines and reputation can be enormous.

Attack

In *computer* and *computer networks* an attack is any attempt to expose, alter, disable, destroy, steal or gain unauthorized access to or make unauthorized use of an Asset.

Definitions

IETF

Internet Engineering Task Force defines attack in RFC 2828 as:

> *An assault on system security that derives from an intelligent threat, i.e., an intelligent act that is a deliberate attempt (especially in the sense of a method or technique) to evade security services and violate the security policy of a system.*

US Government

CNSS Instruction No. 4009 dated 26 April 2010 by Committee on National Security Systems of United States of America defines an attack as:

Any kind of malicious activity that attempts to collect, disrupt, deny, degrade, or destroy information system resources or the information itself.

The increasing dependencies of modern society on information and computers networks (both in private and public sectors, including military) has led to new terms like cyber attack and cyberwarfare.

CNSS Instruction No. 4009 define a cyber attack as:

An attack, via cyberspace, targeting an enterprise's use of cyberspace for the purpose of disrupting, disabling, destroying, or maliciously controlling a computing environment/infrastructure; or destroying the integrity of the data or stealing controlled information.

Types of Attack

An attack can be *active* or *passive*.

An "active attack" attempts to alter system resources or affect their operation.

A "passive attack" attempts to learn or make use of information from the system but does not affect system resources (e.g., wiretapping).

An attack can be perpetrated by an *insider* or from *outside* the organization;

An "inside attack" is an attack initiated by an entity inside the security perimeter (an "insider"), i.e., an entity that is authorized to access system resources but uses them in a way not approved by those who granted the authorization.

An "outside attack" is initiated from outside the perimeter, by an unauthorized or illegitimate user of the system (an "outsider"). In the Internet, potential outside attackers range from amateur pranksters to organized criminals, international terrorists, and hostile governments.

The term "attack" relates to some other basic security terms as shown in the following diagram:

```
+ - - - - - - - - - - - - +  + - - - - +  + - - - - - - - - - - - -+
| An Attack:              |  |Counter- |  | A System Resource:     |
| i.e., A Threat Action   |  | measure |  | Target of the Attack   |
| +----------+            |  | |       |  | | +----------------+   |
```

```
| | Attacker  |<=================||<=========              | |
| |   i.e.,   |   Passive  | |             | | | Vulnerability | |
| | A Threat  |<================>||<========>              | |
| |  Agent    |  or Active | |             | | +-------|||-------+ |
| +----------+   Attack   | |             | |        VVV         |
|                         | |             | | Threat Consequences |
+ - - - - - - - - - - - - + + - - - - + + - - - - - - - - - - -+
```

A resource (both physical or logical), called an asset, can have one or more vulnerabilities that can be exploited by a threat agent in a threat action. As a result, the confidentiality, integrity or availability of resources may be compromised. Potentially, the damage may extend to resources in addition to the one initially identified as vulnerable, including further resources of the organization, and the resources of other involved parties (customers, suppliers).

The so-called CIA triad is the basis of information security.

The attack can be *active* when it attempts to alter system resources or affect their operation: so it compromises integrity or availability. A "*passive attack*" attempts to learn or make use of information from the system but does not affect system resources: so it compromises confidentiality.

A threat is a potential for violation of security, which exists when there is a circumstance, capability, action, or event that could breach security and cause harm. That is, a threat is a possible danger that might exploit a vulnerability. A threat can be either "intentional" (i.e., intelligent; e.g., an individual cracker or a criminal organization) or "accidental" (e.g., the possibility of a computer malfunctioning, or the possibility of an "act of God" such as an earthquake, a fire, or a tornado).

A set of policies concerned with information security management, the information security management systems (ISMS), has been developed to manage, according to risk management principles, the countermeasures in order to accomplish to a security strategy set up following rules and regulations applicable in a country.

An attack should led to a *security incident* i.e. a *security event* that involves a *security violation*. In other words, a security-relevant system event in which the system's security policy is disobeyed or otherwise breached.

The overall picture represents the risk factors of the risk scenario.

An organization should make steps to detect, classify and manage security incidents. The first logical step is to set up an incident response plan and eventually a computer emergency response team.

In order to detect attacks, a number of countermeasures can be set up at organizational, procedural and technical levels. Computer emergency response team, information technology security audit and intrusion detection system are example of these.

An attack usually is perpetrated by someone with bad intentions: black hatted attacks falls in this category, while other perform penetration testing on an organization information system to find out if all foreseen controls are in place.

The attacks can be classified according to their origin: i.e. if it is conducted using one or more computers: in the last case is called a distributed attack. Botnets are used to conduct distributed attacks.

Other classifications are according to the procedures used or the type of vulnerabilities exploited: attacks can be concentrated on network mechanisms or host features.

Some attacks are physical: i.e. theft or damage of computers and other equipment. Others are attempts to force changes in the logic used by computers or network protocols in order to achieve unforeseen (by the original designer) result but useful for the attacker. Software used to for logical attacks on computers is called malware.

The following is a partial short list of attacks:

- Passive
  - Network
    - Wiretapping
    - Port scan
    - Idle scan
- Active
  - Denial-of-service attack
  - Spoofing
  - Network
    - Man in the middle
    - ARP poisoning
    - Ping flood
    - Ping of death
    - Smurf attack

- o Host
  - Buffer overflow
  - Heap overflow
  - Stack overflow
  - Format string attack

Consequence of a Potential Attack

A whole industry is working trying to minimize the likelihood and the consequence of an information attack.

For a partial list: Computer security software companies.

They offer different products and services, aimed at:

- study all possible attacks category
- publish books and articles about the subject
- discovering vulnerabilities
- evaluating the risks
- fixing vulnerabilities
- invent, design and deploy countermeasures
- set up contingency plan in order to be ready to respond

Many organization are trying to classify vulnerability and their consequence: the most famous vulnerability database is the Common Vulnerabilities and Exposures.

Computer emergency response teams are set up by government and large organization to handle computer security incidents.

Attack Surface

The attack surface of a software environment is the sum of the different points (the "attack vectors") where an unauthorized user (the "attacker") can try to enter data to or extract data from an environment. Keeping the attack surface as small as possible is a basic security measure.

Examples of Attack Vectors

Examples of attack vectors include user input fields, protocols, interfaces, and services.

Understanding an Attack Surface

Due to the increase in the countless potential vulnerable points each enterprise has, there has been increasing advantage for hackers and attackers as they only need to find one vulnerable point to succeed in their attack.

According to the white paper of SkyBox Security, there are three steps towards understanding and visualizing an attack surface:

Step 1: Visualize. Visualize the system of an enterprise is the first step, by mapping out all the devices, paths and networks.

Step 2: Find Indicators of Exposures. The second step is to correspond each indicator of a vulnerability being potentially exposed to the visualized map in the last step. One IOE can be "missing security controls in systems and software".

Step 3: Find Indicators of Compromise. This is an indicator that an attack has already succeeded.

Surface Reduction

The basic strategies of attack surface reduction include the following: reduce the amount of code running, reduce entry points available to untrusted users, and eliminate services requested by relatively few users. One approach to improving information security is to reduce the attack surface of a system or software. By turning off unnecessary functionality, there are fewer security risks. By having less code available to unauthorized actors, there will tend to be fewer failures. Although attack surface reduction helps prevent security failures, it does not mitigate the amount of damage an attacker could inflict once a vulnerability is found.

Attack Surface Analyzer

Attack Surface Analyzer is a tool created for the analysis of changes made to the attack surface of the operating systems since Windows Vista and beyond. It is a tool recommended by Microsoft in its SDL guidelines in the verification stage of the development.

Features

Analysis of Different Threat Categories

Attack Surface Analyzer is all in one tool for analysis of changes made to the various parts of the attack surface of Windows 6 series Operating System (includes Windows Vista and Windows 7). Using this one tool, you can analyze the changes made to the Registry, File permissions, Windows IIS Server, GAC assemblies and a lot more can be done. According to Microsoft, it is the same tool in use by the engineers of the security team at Microsoft to analyze the effects of software installation on the Windows Operating System.

It would not have been possible when there was no all in one tool. You would have had to use different software for all the different parts of Windows and then combine the effects logically by yourself. The tool enlists the various elements it enumerates while running a system scan. The elements are:

- files
- registry keys
- memory information
- windows
- Windows firewall
- GAC Assemblies
- network shares
- Logon sessions
- ports
- named pipes
- autorun tasks
- RPC endpoints
- processes
- threads
- desktops
- handles
- Microsoft Internet Information Services Server

The above list is a comprehensive set of elements that are both possible as well as important elements that can be changes when new software is installed on the system. While some software might change only a few elements in the list, some other can change a few more and different elements on the system. Attack Surface Analyzer combines all of them so that it is easier to analyze all parts.

Enlisting Threats

While Attack Surface Analyzer can tell you the changes for sure, in some cases, it will also be able to tell you that a particular change in the configuration is causing a threat.

As of now, the tool does not enlist the threats in all the categories (or parts of the Operating System) it scans but only a few, the most noticeable of which are the issues in services configurations, File system ACLs and issues related to the processes running on the system.

Determining Threat Severity

Getting the list of threats to the system is a great thing when you have it from software released by Microsoft itself. After all, no one knows Windows better than Microsoft. With the improved concerns over security shown by Microsoft, it is important that the severity of a threat is also known to the IT team of an enterprise. The Attack Surface Analyzer also shows the severity of the threats that it finds. However, it seems not to report the severity of each and every threat. Instead it shows the severity of the threat by its category. For example, the severity of threat caused by "Executables With Weak ACLs" (threat severity of level 1) is less than that caused by "Processes With Impersonation Tokens" (threat severity of level 2). It is surely a desirable feature to enlist the level of severity caused by each threat rather by the category to which it belongs. There however, is no news about when that might be available.

Built in Help

Every organization has its experts on various domains of security. There may be a case when a network security expert in an organization is not aware of the details and terminology of some other domain (say Windows Services). However, the two issues may be connected to each other. While it is not possible (and in some case not important) for the experts of two security expert teams to know everything about the terms in use by each other, it might be required in a few cases. A brief description (along with a link to technet library describing the term in detail) of all threats and changes to the attack surface are enlisted in the report generated by the Attack Surface Analyzer. While the brief description is usually enough for the experts, it might be needed in other cases. Microsoft has made it easy to find the right resource for the term rather than relying upon the web search engines.

Organization of Changes made to the Attack Surface

Attack Surface of Windows Operating System concerns various parts of the Operating System. It would have been difficult for anyone to understand the report if all of the changes were listed in serial order. Attack Surface Analyzer makes it easy for the user to browse through the report by listing the threats in categories and providing a Table of contents in an HTML page.

Report Generation

Attack Surface Analyzer can compare two scan data (generated by itself on two different scans) and generate a report, which can then be viewed in the HTML format. It is also possible to run the scans on one system and then generate on another system using the same tool. This is good for Windows Vista Clients because it is not possible to generate report using the current version of Attack Surface Analyzer on Windows Vista. In such a case, Attack Surface Analyzer can be used to run scans on the Windows Vista Client, transfer the scan result files to a computer running Windows 7 and then generate and browse the report on the Windows 7 based computer.

System Requirements

Attack Surface Analyzer works on the Windows 6.X series of Operating Systems but report generation can only be done on 6.1 version Operating Systems. Following are the system requirements of Attack Surface Analyzer (from the official download page):

Installable on: Windows Vista, Windows 7, Windows Server 2008 and Windows Server 2008 R2

Collection of Attack Surface Data: Windows Vista, Windows 7, Windows Server 2008 and Windows Server 2008 R2

Analysis of Attack Surface data and report generation: Windows 7 or Windows Server 2008 R2 with Microsoft .Net 3.5 SP1

Microsoft has not enlisted any hardware requirements separately. The tool should be able to perform its job on any machine meeting the hardware requirements of the in-stalled Operating System. Note, however, that the running time for generation of scan data and report depends on the hardware capabilities (better hardware would get the work done faster).

Scans

Attack Surface Analyzer list two types of scans namely baseline scan and product scan. In strict technical terms both the scans are same. The difference between them is logi-cal, not technical.

Baseline Scan

This is the scan run that the user will run to generate the data on the initial sys-tem. This data is then compared with the product scan. After running the baseline scan, the product whose effect on the attack surface of the Operating System is to be checked is installed. The installation changes the system configuration (possibly) by installing services, changing firewall rules, installing new .NET assemblies and so on. Baseline scan is a logical scan run by the user using Attack Surface Analyzer that generates the file containing the configuration of the system before this software is installed.

Product Scan

Product scan signifies the state of the system after the 'product' was installed. In this context, the product is the software whose effects on the system upon installation are to be checked. To generate a report, two scans are required in minimum. The product scan would capture the changes made to the system by the installation of the software product under testing. The scan data generated in this scan is compared with the baseline scan data to find the changes made to the system configurations on different points. It is worth a note that more than one system state can be captured using Attack Surface Analyzer and any combination of them can be used for the report generation. However the 'Baseline Scan' should be the one that was taken before the other. The other can automatically be called as the product scan.

Passive Attack

Port Scan

A port scanner is an application designed to probe a server or host for open ports. This is often used by administrators to verify security policies of their networks and by attackers to identify network services running on a host and exploit vulnerabilities.

A port scan or portscan is a process that sends client requests to a range of server port addresses on a host, with the goal of finding an active port; this is not a nefarious process in and of itself. The majority of uses of a port scan are not attacks, but rather simple probes to determine services available on a remote machine.

To portsweep is to scan multiple hosts for a specific listening port. The latter is typically used to search for a specific service, for example, an SQL-based computer worm may portsweep looking for hosts listening on TCP port 1433.

TCP/IP Basics

The design and operation of the Internet is based on the Internet Protocol Suite, commonly also called TCP/IP. In this system, network services are referenced using two components: a host address and a port number. There are 65536 distinct and usable port numbers. Most services use a limited range of port numbers.

Some port scanners scan only the most common port numbers, or ports most commonly associated with vulnerable services, on a given host.

The result of a scan on a port is usually generalized into one of three categories:

1. *Open* or *Accepted*: The host sent a reply indicating that a service is listening on the port.

2. *Closed* or *Denied* or *Not Listening*: The host sent a reply indicating that connections will be denied to the port.

3. *Filtered*, *Dropped* or *Blocked*: There was no reply from the host.

Open ports present two vulnerabilities of which administrators must be wary:

1. Security and stability concerns associated with the program responsible for delivering the service - Open ports.

2. Security and stability concerns associated with the operating system that is running on the host - Open or Closed ports.

Filtered ports do not tend to present vulnerabilities.

Assumptions

All forms of port scanning rely on the assumption that the targeted host is compliant with RFC 793 - Transmission Control Protocol. Although this is the case most of the time, there is still a chance a host might send back strange packets or even generate false positives when the TCP/IP stack of the host is non-RFC-compliant or has been altered. This is especially true for less common scan techniques that are OS-dependent (FIN scanning, for example). The TCP/IP stack fingerprinting method also relies on these types of different network responses from a specific stimulus to guess the type of the operating system the host is running.

Types

TCP Scanning

The simplest port scanners use the operating system's network functions and are generally the next option to go to when SYN is not a feasible option (described next). Nmap calls this mode connect scan, named after the Unix connect() system call. If a port is open, the operating system completes the TCP three-way handshake, and the port scanner immediately closes the connection to avoid performing a Denial-of-service attack. Otherwise an error code is returned. This scan mode has the advantage that the user does not require special privileges. However, using the OS network functions prevents low-level control, so this scan type is less common. This method is "noisy", particularly if it is a "*portsweep*": the services can log the sender IP address and Intrusion detection systems can raise an alarm.

SYN Scanning

SYN scan is another form of TCP scanning. Rather than use the operating system's network functions, the port scanner generates raw IP packets itself, and monitors for responses. This scan type is also known as "half-open scanning", because it never actually opens a full TCP connection. The port scanner generates a SYN packet. If the target port is open, it will respond with a SYN-ACK packet. The scanner host responds with an RST packet, closing the connection before the handshake is completed. If the port is closed but unfiltered, the target will instantly respond with an RST packet.

The use of raw networking has several advantages, giving the scanner full control of the packets sent and the timeout for responses, and allowing detailed reporting of the responses. There is debate over which scan is less intrusive on the target host. SYN scan has the advantage that the individual services never actually receive a connection. However, the RST during the handshake can cause problems for some network stacks, in particular simple devices like printers. There are no conclusive arguments either way.

UDP Scanning

UDP scanning is also possible, although there are technical challenges. UDP is a connectionless protocol so there is no equivalent to a TCP SYN packet. However, if a UDP packet is sent to a port that is not open, the system will respond with an ICMP port unreachable message. Most UDP port scanners use this scanning method, and use the absence of a response to infer that a port is open. However, if a port is blocked by a firewall, this method will falsely report that the port is open. If the port unreachable message is blocked, all ports will appear open. This method is also affected by ICMP rate limiting.

An alternative approach is to send application-specific UDP packets, hoping to generate an application layer response. For example, sending a DNS query to port 53 will result in a response, if a DNS server is present. This method is much more reliable at identifying open ports. However, it is limited to scanning ports for which an application specific probe packet is available. Some tools (e.g., nmap) generally have probes for less than 20 UDP services, while some commercial tools (e.g., nessus) have as many as 70. In some cases, a service may be listening on the port, but configured not to respond to the particular probe packet.

ACK Scanning

ACK scanning is one of the more unusual scan types, as it does not exactly determine whether the port is open or closed, but whether the port is filtered or unfiltered. This is especially good when attempting to probe for the existence of a firewall and its rulesets. Simple packet filtering will allow established connections (packets with the ACK bit set), whereas a more sophisticated stateful firewall might not.

Window Scanning

Rarely used because of its outdated nature, window scanning is fairly untrustworthy in determining whether a port is opened or closed. It generates the same packet as an

ACK scan, but checks whether the window field of the packet has been modified. When the packet reaches its destination, a design flaw attempts to create a window size for the packet if the port is open, flagging the window field of the packet with 1's before it returns to the sender. Using this scanning technique with systems that no longer support this implementation returns 0's for the window field, labeling open ports as closed.

FIN Scanning

Since SYN scans are not surreptitious enough, firewalls are, in general, scanning for and blocking packets in the form of SYN packets. FIN packets can bypass firewalls without modification. Closed ports reply to a FIN packet with the appropriate RST packet, whereas open ports ignore the packet on hand. This is typical behavior due to the nature of TCP, and is in some ways an inescapable downfall.

Other Scan Types

Some more unusual scan types exist. These have various limitations and are not widely used. Nmap supports most of these.

- X-mas and Null Scan - are similar to FIN scanning, but:

  o X-mas sends packets with FIN, URG and PUSH flags turned on like a Christmas tree

  o Null sends a packet with no TCP flags set

- Protocol scan - determines what IP level protocols (TCP, UDP, GRE, etc.) are enabled.

- Proxy scan - a proxy (SOCKS or HTTP) is used to perform the scan. The target will see the proxy's IP address as the source. This can also be done using some FTP servers.

- Idle scan - Another method of scanning without revealing one's IP address, taking advantage of the predictable IP ID flaw.

- CatSCAN - Checks ports for erroneous packets.

- ICMP scan - determines if a host responds to ICMP requests, such as echo (ping), netmask, etc.

Port Filtering by ISPs

Many Internet service providers restrict their customers' ability to perform port scans to destinations outside of their home networks. This is usually covered in the terms of service or acceptable use policy to which the customer must agree. Some ISPs implement packet filters or transparent proxies that prevent outgoing service requests to certain ports. For example, if an ISP provides a transparent HTTP proxy on port 80, port scans of any address will appear to have port 80 open, regardless of the target host's actual configuration.

Ethics

The information gathered by a port scan has many legitimate uses including network inventory and the verification of the security of a network. Port scanning can, however, also be used to compromise security. Many exploits rely upon port scans to find open ports and send specific data patterns in an attempt to trigger a condition known as a buffer overflow. Such behavior can compromise the security of a network and the computers therein, resulting in the loss or exposure of sensitive information and the ability to do work.

The threat level caused by a port scan can vary greatly according to the method used to scan, the kind of port scanned, its number, the value of the targeted host and the administrator who monitors the host. But a port scan is often viewed as a first step for an attack, and is therefore taken seriously because it can disclose much sensitive information about the host. Despite this, the probability of a port scan alone followed by a real attack is small. The probability of an attack is much higher when the port scan is associated with a vulnerability scan.

Legal Implications

Because of the inherently open and decentralized architecture of the Internet, lawmakers have struggled since its creation to define legal boundaries that permit effective prosecution of cybercriminals. Cases involving port scanning activities are an example of the difficulties encountered in judging violations. Although these cases are rare, most of the time the legal process involves proving that an intent to commit a break-in or unauthorized access existed, rather than just the performance of a port scan:

- In June 2003, an Israeli, Avi Mizrahi, was accused by the Israeli authorities of the offense of attempting the unauthorized access of computer material. He had port scanned the Mossad website. He was acquitted of all charges on February 29, 2004. The judge ruled that these kinds of actions should not be discouraged when they are performed in a positive way.

- A 17-year-old Finn was accused of attempted computer break-in by a major Finnish bank. On April 9, 2003, he was convicted of the charge by the Supreme Court of Finland and ordered to pay US$12,000 for the expense of the forensic analysis made by the bank. In 1998, he had port scanned the bank network in an attempt to access the closed network, but failed to do so.

- In December 1999, Scott Moulton was arrested by the FBI and accused of attempted computer trespassing under Georgia's Computer Systems Protection

Act and Computer Fraud and Abuse Act of America. At this time, his IT service company had an ongoing contract with Cherokee County of Georgia to maintain and upgrade the 911 center security. He performed several port scans on Cherokee County servers to check their security and eventually port scanned a web server monitored by another IT company, provoking a tiff which ended up in a tribunal. He was acquitted in 2000, the judge ruling there was no damage impairing the integrity and availability of the network.

In 2006, the UK Parliament had voted an amendment to the Computer Misuse Act 1990 such that a person is guilty of an offence who "makes, adapts, supplies or offers to supply any article knowing that it is designed or adapted for use in the course of or in connection with an offence under section 1 or 3 [of the CMA]". Nevertheless, the area of effect of this amendment is blurred, and widely criticized by Security experts as such.

Germany, with the Strafgesetzbuch 202a,b,c also has a similar law, and the Council of the European Union has issued a press release stating they plan to pass a similar one too, albeit more precise.

Idle Scan

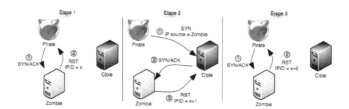

Idle scan on an open port

The idle scan is a TCP port scan method that consists of sending spoofed packets to a computer to find out what services are available. This is accomplished by impersonating another computer called a "*zombie*" (that is not transmitting or receiving information) and observing the behavior of the "zombie" system.

Information

This action can be done through common software network utilities such as nmap and hping. The attack involves sending forged packets to a specific machine *target* in an effort to find distinct characteristics of another *zombie* machine. The attack is sophisticated because there is no interaction between the attacker computer and the target: the attacker interacts only with the "*zombie*" computer.

This exploit functions with two purposes, as a port scanner and a mapper of trusted IP relationships between machines. The target system interacts with the "*zombie*" computer and difference in behaviour can be observed using different "zombies" with evidence of different privileges granted by the target to different computers.

Discovered by Salvatore Sanfilippo (also known by his handle "Antirez") in 1998, the idle scan has been used by many black hat "hackers" to covertly identify open ports on a target computer in preparation for attacking it. Although it was originally named *dumb scan*, the term *idle scan* was coined in 1999, after the publication of a proof of concept 16-bit identification field (IPID) scanner named *idlescan*, by Filipe Almeida (aka LiquidK). This type of scan can also be referenced as *zombie scan*; all the nomenclatures are due to the nature of one of the computers involved in the attack.

TCP/IP Basics

The design and operation of the Internet is based on the Internet Protocol Suite, commonly also called TCP/IP. IP is the primary protocol in the Internet Layer of the Internet Protocol Suite and has the task of delivering datagrams from the source host to the destination host solely based on their addresses. For this purpose, IP defines addressing methods and structures for datagram encapsulation. It is a connectionless protocol and relies on the transmission of packets. Every IP packet from a given source has an ID that uniquely identifies IP datagram.

TCP provides reliable, ordered delivery of a stream of bytes from a program on one computer to another program on another computer. TCP is the protocol that major Internet applications rely on, such as the World Wide Web, e-mail, and file transfer. Each of these applications (web server, email server, FTP server) is called a network service. In this system, network services are identified using two components: a host address and a port number. There are 65536 distinct and usable port numbers per host. Most services use a limited range of numbers by default, and the default port number for a service is almost always used.

Some port scanners scan only the most common port numbers, or ports most commonly associated with vulnerable services, on a given host. List of TCP and UDP port numbers.

The result of a scan on a port is usually generalized into one of three categories:

- Open or Accepted: The host sent a reply indicating that a service is listening on the port.

- Closed or Denied or Not Listening: The host sent a reply indicating that connections will be denied to the port.

- Filtered, Dropped or Blocked: There was no reply from the host.

Open ports present two vulnerabilities of which administrators must be wary:

1. Security and stability concerns associated with the program responsible for delivering the service - Open ports.

2. Security and stability concerns associated with the operating system that is running on the host - Open or Closed ports.

Filtered ports do not tend to present vulnerabilities. The host in a local network can be protected by a firewall that filters, according with rules that its administrator set up, packets. This is done to deny services to hosts not known and prevent intrusion in the inside network. The IP protocol is network layer transmission protocol.

Basic Mechanics

Idle scans take advantage of predictable Identification field value from IP header: every IP packet from a given source has an ID that uniquely identifies fragments of an original IP datagram; the protocol implementation assigns values to this mandatory field generally by a fixed value (1) increment. Because transmitted packets are numbered in a sequence you can say how many packets are transmitted between two packets that you receive.

An attacker would first scan for a host with a sequential and predictable sequence number (IPID). The latest versions of Linux, Solaris, OpenBSD, and Windows Vista are not suitable as zombie, since the IPID has been implemented with patches that randomized the IPID. Computers chosen to be used in this stage are known as "zombies".

Once a suitable zombie is found the next step would be to try to establish a TCP connection with a given service (port) of the target system, impersonating the zombie. It is done by sending a SYN packet to the target computer, spoofing the IP address from the zombie, i.e. with the source address equal to zombie IP address.

If the port of the target computer is open it will accept the connection for the service, responding with a SYN/ACK packet back to the zombie.

The zombie computer will then send a RST packet to the target computer (to reset the connection) because it did not actually send the SYN packet in the first place.

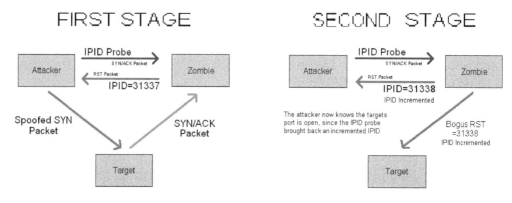

The first stage of an idle scan   The second stage of an idle scan

Since the zombie had to send the RST packet it will increment its IPID. This is how an attacker would find out if the targets port is open. The attacker will send another packet to the zombie. If the IPID is incremented only by a step then the attacker would know that the particular port is closed.

The method assumes that zombie has no other interactions: if there is any message sent for other reasons between the first interaction of the attacker with the zombie and the second interaction other than RST message, there will be a false positive.

Finding a Zombie Host

The first step in executing an idle scan is to find an appropriate zombie. It needs to assign IP ID packets incrementally on a global (rather than per-host it communicates with) basis. It should be idle (hence the scan name), as extraneous traffic will bump up its IP ID sequence, confusing the scan logic. The lower the latency between the attacker and the zombie, and between the zombie and the target, the faster the scan will proceed.

Note that when a port is open, IPIDs increment by 2. Following is the sequence:

1. Attacker to target -> SYN, target to zombie ->SYN/ACK, Zombie to target -> RST (IPID increment by 1)

2. Now attacker tries to probe zombie for result. Attacker to Zombie ->SYN/ACK, Zombie to Attacker -> RST (IPID increment by 1)

So, in this process IPID increments by 2 finally.

When an idle scan is attempted, tools (for example nmap) tests the proposed zombie and reports any problems with it. If one doesn't work, try another. Enough Internet hosts are vulnerable that zombie candidates aren't hard to find. A common approach is to simply execute a ping sweep of some network. Choosing a network near your source address, or near the target, produces better results. You can try an idle scan using each available host from the ping sweep results until you find one that works. As usual, it is best to ask permission before using someone's machines for unexpected purposes such as idle scanning.

Simple network devices often make great zombies because they are commonly both underused (idle) and built with simple network stacks which are vulnerable to IP ID traffic detection.

While identifying a suitable zombie takes some initial work, you can keep re-using the good ones. Alternatively, there have been some research on utilizing unintended public web services as zombie hosts to perform similar idle scans. Leveraging the way some of these services perform outbound connections upon user submissions can serve as some kind of poor's man idle scanning.

Using Hping

The hping method for idle scanning provides a lower level example for how idle scanning is performed. In this example the target host (172.16.0.100) will be scanned using an idle host (172.16.0.105). An open and a closed port will be tested to see how each scenario plays out.

First, establish that the idle host is actually idle, send packets using hping2 and observe the id numbers increase incrementally by one. If the id numbers increase haphazardly, the host is not actually idle or has an OS that has no predictable IP ID.

```
[root@localhost hping2-rc3]# ./hping2 -S 172.16.0.105

HPING 172.16.0.105 (eth0 172.16.0.105): S set, 40 headers + 0 data bytes

len=46 ip=172.16.0.105 ttl=128 id=1371 sport=0 flags=RA seq=0 win=0 rtt=0.3 ms

len=46 ip=172.16.0.105 ttl=128 id=1372 sport=0 flags=RA seq=1 win=0 rtt=0.2 ms

len=46 ip=172.16.0.105 ttl=128 id=1373 sport=0 flags=RA seq=2 win=0 rtt=0.3 ms

len=46 ip=172.16.0.105 ttl=128 id=1374 sport=0 flags=RA seq=3 win=0 rtt=0.2 ms

len=46 ip=172.16.0.105 ttl=128 id=1375 sport=0 flags=RA seq=4 win=0 rtt=0.2 ms

len=46 ip=172.16.0.105 ttl=128 id=1376 sport=0 flags=RA seq=5 win=0 rtt=0.2 ms

len=46 ip=172.16.0.105 ttl=128 id=1377 sport=0 flags=RA seq=6 win=0 rtt=0.2 ms

len=46 ip=172.16.0.105 ttl=128 id=1378 sport=0 flags=RA seq=7 win=0 rtt=0.2 ms

len=46 ip=172.16.0.105 ttl=128 id=1379 sport=0 flags=RA seq=8 win=0 rtt=0.4 ms
```

Send a spoofed SYN packet to the target host on a port you expect to be open. In this case, port 22 (ssh) is being tested.

```
# hping2 —spoof 172.16.0.105 -S 172.16.0.100 -p 22 -c 1

HPING 172.16.0.100 (eth0 172.16.0.100): S set, 40 headers + 0 data bytes

--- 172.16.0.100 hping statistic ---

1 packets transmitted, 0 packets received, 100% packet loss

round-trip min/avg/max = 0.0/0.0/0.0 ms
```

Since we spoofed the packet, we did not receive a reply and hping reports 100% packet loss. The target host replied directly to the idle host with a syn/ack packet. Now, check the idle host to see if the id number has increased.

```
# hping2 -S 172.16.0.105 -p 445 -c 1

HPING 172.16.0.105 (eth0 172.16.0.105): S set, 40 headers + 0 data bytes

len=46 ip=172.16.0.105 ttl=128 DF id=1381 sport=445 flags=SA seq=0 win=64320
rtt=0.3 ms

--- 172.16.0.105 hping statistic ---
```

```
1 packets tramitted, 1 packets received, 0% packet loss

round-trip min/avg/max = 0.3/0.3/0.3 ms
```

Notice that the proxy hosts id increased from id=1379 to id=1381. 1380 was consumed when the idle host replied to the target host's syn/ack packet with an rst packet.

Run through the same processes again testing a port that is likely closed. Here we are testing port 23 (telnet).

```
# hping2 -S 172.16.0.105 -p 445 -c 1; hping2-spoof 172.16.0.105 -S 172.16.0.100
-p 23 -c 1; hping2 -S 172.16.0.105 -p 445 -c 1

HPING 172.16.0.105 (eth0 172.16.0.105): S set, 40 headers + 0 data bytes

len=46 ip=172.16.0.105 ttl=128 DF id=1382 sport=445 flags=SA seq=0 win=64320
rtt=2.1 ms

--- 172.16.0.105 hping statistic ---

1 packets tramitted, 1 packets received, 0% packet loss

round-trip min/avg/max = 2.1/2.1/2.1 ms

HPING 172.16.0.100 (eth0 172.16.0.100): S set, 40 headers + 0 data bytes

--- 172.16.0.100 hping statistic ---

1 packets tramitted, 0 packets received, 100% packet loss

round-trip min/avg/max = 0.0/0.0/0.0 ms

HPING 172.16.0.105 (eth0 172.16.0.105): S set, 40 headers + 0 data bytes

len=46 ip=172.16.0.105 ttl=128 DF id=1383 sport=445 flags=SA seq=0 win=64320
rtt=0.3 ms

--- 172.16.0.105 hping statistic ---

1 packets tramitted, 1 packets received, 0% packet loss

round-trip min/avg/max = 0.3/0.3/0.3 ms
```

Notice that this time, the id did not increase because the port was closed. When we sent the spoofed packet to the target host, it replied to the idle host with an rst packet which did not increase the id counter.

Using Nmap

The first thing the user would do is to find a suitable zombie on the LAN:

Performing a port scan and OS identification (-O option in nmap) on the zombie candidate network rather than just a ping scan helps in selecting a good zombie. As long as verbose mode (-v) is enabled, OS detection will usually determine the IP ID sequence generation method and print a line such as "IP ID Sequence Generation: Incremental". If the type is given as Incremental or Broken little-endian incremental, the machine is a good zombie candidate. That is still no guarantee that it will work, as Solaris and some other systems create a new IP ID sequence for each host they communicate with. The host could also be too busy. OS detection and the open port list can also help in identifying systems that are likely to be idle.

Another approach to identifying zombie candidates is the run the ipidseq NSE script against a host. This script probes a host to classify its IP ID generation method, then prints the IP ID classification much like the OS detection does. Like most NSE scripts, ipidseq.nse can be run against many hosts in parallel, making it another good choice when scanning entire networks looking for suitable hosts.

```
nmap -v -O -sS 192.168.1.0/24
```

This tells nmap to do a ping sweep and show all hosts that are up in the given IP range. Once you have found a zombie, next you would send the spoofed packets:

```
nmap -P0 -p <port> -sI <zombie IP> <target IP>
```

The images juxtaposition show both of these stages in a successful scenario.

Effectiveness

Although many Operating Systems are now immune from being used in this attack, Some popular systems are still vulnerable; making the idle scan still very effective. Once a successful scan is completed there is no trace of the attacker's IP address on the target's firewall or Intrusion-detection system log. Another useful possibility is the chance of by-passing a firewall because you are scanning the target from the zombie's computer, which might have extra rights than the attacker's.

Active Attack

Denial-of-service Attack

In computing, a denial-of-service attack (DoS attack) is a cyber-attack where the perpetrator seeks to make a machine or network resource unavailable to its intended users by temporarily or indefinitely disrupting services of a host connected to the Internet. Denial of service is typically accomplished by flooding the targeted machine or resource with superfluous requests in an attempt to overload systems and prevent some or all legitimate requests from being fulfilled.

In a distributed denial-of-service attack (DDoS attack), the incoming traffic flooding the victim originates from many different sources. This effectively makes it impossible to stop the attack simply by blocking a single source.

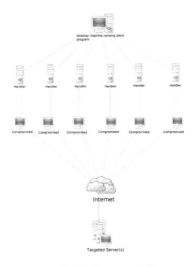

DDoS Stacheldraht attack diagram.

A DoS or DDoS attack is analogous to a group of people crowding the entry door or gate to a shop or business, and not letting legitimate parties enter into the shop or business, disrupting normal operations.

Criminal perpetrators of DoS attacks often target sites or services hosted on high-profile web servers such as banks or credit card payment gateways. Revenge, blackmail and activism can motivate these attacks.

Types

Denial-of-service attacks are characterized by an explicit attempt by attackers to prevent legitimate users of a service from using that service. There are two general forms of DoS attacks: those that crash services and those that flood services. The most serious attacks are distributed.

Distributed DoS

A distributed denial-of-service (DDoS) is a DoS attack where the perpetrator uses more than one unique IP address, often thousands of them. Since the incoming traffic flooding the victim originates from many different sources, it is impossible to stop the attack simply by using ingress filtering. It also makes it very difficult to distinguish legitimate user traffic from attack traffic when spread across so many points of origin. As an alternative or augmentation of a DDoS, attacks may involve forging of IP sender addresses (IP address spoofing) further complicating identifying and defeating the attack.

The scale of DDoS attacks has continued to rise over recent years, by 2016 exceeding a terabit per second.

Application Layer Attacks

An application layer DDoS attack (sometimes referred to as layer 7 DDoS attack) is a form of DDoS attack where attackers target the application layer of the OSI model. The attack over-exercises specific functions or features of a website with the intention to disable those functions or features. This application-layer attack is different from an entire network attack, and is often used against financial institutions to distract IT and security personnel from security breaches. As of 2013, application layer DDoS attacks represent 20% of all DDoS attacks. According to research by the company Akamai, there have been "51 percent more application layer attacks" from Q4 2013 to Q4 2014 and "16 percent more" from Q3 2014 over Q4 2014. In November 2017; Junade Ali, a Computer Scientist at Cloudflare noted that whilst network-level attacks continue to be of high capacity, they are occurring less frequently. Ali further notes that although network-level attacks are becoming less frequent, data from Cloudflare demonstrates that application-layer attacks are still showing no sign of slowing down.

Application Layer

The Open Systems Interconnection (OSI) model (ISO/IEC 7498-1) is a conceptual model that characterizes and standardizes the internal functions of a communication system by partitioning it into abstraction layers. The model is a product of the Open Systems Interconnection project at the International Organization for Standardization (ISO). The model groups similar communication functions into one of seven logical layers. A layer serves the layer above it and is served by the layer below it. For example, a layer that provides error-free communications across a network provides the path needed by applications above it, while it calls the next lower layer to send and receive packets that make up the contents of that path. Two instances at one layer are connected by a horizontal connection on that layer.

In the OSI model, the definition of its application layer is narrower in scope. The OSI model defines the application layer as being the user interface. The OSI application layer is responsible for displaying data and images to the user in a human-recognizable format and to interface with the presentation layer below it.

Method of Attack

An application layer DDoS attack is done mainly for specific targeted purposes, including disrupting transactions and access to databases. It requires less resources and often accompanies network layer attacks. An attack is disguised to look like legitimate traffic, except it targets specific application packets. The attack on the application layer can disrupt services such as the retrieval of information or search function as well as web browser function, email services and photo applications. In order to be deemed a *distributed* denial of service attack, more than around 3–5 nodes on different networks should be used; using fewer than 3–5 nodes qualifies as a Denial-of-service attack and not a DDoS.

Advanced Persistent DoS

An advanced persistent DoS (APDoS) is more likely to be perpetrated by an advanced persistent threat (APT): actors who are well-resourced, exceptionally skilled and have access to substantial commercial grade computer resources and capacity. APDoS attacks represent a clear and emerging threat needing specialised monitoring and incident response services and the defensive capabilities of specialised DDoS mitigation service providers.

This type of attack involves massive network layer DDoS attacks through to focused application layer (HTTP) floods, followed by repeated (at varying intervals) SQLi and XSS attacks.[Typically, the perpetrators can simultaneously use from 2 to 5 attack vectors involving up to several tens of millions of requests per second, often accompanied by large SYN floods that can not only attack the victim but also any service provider implementing any sort of managed DDoS mitigation capability. These attacks can persist for several weeks- the longest continuous period noted so far lasted 38 days. This APDoS attack involved approximately 50+ petabits (50,000+ terabits) of malicious traffic.

Attackers in this scenario may (or often will) tactically switch between several targets to create a diversion to evade defensive DDoS countermeasures but all the while eventually concentrating the main thrust of the attack onto a single victim. In this scenario, threat actors with continuous access to several very powerful network resources are capable of sustaining a prolonged campaign generating enormous levels of un-amplified DDoS traffic.

APDoS attacks are characterised by:

- advanced reconnaissance (pre-attack OSINT and extensive decoyed scanning crafted to evade detection over long periods)

- tactical execution (attack with a primary and secondary victims but focus is on primary)

- explicit motivation (a calculated end game/goal target)

- large computing capacity (access to substantial computer power and network bandwidth resources)

- simultaneous multi-threaded OSI layer attacks (sophisticated tools operating at layers 3 through 7)

- persistence over extended periods (using all the above into a concerted, well managed attack across a range of targets)

Denial-of-service as a Service

Some vendors provide so-called "booter" or "stresser" services, which have simple web-based front ends, and accept payment over the web. Marketed and promoted as stress-testing tools, they can be used to perform unauthorized denial-of-service attacks, and allow technically unsophisticated attackers access to sophisticated attack tools without the need for the attacker to understand their use. Usually powered by a botnet, the traffic produced by a consumer stresser can range anywhere from 5-50 Gbit/s, which can, in most cases, deny the average home user internet access.

Symptoms

The United States Computer Emergency Readiness Team (US-CERT) has identified symptoms of a denial-of-service attack to include:

- unusually slow network performance (opening files or accessing web sites)

- unavailability of a particular web site

- inability to access any web site

- dramatic increase in the number of spam emails received (this type of DoS attack is considered an e-mail bomb)

Additional symptoms may include:

- disconnection of a wireless or wired internet connection

- long-term denial of access to the web or any internet services

If the attack is conducted on a sufficiently large scale, entire geographical regions of Internet connectivity can be compromised without the attacker's knowledge or intent by incorrectly configured or flimsy network infrastructure equipment.

Attack Techniques

A wide array of programs are used to launch DoS-attacks.

Attack Tools

In cases such as MyDoom the tools are embedded in malware, and launch their attacks without the knowledge of the system owner. Stacheldraht is a classic example of a DDoS tool. It uses a layered structure where the attacker uses a client program to connect to handlers, which are compromised systems that issue commands to the zombie agents, which in turn facilitate the DDoS attack. Agents are compromised via the handlers by the attacker, using automated routines to exploit vulnerabilities in programs that accept remote connections running on the targeted remote hosts. Each handler can control up to a thousand agents.

In other cases a machine may become part of a DDoS attack with the owner's consent, for example, in Operation Payback, organized by the group Anonymous. The LOIC has typically been used in this way. Along with HOIC a wide variety of DDoS tools are available today, including paid and free versions, with different features available. There is an underground market for these in hacker related forums and IRC channels.

UK's GCHQ has tools built for DDoS, named PREDATORS FACE and ROLLING THUNDER.

Application-layer Floods

Various DoS-causing exploits such as buffer overflow can cause server-running software to get confused and fill the disk space or consume all available memory or CPU time.

Other kinds of DoS rely primarily on brute force, flooding the target with an overwhelming flux of packets, oversaturating its connection bandwidth or depleting the target's system resources. Bandwidth-saturating floods rely on the attacker having higher bandwidth available than the victim; a common way of achieving this today is via distributed denial-of-service, employing a botnet. Another target of DDoS attacks may be to produce added costs for the application operator, when the latter uses resources based on cloud computing. In this case normally application used resources are tied to a needed Quality of Service level (e.g. responses should be less than 200 ms) and this rule is usually linked to automated software (e.g. Amazon CloudWatch) to raise more virtual resources from the provider in order to meet the defined QoS levels for the increased requests.The main incentive behind such attacks may be to drive the application owner to raise the elasticity levels in order to handle the increased application traffic, in order to cause financial losses or force them to become less competitive. Other floods may use specific packet types or connection requests to saturate finite resources by, for example, occupying the maximum number of open connections or filling the victim's disk space with logs.

A "banana attack" is another particular type of DoS. It involves redirecting outgoing messages from the client back onto the client, preventing outside access, as well as flooding the client with the sent packets. A LAND attack is of this type.

An attacker with shell-level access to a victim's computer may slow it until it is unusable or crash it by using a fork bomb.

A kind of application-level DoS attack is XDoS (or XML DoS) which can be controlled by modern web application firewalls (WAFs).

Degradation-of-service Attacks

"Pulsing" zombies are compromised computers that are directed to launch intermittent and short-lived floodings of victim websites with the intent of merely slowing it rather than crashing it. This type of attack, referred to as "degradation-of-service" rather than "denial-of-service", can be more difficult to detect than regular zombie invasions and can disrupt and hamper connection to websites for prolonged periods of time, potentially causing more disruption than concentrated floods. Exposure of degradation-of-service attacks is complicated further by the matter of discerning whether the server is really being attacked or under normal traffic loads.

Denial-of-service Level II

The goal of DoS L2 (possibly DDoS) attack is to cause a launching of a defense mechanism which blocks the network segment from which the attack originated. In case of distributed attack or IP header modification (that depends on the kind of security behavior) it will fully block the attacked network from the Internet, but without system crash.

Distributed DoS Attack

A distributed denial-of-service (DDoS) attack occurs when multiple systems flood the bandwidth or resources of a targeted system, usually one or more web servers. Such an attack is often the result of multiple compromised systems (for example, a botnet) flooding the targeted system with traffic. A botnet is a network of zombie computers programmed to receive commands without the owners' knowledge. When a server is overloaded with connections, new connections can no longer be accepted. The major advantages to an attacker of using a distributed denial-of-service attack are that multiple machines can generate more attack traffic than one machine, multiple attack machines are harder to turn off than one attack machine, and that the behavior of each attack machine can be stealthier, making it harder to track and shut down. These attacker advantages cause challenges for defense mechanisms. For example, merely purchasing more incoming bandwidth than the current volume of the attack might not help, because the attacker might be able to simply add more attack machines. This, after all, will end up completely crashing a website for periods of time.

Malware can carry DDoS attack mechanisms; one of the better-known examples of this was MyDoom. Its DoS mechanism was triggered on a specific date and time. This type of DDoS involved hardcoding the target IP address prior to release of the malware and no further interaction was necessary to launch the attack.

A system may also be compromised with a trojan, allowing the attacker to download a zombie agent, or the trojan may contain one. Attackers can also break into systems using automated tools that exploit flaws in programs that listen for connections from remote hosts. This scenario primarily concerns systems acting as servers on the web. Stacheldraht is a classic example of a DDoS tool. It uses a layered structure where the attacker uses a client program to connect to handlers, which are compromised systems that issue commands to the zombie agents, which in turn facilitate the DDoS attack. Agents are compromised via the handlers by the attacker, using automated routines to exploit vulnerabilities in programs that accept remote connections running on the targeted remote hosts. Each handler can control up to a thousand agents. In some cases a machine may become part of a DDoS attack with the owner's consent, for example, in Operation Payback, organized by the group Anonymous. These attacks can use different types of internet packets such as: TCP, UDP, ICMP etc.

These collections of systems compromisers are known as botnets / rootservers. DDoS tools like Stacheldraht still use classic DoS attack methods centered on IP spoofing and amplification like smurf attacks and fraggle attacks (these are also known as bandwidth consumption attacks). SYN floods (also known as resource starvation attacks) may also be used. Newer tools can use DNS servers for DoS purposes. Unlike MyDoom's DDoS mechanism, botnets can be turned against any IP address. Script kiddies use them to deny the availability of well known websites to legitimate users. More sophisticated attackers use DDoS tools for the purposes of extortion – even against their business rivals.

Simple attacks such as SYN floods may appear with a wide range of source IP addresses, giving the appearance of a well distributed DoS. These flood attacks do not require completion of the TCP three way handshake and attempt to exhaust the destination SYN queue or the server bandwidth. Because the source IP addresses can be trivially spoofed, an attack could come from a limited set of sources, or may even originate from a single host. Stack enhancements such as syn cookies may be effective mitigation against SYN queue flooding, however complete bandwidth exhaustion may require involvement.

If an attacker mounts an attack from a single host it would be classified as a DoS attack. In fact, any attack against availability would be classed as a denial-of-service attack. On the other hand, if an attacker uses many systems to simultaneously launch attacks against a remote host, this would be classified as a DDoS attack.

It has been reported that there are new attacks from internet of things which have been involved in denial of service attacks. In one noted attack that was made peaked at around 20,000 requests per second which came from around 900 CCTV cameras.

UK's GCHQ has tools built for DDoS, named PREDATORS FACE and ROLLING THUNDER.

DDoS Extortion

In 2015, DDoS botnets such as DD4BC grew in prominence, taking aim at financial institutions. Cyber-extortionists typically begin with a low-level attack and a warning that a larger attack will be carried out if a ransom is not paid in Bitcoin. Security experts recommend targeted websites to not pay the ransom. The attackers tend to get into an extended extortion scheme once they recognize that the target is ready to pay.

HTTP POST DoS Attack

First discovered in 2009, the HTTP POST attack sends a complete, legitimate HTTP POST header, which includes a 'Content-Length' field to specify the size of the message body to follow. However, the attacker then proceeds to send the actual message body at an extremely slow rate (e.g. 1 byte/110 seconds). Due to the entire message being correct and complete, the target server will attempt to obey the 'Content-Length' field in the header, and wait for the entire body of the message to be transmitted, which can take a very long time. The attacker establishes hundreds or even thousands of such connections, until all resources for incoming connections on the server (the victim) are used up, hence making any further (including legitimate) connections impossible until all data has been sent. It is notable that unlike many other (D)DoS attacks, which try to subdue the server by overloading its network or CPU, a HTTP POST attack targets the *logical* resources of the victim, which means the victim would still have enough network bandwidth and processing power to operate. Further combined with the fact that Apache will, by default, accept requests up to 2GB in size, this attack can be particularly powerful. HTTP POST attacks are difficult to differentiate from legitimate connections, and are therefore able to bypass some protection systems. OWASP, an open source web application security project, has released a testing tool to test the security of servers against this type of attacks.

Internet Control Message Protocol (ICMP) Flood

A smurf attack relies on misconfigured network devices that allow packets to be sent to all computer hosts on a particular network via the broadcast address of the network, rather than a specific machine. The attacker will send large numbers of IP packets with the source address faked to appear to be the address of the victim. The network's bandwidth is quickly used up, preventing legitimate packets from getting through to their destination.

Ping flood is based on sending the victim an overwhelming number of ping packets, usually using the "ping" command from Unix-like hosts (the -t flag on Windows systems is much less capable of overwhelming a target, also the -l (size) flag does not allow sent packet size greater than 65500 in Windows). It is very simple to launch, the primary requirement being access to greater bandwidth than the victim.

Ping of death is based on sending the victim a malformed ping packet, which will lead to a system crash on a vulnerable system.

The BlackNurse attack is an example of an attack taking advantage of the required Destination Port Unreachable ICMP packets.

Nuke

A Nuke is an old denial-of-service attack against computer networks consisting of fragmented or otherwise invalid ICMP packets sent to the target, achieved by using a modified ping utility to repeatedly send this corrupt data, thus slowing down the affected computer until it comes to a complete stop.

A specific example of a nuke attack that gained some prominence is the WinNuke, which exploited the vulnerability in the NetBIOS handler in Windows 95. A string of out-of-band data was sent to TCP port 139 of the victim's machine, causing it to lock up and display a Blue Screen of Death (BSOD).

Peer-to-peer Attacks

Attackers have found a way to exploit a number of bugs in peer-to-peer servers to initiate DDoS attacks. The most aggressive of these peer-to-peer-DDoS attacks exploits DC++. With peer-to-peer there is no botnet and the attacker does not have to communicate with the clients it subverts. Instead, the attacker acts as a "puppet master," instructing clients of large peer-to-peer file sharing hubs to disconnect from their peer-to-peer network and to connect to the victim's website instead.

Permanent Denial-of-service Attacks

Permanent denial-of-service (PDoS), also known loosely as phlashing, is an attack that damages a system so badly that it requires replacement or reinstallation of hardware. Unlike the distributed denial-of-service attack, a PDoS attack exploits security flaws which allow remote administration on the management interfaces of the victim's hardware, such as routers, printers, or other networking hardware. The attacker uses these vulnerabilities to replace a device's firmware with a modified, corrupt, or defective firmware image—a process which when done legitimately is known as *flashing*. This therefore "bricks" the device, rendering it unusable for its original purpose until it can be repaired or replaced.

The PDoS is a pure hardware targeted attack which can be much faster and requires fewer resources than using a botnet or a root/vserver in a DDoS attack. Because of these features, and the potential and high probability of security exploits on Network Enabled Embedded Devices (NEEDs), this technique has come to the attention of numerous hacking communities.

PhlashDance is a tool created by Rich Smith (an employee of Hewlett-Packard's Systems Security Lab) used to detect and demonstrate PDoS vulnerabilities at the 2008 EUSecWest Applied Security Conference in London.

Reflected / Spoofed Attack

A distributed denial-of-service attack may involve sending forged requests of some type to a very large number of computers that will reply to the requests. Using Internet Protocol address spoofing, the source address is set to that of the targeted victim, which means all the replies will go to (and flood) the target. (This reflected attack form is sometimes called a "DRDOS".)

ICMP Echo Request attacks (Smurf attack) can be considered one form of reflected attack, as the flooding host(s) send Echo Requests to the broadcast addresses of mis-configured networks, thereby enticing hosts to send Echo Reply packets to the victim. Some early DDoS programs implemented a distributed form of this attack.

Amplification

Amplification attacks are used to magnify the bandwidth that is sent to a victim. This is typically done through publicly accessible DNS servers that are used to cause congestion on the target system using DNS response traffic. Many services can be exploited to act as reflectors, some harder to block than others. US-CERT have observed that different services implies in different amplification factors, as you can see below:

UDP-based Amplification Attacks	
Protocol	Bandwidth Amplification Factor
NTP	556.9
CharGen	358.8
DNS	up to 179
QOTD	140.3
Quake Network Protocol	63.9
BitTorrent	4.0 - 54.3
SSDP	30.8
Kad	16.3
SNMPv2	6.3
Steam Protocol	5.5
NetBIOS	3.8

DNS amplification attacks involve a new mechanism that increased the amplification effect, using a much larger list of DNS servers than seen earlier. The process typically involves an attacker sending a DNS name look up request to a public DNS server, spoofing the source IP address of the targeted victim. The attacker tries to request as much zone information as possible, thus amplifying the DNS record response that is sent to the targeted victim. Since the size of the request is significantly smaller than the response, the attacker is easily able to increase the amount of traffic directed at the target. SNMP and NTP can also be exploited as reflector in an amplification attack.

An example of an amplified DDoS attack through NTP is through a command called monlist, which sends the details of the last 600 people who have requested the time from that computer back to the requester. A small request to this time server can be sent using a spoofed source IP address of some victim, which results in 556.9 times the amount of data that was requested back to the victim. This becomes amplified when using botnets that all send requests with the same spoofed IP source, which will send a massive amount of data back to the victim.

It is very difficult to defend against these types of attacks because the response data is coming from legitimate servers. These attack requests are also sent through UDP, which does not require a connection to the server. This means that the source IP is not verified when a request is received by the server. In order to bring awareness of these vulnerabilities, campaigns have been started that are dedicated to finding amplification vectors which has led to people fixing their resolvers or having the resolvers shut down completely.

R-U-Dead-Yet? (RUDY)

RUDY attack targets web applications by starvation of available sessions on the web server. Much like Slowloris, RUDY keeps sessions at halt using never-ending POST transmissions and sending an arbitrarily large content-length header value.

Shrew Attack

The shrew attack is a denial-of-service attack on the Transmission Control Protocol. It uses short synchronized bursts of traffic to disrupt TCP connections on the same link, by exploiting a weakness in TCP's retransmission timeout mechanism.

Slow Read Attack

A slow read attack sends legitimate application layer requests, but reads responses very slowly, thus trying to exhaust the server's connection pool. It is achieved by advertising a very small number for the TCP Receive Window size, and at the same time emptying clients' TCP receive buffer slowly, which causes a very low data flow rate.

Sophisticated Low-bandwidth Distributed Denial-of-Service Attack

A sophisticated low-bandwidth DDoS attack is a form of DoS that uses less traffic and increases their effectiveness by aiming at a weak point in the victim's system design, i.e., the attacker sends traffic consisting of complicated requests to the system. Essentially, a sophisticated DDoS attack is lower in cost due to its use of less traffic, is smaller in size making it more difficult to identify, and it has the ability to hurt systems which are protected by flow control mechanisms.

(S)SYN Flood

A SYN flood occurs when a host sends a flood of TCP/SYN packets, often with a forged sender address. Each of these packets are handled like a connection request, causing the server to spawn a half-open connection, by sending back a TCP/SYN-ACK packet

(Acknowledge), and waiting for a packet in response from the sender address (response to the ACK Packet). However, because the sender address is forged, the response never comes. These half-open connections saturate the number of available connections the server can make, keeping it from responding to legitimate requests until after the attack ends.

Teardrop Attacks

A teardrop attack involves sending mangled IP fragments with overlapping, oversized payloads to the target machine. This can crash various operating systems because of a bug in their TCP/IP fragmentation re-assembly code. Windows 3.1x, Windows 95 and Windows NT operating systems, as well as versions of Linux prior to versions 2.0.32 and 2.1.63 are vulnerable to this attack.

(Although in September 2009, a vulnerability in Windows Vista was referred to as a "teardrop attack", this targeted SMB2 which is a higher layer than the TCP packets that teardrop used).

One of the fields in an IP header is the "fragment offset" field, indicating the starting position, or offset, of the data contained in a fragmented packet relative to the data in the original packet. If the sum of the offset and size of one fragmented packet differs from that of the next fragmented packet, the packets overlap. When this happens, a server vulnerable to teardrop attacks is unable to reassemble the packets - resulting in a denial-of-service condition.

Telephony Denial-of-service (TDoS)

Voice over IP has made abusive origination of large numbers of telephone voice calls inexpensive and readily automated while permitting call origins to be misrepresented through caller ID spoofing.

According to the US Federal Bureau of Investigation, telephony denial-of-service (TDoS) has appeared as part of various fraudulent schemes:

- A scammer contacts the victim's banker or broker, impersonating the victim to request a funds transfer. The banker's attempt to contact the victim for verification of the transfer fails as the victim's telephone lines are being flooded with thousands of bogus calls, rendering the victim unreachable.

- A scammer contacts consumers with a bogus claim to collect an outstanding payday loan for thousands of dollars. When the consumer objects, the scammer retaliates by flooding the victim's employer with thousands of automated calls. In some cases, displayed caller ID is spoofed to impersonate police or law enforcement agencies.

- A scammer contacts consumers with a bogus debt collection demand and threatens to send police; when the victim balks, the scammer floods local police numbers with calls on which caller ID is spoofed to display the victims number. Police soon arrive at the victim's residence attempting to find the origin of the calls.

Telephony denial-of-service can exist even without Internet telephony. In the 2002 New Hampshire Senate election phone jamming scandal, telemarketers were used to flood political opponents with spurious calls to jam phone banks on election day. Widespread publication of a number can also flood it with enough calls to render it unusable, as happened by accident in 1981 with multiple +1-area code-867-5309 subscribers inundated by hundreds of misdialed calls daily in response to the song 867-5309/Jenny.

TDoS differs from other telephone harassment (such as prank calls and obscene phone calls) by the number of calls originated; by occupying lines continuously with repeated automated calls, the victim is prevented from making or receiving both routine and emergency telephone calls.

Related exploits include SMS flooding attacks and black fax or fax loop transmission.

Defense Techniques

Defensive responses to denial-of-service attacks typically involve the use of a combination of attack detection, traffic classification and response tools, aiming to block traffic that they identify as illegitimate and allow traffic that they identify as legitimate. A list of prevention and response tools is provided below:

Application Front end Hardware

Application front-end hardware is intelligent hardware placed on the network before traffic reaches the servers. It can be used on networks in conjunction with routers and switches. Application front end hardware analyzes data packets as they enter the system, and then identifies them as priority, regular, or dangerous. There are more than 25 bandwidth management vendors.

Application Level Key Completion Indicators

In order to meet the case of application level DDoS attacks against cloud-based applications, approaches may be based on an application layer analysis, to indicate whether an incoming traffic bulk is legitimate or not and thus enable the triggering of elasticity decisions without the economical implications of a DDoS attack. These approaches mainly rely on an identified path of value inside the application and monitor the macroscopic progress of the requests in this path, towards the final generation of profit, through markers denoted as Key Completion Indicators.

In essence, this technique is a statistical method of assessing the behavior of incoming requests to detect if something unusual or abnormal is going on. Imagine if you were to observe the behavior of normal, paying customers at a brick-and-mortar department store. On average, they would spend in aggregate a known percentage of time on different activities such as picking up items and examining them, putting them back on shelves, trying on clothes, filling a basket, waiting in line, paying for their purchases, and leaving. These high-level activities correspond to the Key Completion Indicators in a service or site, and once normal behavior is determined, abnormal behavior can be identified. For example, if a huge number of customers arrive and spend all their time picking up items and setting them down, but never making any purchases, this can be flagged as unusual behavior.

In the case of elastic cloud services where a huge and abnormal additional workload may incur significant charges from the cloud service provider, this technique can be used to stop or even scale back the elastic expansion of server availability in order to protect from economic loss. In the example analogy, imagine that the department store had the ability to bring in additional employees on a few minutes' notice and routinely did this during "rushes" of unusual customer volume. If a mob shows up that never does any buying, after a relatively short time of paying for the additional employee costs, the store can scale back the number of employees, understanding that the non-buying customers provide no profit for the store and thus should not be serviced. While this may prevent the store from making sales to legitimate customers during the period of attack, it saves the potentially ruinous cost of calling up huge numbers of employees to service an illegitimate load.

Blackholing and Sinkholing

With blackhole routing, all the traffic to the attacked DNS or IP address is sent to a "black hole" (null interface or a non-existent server). To be more efficient and avoid affecting network connectivity, it can be managed by the ISP.

A DNS sinkhole routes traffic to a valid IP address which analyzes traffic and rejects bad packets. Sinkholing is not efficient for most severe attacks.

IPS based Prevention

Intrusion prevention systems (IPS) are effective if the attacks have signatures associated with them. However, the trend among the attacks is to have legitimate content but bad intent. Intrusion-prevention systems which work on content recognition cannot block behavior-based DoS attacks.

An ASIC based IPS may detect and block denial-of-service attacks because they have the processing power and the granularity to analyze the attacks and act like a circuit breaker in an automated way.

A rate-based IPS (RBIPS) must analyze traffic granularly and continuously monitor the traffic pattern and determine if there is traffic anomaly. It must let the legitimate traffic flow while blocking the DoS attack traffic.

DDS based Defense

More focused on the problem than IPS, a DoS defense system (DDS) can block connection-based DoS attacks and those with legitimate content but bad intent. A DDS can also address both protocol attacks (such as teardrop and ping of death) and rate-based attacks (such as ICMP floods and SYN floods).

Firewalls

In the case of a simple attack, a firewall could have a simple rule added to deny all incoming traffic from the attackers, based on protocols, ports or the originating IP addresses.

More complex attacks will however be hard to block with simple rules: for example, if there is an ongoing attack on port 80 (web service), it is not possible to drop all incoming traffic on this port because doing so will prevent the server from serving legitimate traffic. Additionally, firewalls may be too deep in the network hierarchy, with routers being adversely affected before the traffic gets to the firewall.

Routers

Similar to switches, routers have some rate-limiting and ACL capability. They, too, are manually set. Most routers can be easily overwhelmed under a DoS attack. Cisco IOS has optional features that can reduce the impact of flooding.

Switches

Most switches have some rate-limiting and ACL capability. Some switches provide automatic and/or system-wide rate limiting, traffic shaping, delayed binding (TCP splicing), deep packet inspection and Bogon filtering (bogus IP filtering) to detect and remediate DoS attacks through automatic rate filtering and WAN Link failover and balancing.

These schemes will work as long as the DoS attacks can be prevented by using them. For example, SYN flood can be prevented using delayed binding or TCP splicing. Similarly content based DoS may be prevented using deep packet inspection. Attacks originating from dark addresses or going to dark addresses can be prevented using bogon filtering. Automatic rate filtering can work as long as set rate-thresholds have been set correctly. Wan-link failover will work as long as both links have DoS/DDoS prevention mechanism.

Upstream Filtering

All traffic is passed through a "cleaning center" or a "scrubbing center" via various methods such as proxies, tunnels, digital cross connects, or even direct circuits, which separates "bad" traffic (DDoS and also other common internet attacks) and only sends good traffic beyond to the server. The provider needs central connectivity to the Internet to manage this kind of service unless they happen to be located within the same facility as the "cleaning center" or "scrubbing center".

Examples of providers of this service:

- Akamai Technologies
- CloudFlare
- Level 3 Communications
- Radware
- Arbor Networks
- AT&T
- Allot
- F5 Networks
- Incapsula
- Neustar Inc
- Tata Communications
- Verisign
- Verizon

Unintentional Denial-of-service

An unintentional denial-of-service can occur when a system ends up denied, not due to a deliberate attack by a single individual or group of individuals, but simply due to a sudden enormous spike in popularity. This can happen when an extremely popular website posts a prominent link to a second, less well-prepared site, for example, as part of a news story. The result is that a significant proportion of the primary site's regular users – potentially hundreds of thousands of people – click that link in the space of a few hours, having the same effect on the target website as a DDoS attack. A VIPDoS is the same, but specifically when the link was posted by a celebrity.

When Michael Jackson died in 2009, websites such as Google and Twitter slowed down or even crashed. Many sites' servers thought the requests were from a virus or spyware trying to cause a denial-of-service attack, warning users that their queries looked like "automated requests from a computer virus or spyware application".

News sites and link sites – sites whose primary function is to provide links to interesting content elsewhere on the Internet – are most likely to cause this phenomenon. The canonical example is the Slashdot effect when receiving traffic from Slashdot. It is also known as "the Reddit hug of death" and "the Digg effect".

Routers have also been known to create unintentional DoS attacks, as both D-Link and Netgear routers have overloaded NTP servers by flooding NTP servers without respecting the restrictions of client types or geographical limitations.

Similar unintentional denials-of-service can also occur via other media, e.g. when a URL is mentioned on television. If a server is being indexed by Google or another search engine during peak periods of activity, or does not have a lot of available bandwidth while being indexed, it can also experience the effects of a DoS attack.

Legal action has been taken in at least one such case. In 2006, Universal Tube & Rollform Equipment Corporation sued YouTube: massive numbers of would-be youtube.com users accidentally typed the tube company's URL, utube.com. As a result, the tube company ended up having to spend large amounts of money on upgrading their bandwidth. The company appears to have taken advantage of the situation, with utube.com now containing ads for advertisement revenue.

In March 2014, after Malaysia Airlines Flight 370 went missing, DigitalGlobe launched a crowdsourcing service on which users could help search for the missing jet in satellite images. The response overwhelmed the company's servers.

An unintentional denial-of-service may also result from a prescheduled event created by the website itself, as was the case of the Census in Australia in 2016.This could be caused when a server provides some service at a specific time. This might be a university website setting the grades to be available where it will result in many more login requests at that time than any other.

Side Effects of Attacks

Backscatter

In computer network security, backscatter is a side-effect of a spoofed denial-of-service attack. In this kind of attack, the attacker spoofs (or forges) the source address in IP packets sent to the victim. In general, the victim machine cannot distinguish between the spoofed packets and legitimate packets, so the victim responds to the spoofed packets as it normally would. These response packets are known as backscatter.

If the attacker is spoofing source addresses randomly, the backscatter response packets from the victim will be sent back to random destinations. This effect can be used by network telescopes as indirect evidence of such attacks.

The term "backscatter analysis" refers to observing backscatter packets arriving at a statistically significant portion of the IP address space to determine characteristics of DoS attacks and victims.

Legality

Many jurisdictions have laws under which denial-of-service attacks are illegal.

- In the US, denial-of-service attacks may be considered a federal crime under the Computer Fraud and Abuse Act with penalties that include years of imprisonment. The Computer Crime and Intellectual Property Section of the US Department of Justice handles cases of (D)DoS.

- In European countries, committing criminal denial-of-service attacks may, as a minimum, lead to arrest. The United Kingdom is unusual in that it specifically outlawed denial-of-service attacks and set a maximum penalty of 10 years in prison with the Police and Justice Act 2006, which amended Section 3 of the Computer Misuse Act 1990.

On January 7, 2013, Anonymous posted a petition on the whitehouse.gov site asking that DDoS be recognized as a legal form of protest similar to the Occupy protests, the claim being that the similarity in purpose of both are same.

Spoofing Attack

In the context of network security, a spoofing attack is a situation in which one person or program successfully masquerades as another by falsifying data, thereby gaining an illegitimate advantage.

Spoofing and TCP/IP

Many of the protocols in the TCP/IP suite do not provide mechanisms for authenticating the source or destination of a message. They are thus vulnerable to spoofing attacks when extra precautions are not taken by applications to verify the identity of the sending or receiving host. IP spoofing and ARP spoofing in particular may be used to leverage man-in-the-middle attacks against hosts on a computer network. Spoofing attacks which take advantage of TCP/IP suite protocols may be mitigated with the use of firewalls capable of deep packet inspection or by taking measures to verify the identity of the sender or recipient of a message.

Referrer Spoofing

Some websites, especially pornographic paysites, allow access to their materials only from certain approved (login-) pages. This is enforced by checking the referrer header of the HTTP request. This referrer header however can be changed (known as "referrer spoofing" or "Ref-tar spoofing"), allowing users to gain unauthorized access to the materials.

Poisoning of File-sharing Networks

"Spoofing" can also refer to copyright holders placing distorted or unlistenable versions of works on file-sharing networks.

Caller ID Spoofing

Public telephone networks often provide Caller ID information, which includes the caller's name and number, with each call. However, some technologies (especially in Voice over IP (VoIP) networks) allow callers to forge Caller ID information and present false names and numbers. Gateways between networks that allow such spoofing and other public networks then forward that false information. Since spoofed calls can originate from other countries, the laws in the receiver's country may not apply to the caller. This limits laws' effectiveness against the use of spoofed Caller ID information to further a scam.

E-mail Address Spoofing

The sender information shown in e-mails (the "From" field) can be spoofed easily. This technique is commonly used by spammers to hide the origin of their e-mails and leads to problems such as misdirected bounces (i.e. e-mail spam backscatter).

E-mail address spoofing is done in quite the same way as writing a forged return address using snail mail. As long as the letter fits the protocol, (i.e. stamp, postal code) the SMTP protocol will send the message. It can be done using a mail server with telnet.

GPS Spoofing

A GPS spoofing attack attempts to deceive a GPS receiver by broadcasting incorrect GPS signals, structured to resemble a set of normal GPS signals, or by rebroadcasting genuine signals captured elsewhere or at a different time. These spoofed signals may be modified in such a way as to cause the receiver to estimate its position to be somewhere other than where it actually is, or to be located where it is but at a different time, as determined by the attacker. One common form of a GPS spoofing attack, commonly termed a carry-off attack, begins by broadcasting signals synchronized with the genuine signals observed by the target receiver. The power of the counterfeit signals is then gradually increased and drawn away from the genuine signals. It has been suggested that the capture of a Lockheed RQ-170 drone aircraft in northeastern Iran in December, 2011 was the result of such an attack. GPS spoofing attacks had been predicted and discussed in the GPS community previously, but no known example of a malicious spoofing attack has yet been confirmed. A "proof-of-concept" attack was successfully performed in June, 2013, when the luxury yacht "White Rose" was misdirected with spoofed GPS signals from Monaco to the island of Rhodes by a group of aerospace engineering students from the Cockrell School of Engineering at the University of Texas in Austin. The students were aboard the yacht, allowing their spoofing equipment to gradually overpower the signal strengths of the actual GPS constellation satellites, altering the course of the yacht.

Russian GPS Spoofing

In June 2017, approximately twenty ships in the Black Sea complained of GPS anomalies, showing vessels to be transpositioned miles from their actual location, in what Professor Todd Humphreys believed was most likely a spoofing attack. GPS anomalies around Putin's Palace and the Moscow Kremlin have lead researchers to believe that Russian authorities use GPS spoofing wherever Vladimir Putin is located, affecting maritime traffic.

Preventing GPS Spoofing

There are different ways to prevent GPS spoofing. The Department of Homeland Security, in collaboration with the National Cybersecurity and Communications Integration Center (NCCIC) and the National Coordinating Center for Communications (NCC), released a paper which lists methods to prevent this type of spoofing. Some of the most important and most recommended to use are:

1. Obscure antennas. Install antennas where they are not visible from publicly accessible locations or obscure their exact locations by introducing impediments to hide the antennas.

2. Add a sensor/blocker. Sensors can detect characteristics of interference, jamming, and spoofing signals, provide local indication of an attack or anomalous condition, communicate alerts to a remote monitoring site, and collect and report data to be analyzed for forensic purposes.

3. Extend data spoofing whitelists to sensors. Existing data spoofing whitelists have been and are being implemented in government reference software, and should also be implemented in sensors.

4. Use more GPS signal types. Modernized civil GPS signals are more robust than the L1 signal and should be leveraged for increased resistance to interference, jamming, and spoofing.

5. Reduce latency in recognition and reporting of interference, jamming, and spoofing. If a receiver is misled by an attack before the attack is recognized and

reported, then backup devices may be corrupted by the receiver before hand over.

These installation and operation strategies and development opportunities described herein can significantly enhance the ability of GNSS receivers and associated equipment to defend against a range of interference, jamming, and spoofing attacks.

Man-in-the-middle Attack

In cryptography and computer security, a man-in-the-middle attack (MITM) is an attack where the attacker secretly relays and possibly alters the communication between two parties who believe they are directly communicating with each other. One example of man-in-the-middle attacks is active eavesdropping, in which the attacker makes independent connections with the victims and relays messages between them to make them believe they are talking directly to each other over a private connection, when in fact the entire conversation is controlled by the attacker. The attacker must be able to intercept all relevant messages passing between the two victims and inject new ones. This is straightforward in many circumstances; for example, an attacker within reception range of an unencrypted wireless access point (Wi-Fi) could insert himself as a man-in-the-middle.

As an attack that aims at circumventing mutual authentication, or lack thereof, a man-in-the-middle attack can succeed only when the attacker can impersonate each endpoint to their satisfaction as expected from the legitimate ends. Most cryptographic protocols include some form of endpoint authentication specifically to prevent MITM attacks. For example, TLS can authenticate one or both parties using a mutually trusted certificate authority.

Example

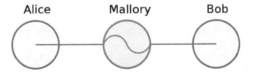

Alice   Mallory   Bob

An illustration of the man-in-the-middle attack

Suppose Alice wishes to communicate with Bob. Meanwhile, Mallory wishes to intercept the conversation to eavesdrop and optionally to deliver a false message to Bob.

First, Alice asks Bob for his public key. If Bob sends his public key to Alice, but Mallory is able to intercept it, a man-in-the-middle attack can begin. Mallory sends a forged message to Alice that purports to come from Bob, but instead includes Mallory's public key.

Alice, believing this public key to be Bob's, encrypts her message with Mallory's key and sends the enciphered message back to Bob. Mallory again intercepts, deciphers the message using her private key, possibly alters it if she wants, and re-enciphers it using the public key Bob originally sent to Alice. When Bob receives the newly enciphered message, he believes it came from Alice.

1. Alice sends a message to Bob, which is intercepted by Mallory:

   Alice *"Hi Bob, it's Alice. Give me your key."* → Mallory Bob

2. Mallory relays this message to Bob; Bob cannot tell it is not really from Alice:

   Alice Mallory *"Hi Bob, it's Alice. Give me your key."* → Bob

3. Bob responds with his encryption key:

   Alice Mallory ← *[Bob's key]* Bob

4. Mallory replaces Bob's key with her own, and relays this to Alice, claiming that it is Bob's key:

   Alice ← *[Mallory's key]* Mallory Bob

5. Alice encrypts a message with what she believes to be Bob's key, thinking that only Bob can read it:

   Alice *"Meet me at the bus stop!" [encrypted with Mallory's key]* → Mallory Bob

6. However, because it was actually encrypted with Mallory's key, Mallory can decrypt it, read it, modify it (if desired), re-encrypt with Bob's key, and forward it to Bob:

   Alice Mallory *"Meet me at the van down by the river!" [encrypted with Bob's key]* → Bob

7. Bob thinks that this message is a secure communication from Alice.

8. Bob goes to the van down by the river and gets robbed by Mallory.

9. Alice does not know that Bob was robbed by Mallory thinking Bob is late.

10. Not seeing Bob for a while, she determines something happened to Bob.

This example shows the need for Alice and Bob to have some way to ensure that they are truly each using each other's public keys, rather than the public key of an attacker. Otherwise, such attacks are generally possible, in principle, against any message sent using public-key technology. A variety of techniques can help defend against MITM attacks.

Defense and Detection

MITM attacks can be prevented or detected by two means: authentication and tamper detection. Authentication provides some degree of certainty that a given message has come from a legitimate source. Tamper detection merely shows evidence that a message may have been altered.

Authentication

All cryptographic systems that are secure against MITM attacks provide some method of authentication for messages. Most require an exchange of information (such as public keys) in addition to the message over a secure channel. Such protocols often use key-agreement protocols have been developed, with different security requirements for the secure channel, though some have attempted to remove the requirement for any secure channel at all.

A public key infrastructure, such as Transport Layer Security, may harden Transmission Control Protocol against Man-in-the-middle-attacks. In such structures, clients and servers exchange certificates which are issued and verified by a trusted third party called a certificate authority (CA). If the original key to authenticate this CA has not been itself the subject of a MITM attack, then the certificates issued by the CA may be used to authenticate the messages sent by the owner of that certificate. Use of mutual authentication, in which both the server and the client validate the other's communication, covers both ends of a MITM attack, though the default behavior of most connections is to only authenticate the server.

Attestments, such as verbal communications of a shared value (as in ZRTP), or recorded attestments such as audio/visual recordings of a public key hash are used to ward off MITM attacks, as visual media is much more difficult and time-consuming to imitate than simple data packet communication. However, these methods require a human in the loop in order to successfully initiate the transaction.

HTTP Public Key Pinning, sometimes called "certificate pinning", helps prevent a MITM attack in which the certificate authority itself is compromised, by having the server provide a list of "pinned" public key hashes during the first transaction. Subsequent transactions then require one or more of the keys in the list must be used by the server in order to authenticate that transaction.

DNSSEC extends the DNS protocol to use signatures to authenticate DNS records, preventing simple MITM attacks from directing a client to a malicious IP address.

Tamper Detection

Latency examination can potentially detect the attack in certain situations, such as with long calculations that lead into tens of seconds like hash functions. To detect potential attacks, parties check for discrepancies in response times. For example: Say that two parties normally take a certain amount of time to perform a particular transaction. If one transaction, however, were to take an abnormal length of time to reach the other party, this could be indicative of a third party's interference inserting additional latency in the transaction.

Quantum Cryptography, in theory, provides tamper-evidence for transactions through the no-cloning theorem. Protocols based on quantum cryptography typically authenticate part or all of their classical communication with an unconditionally secure authentication scheme e.g. Wegman-Carter authentication.

Forensic Analysis

Captured network traffic from what is suspected to be an attack can be analyzed in order to determine whether or not there was an attack and determine the source of the attack, if any. Important evidence to analyze when performing network forensics on a suspected attack includes:

- IP address of the server

- DNS name of the server

- X.509 certificate of the server

  o Is the certificate self signed?

  o Is the certificate signed by a trusted CA?

  o Has the certificate been revoked?

  o Has the certificate been changed recently?

  o Do other clients, elsewhere on the Internet, also get the same certificate?

Notable Instances

A notable non-cryptographic man-in-the-middle attack was perpetrated by a Belkin wireless network router in 2003. Periodically, it would take over an HTTP connection being routed through it: this would fail to pass the traffic on to destination, but instead itself respond as the intended server. The reply it sent, in place of the web page the user had requested, was an advertisement for another Belkin product. After an outcry from technically literate users, this 'feature' was removed from later versions of the router's firmware.

In 2011, a security breach of the Dutch certificate authority DigiNotar resulted in the fraudulent issuing of certificates. Subsequently, the fraudulent certificates were used to perform man-in-the-middle attacks.

In 2013, the Nokia's Xpress Browser was revealed to be decrypting HTTPS traffic on Nokia's proxy servers, giving the company clear text access to its customers' encrypted browser traffic. Nokia responded by saying that the content was not stored permanently, and that the company had organizational and technical measures to prevent access to private information.

In 2017, Equifax withdrew its mobile phone apps following concern about man-in-the-middle vulnerabilities.

Other notable real-life implementations include the following:

- DSniff – the first public implementation of MITM attacks against SSL and SSH

- Fiddler2 HTTP(S) diagnostic tool

- NSA impersonation of Google

- Opendium Web Gateway and Opendium UTM Content-control software, used to perform inspection of HTTPS traffic at the gateway

- Superfish malware

- Forcepoint Content Gateway – used to perform inspection of SSL traffic at the proxy

- wsniff – , a tool for 802.11 HTTP/HTTPS based MITM attacks

- Comcast uses MITM attacks to inject JavaScript code to 3rd party web pages, showing their own ads and messages on top of the pages

ARP Spoofing

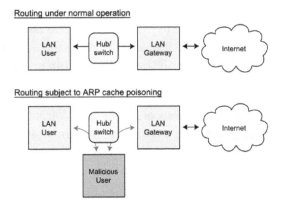

A successful ARP spoofing (poisoning) attack allows an attacker to alter routing on a network, effectively allowing for a man-in-the-middle attack.

In computer networking, ARP spoofing, ARP cache poisoning, or ARP poison routing, is a technique by which an attacker sends (spoofed) Address Resolution Protocol (ARP) messages onto a local area network. Generally, the aim is to associate the attacker's MAC address with the IP address of another host, such as the default gateway, causing any traffic meant for that IP address to be sent to the attacker instead.

ARP spoofing may allow an attacker to intercept data frames on a network, modify the traffic, or stop all traffic. Often the attack is used as an opening for other attacks, such as denial of service, man in the middle, or session hijacking attacks.

The attack can only be used on networks that use ARP, and is confined to and requires the attacker to gain direct access to the local network segment to be attacked.

ARP Vulnerabilities

The Address Resolution Protocol (ARP) is a widely used communications protocol for resolving Internet layer addresses into link layer addresses.

When an Internet Protocol (IP) datagram is sent from one host to another in a local area network, the destination IP address must be resolved to a MAC address for transmission via the data link layer. When another host's IP address is known, and its MAC address is needed, a broadcast packet is sent out on the local network. This packet is known as an *ARP request*. The destination machine with the IP in the ARP request then responds with an *ARP reply* that contains the MAC address for that IP.

ARP is a stateless protocol. Network hosts will automatically cache any ARP replies they receive, regardless of whether network hosts requested them. Even ARP entries that have not yet expired will be overwritten when a new ARP reply packet is received. There is no method in the ARP protocol by which a host can authenticate the peer from which the packet originated. This behavior is the vulnerability that allows ARP spoofing to occur.

Anatomy of an ARP Spoofing Attack

The basic principle behind ARP spoofing is to exploit the lack of authentication in the ARP protocol by sending spoofed ARP messages onto the LAN. ARP spoofing attacks can be run from a compromised host on the LAN, or from an attacker's machine that is connected directly to the target LAN.

Generally, the goal of the attack is to associate the attacker's host MAC address with the IP address of a target host, so that any traffic meant for the target host will be sent to the attacker's host. The attacker may choose to inspect the packets (spying), while forwarding the traffic to the actual default destination to avoid discovery, modify the data before forwarding it (man-in-the-middle attack), or launch a denial-of-service attack by causing some or all of the packets on the network to be dropped.

Defenses

Static ARP Entries

The simplest form of certification is the use of static, read-only entries for critical services in the ARP cache of a host. This prevents only simple attacks and does not scale on a large network, since the mapping has to be set for each pair of machines resulting in n^2-n ARP entries that have to be configured when n machines are present: On every machine there must be an ARP entry for every other machine on the network, which are $n-1$ ARP entries on every of the n machines.

IP address-to-MAC address mappings in the local ARP cache may be statically entered so that hosts ignore all ARP reply packets. While static entries provide some security against spoofing if the operating system handles them correctly, they result in maintenance efforts as address mappings of all systems in the network have to be distributed.

ARP Spoofing Detection and Prevention Software

Software that detects ARP spoofing generally relies on some form of certification or cross-checking of ARP responses. Uncertified ARP responses are then blocked. These techniques may be integrated with the DHCP server so that both dynamic and static IP addresses are certified. This capability may be implemented in individual hosts or may be integrated into Ethernet switches or other network equipment. The existence of multiple IP addresses associated with a single MAC address may indicate an ARP spoof attack, although there are legitimate uses of such a configuration. In a more passive approach a device listens for ARP replies on a network, and sends a notification via email when an ARP entry changes.

AntiARP also provides Windows-based spoofing prevention at the kernel level. ArpStar is a Linux module for kernel 2.6 and Linksys routers that drops invalid packets that violate mapping, and contains an option to repoison/heal.

OS Security

Operating systems react differently. Linux ignores unsolicited replies, but, on the other hand, uses responses to requests from other machines to update its cache. Solaris accepts updates on entries only after a timeout. In Microsoft Windows, the behavior of the ARP cache can be configured through several registry entries under HKEY_LOCAL_MACHINE\SYSTEM\CurrentControlSet\Services\Tcpip\Parameters, ArpCacheLife, ArpCacheMinReferenceLife, ArpUseEtherSNAP, ArpTRSingleRoute, ArpAlwaysSourceRoute, ArpRetryCount.

Legitimate usage

The techniques that are used in ARP spoofing can also be used to implement redundancy of network services. For example, some software allows a backup server to issue a gratuitous ARP request in order to take over for a defective server and transparently offer redundancy. There are two companies known to-date that have tried to commercialize products centered around this strategy, Disney Circle and CUJO. The latter has recently run into significant problems with its ARP-spoofing strategy in consumer's homes; they have now completely removed that capability and replaced it with a DH-CP-based strategy.

ARP spoofing is often used by developers to debug IP traffic between two hosts when a switch is in use: if host A and host B are communicating through an Ethernet switch, their traffic would normally be invisible to a third monitoring host M. The developer configures A to have M's MAC address for B, and B to have M's MAC address for A; and also configures M to forward packets. M can now monitor the traffic, exactly as in a man-in-the-middle attack.

Ping of Death

A ping of death is a type of attack on a computer system that involves sending a mal-formed or otherwise malicious ping to a computer.

A correctly-formed ping packet is typically 56 bytes in size, or 64 bytes when the Internet Protocol header is considered. However, any IPv4 packet (including pings) may be as large as 65,535 bytes. Some computer systems were never designed to properly handle a ping packet larger than the maximum packet size because it vio-lates the Internet Protocol documented in RFC 791. Like other large but well-formed packets, a ping of death is fragmented into groups of 8 octets before transmission. However, when the target computer reassembles the malformed packet, a buffer overflow can occur, causing a system crash and potentially allowing the injection of malicious code.

In early implementations of TCP/IP, this bug is easy to exploit and can affect a wide variety of systems including Unix, Linux, Mac, Windows, and peripheral devices. As systems began filtering out pings of death through firewalls and other detection meth-ods, a different kind of ping attack known as ping flooding later appeared, which floods the victim with so many ping requests that normal traffic fails to reach the system (a basic denial-of-service attack).

Detailed Information

As defined in RFC 791, the maximum packet length of an IPv4 packet including the IP header is 65,535 ($2^{16} - 1$) bytes, a limitation presented by the use of a 16-bit wide IP header field that describes the total packet length.

The underlying Data Link Layer almost always poses limits to the maximum frame size. In Ethernet, this is typically 1500 bytes. In such a case, a large IP packet is split across multiple IP packets (also known as IP fragments), so that each IP fragment will match the imposed limit. The receiver of the IP fragments will reassemble them into the com-plete IP packet, and will continue processing it as usual.

When fragmentation is performed, each IP fragment needs to carry information about which part of the original IP packet it contains. This information is kept in the Fragment Offset field, in the IP header. The field is 13 bits long, and contains the offset of the data in the current IP fragment, in the original IP packet. The offset is given in units of 8 bytes. This allows a maximum offset of 65,528 $((2^{13}-1)*8)$. Then when adding 20 bytes of IP header, the maximum will be 65,548 bytes, which exceeds the maximum frame size. This means that an IP fragment with the maximum offset should have data no larger than 7 bytes, or else it would exceed the limit of the maximum packet length. A malicious user can send an IP fragment with the maximum offset and with much more data than 8 bytes (as large as the physical layer allows it to be).

When the receiver assembles all IP fragments, it will end up with an IP packet which is larger than 65,535 bytes. This may possibly overflow memory buffers which the receiver allocated for the packet, and can cause various problems.

As is evident from the description above, the problem has nothing to do with ICMP, which is used only as payload, big enough to exploit the problem. It is a problem in the reassembly process of IP fragments, which may contain any type of protocol (TCP, UDP, IGMP, etc.).

The correction of the problem is to add checks in the reassembly process. The check for each incoming IP fragment makes sure that the sum of "Fragment Offset" and "Total length" fields in the IP header of each IP fragment is smaller or equal to 65,535. If the sum is greater, then the packet is invalid, and the IP fragment is ignored. This check is performed by some firewalls, to protect hosts that do not have the bug fixed. Another fix for the problem is using a memory buffer larger than 65,535 bytes for the re-assembly of the packet. (This is essentially a breaking of the specification, since it adds support for packets larger than those allowed.)

Ping of Death in IPv6

In 2013, an IPv6 version of the ping of death vulnerability was discovered in Microsoft Windows. Windows TCP/IP stack didn't handle memory allocation correctly when processing incoming malformed ICMPv6 packets, which could cause remote denial of service. This vulnerability was fixed in MS13-065 in August 2013. The CVE-ID for this vulnerability is CVE-2013-3183.

References

- Cortada, James W. (4 December 2003). The Digital Hand: How Computers Changed the Work of American Manufacturing, Transportation, and Retail Industries. USA: Oxford University Press. p. 512. ISBN 0-19-516588-8

- Merkle, Ralph C (April 1978). "Secure Communications Over Insecure Channels". Communications of the ACM. 21 (4): 294–299. doi:10.1145/359460.359473. Received August, 1975; revised September 1977

- S. Karnouskos: Stuxnet Worm Impact on Industrial Cyber-Physical System Security. In:37th

Annual Conference of the IEEE Industrial Electronics Society (IECON 2011), Melbourne, Australia, 7-10 Nov 2011. Retrieved 20 Apr 2014

- Prichard, Janet, and Laurie MacDonald. «Cyber Terrorism: A Study of the Extent of Coverage in Computer Security Textbooks.» Journal of Information Technology Education. 3. (2004): n. page

- Cortada, James W. (3 November 2005). The Digital Hand: Volume II: How Computers Changed the Work of American Financial, Telecommunications, Media, and Entertainment Industries. USA: Oxford University Press. ISBN 978-0-19-516587-6

- Sanaei, M. G., Isnin, I. F., & Bakhtiari, M. (2013). Performance Evaluation of Routing Protocol on AODV and DSR Under Wormhole Attack. International Journal of Computer Networks and Communications Security, Volume 1, Issue 1, ISSN 2308-9830

- Aziz, Benjamin; Hamilton, Geoff (2009). "Detecting man-in-the-middle attacks by precise timing". 2009 Third International Conference on Emerging Security Information, Systems and Technologies: 81–86. Retrieved 2017-02-25

2

Computer Security: Access Control Principles

Access control involves authentication, identification, audit and authorization in computer security. This chapter explores different access control modes such as attribute-based, identity-based and role-based access control, among others. The chapter closely examines the key concepts of access control to provide an extensive understanding of computer security.

Computer Access Control

In computer security, general access control includes identification, authorization, authentication, access approval, and audit. A more narrow definition of access control would cover only access approval, whereby the system makes a decision to grant or reject an access request from an already authenticated subject, based on what the subject is authorized to access. Authentication and access control are often combined into a single operation, so that access is approved based on successful authentication, or based on an anonymous access token. Authentication methods and tokens include passwords, biometric scans, physical keys, electronic keys and devices, hidden paths, social barriers, and monitoring by humans and automated systems.

The two possibilities for imposing computer access control are those based on capabilities and those based on access control lists (ACLs):

- In a capability-based model, holding an unforge-able reference or *capability* to an object provides access to the object (roughly analogous to how possession of one's house key grants one access to one's house); access is conveyed to another party by transmitting such a capability over a secure channel.

- In an ACL-based model, a subject's access to an object depends on whether its identity appears on a list associated with the object (roughly analogous to how a bouncer at a private party would check an ID to see if a name appears on the guest list); access is conveyed by editing the list. (Different ACL systems have a variety of different conventions regarding who or what is responsible for editing the list and how it is edited.)

Both capability-based and ACL-based models have mechanisms to allow access rights to be granted to all members of a *group* of subjects (often the group is itself modeled as a subject).

Services

Access control systems provide the essential services of *authorization, identification and authentication (I&A), access approval,* and *accountability* where:

- authorization specifies what a subject can do

- identification and authentication ensure that only legitimate subjects can log on to a system

- access approval grants access during operations, by association of users with the resources that they are allowed to access, based on the authorization policy

- accountability identifies what a subject (or all subjects associated with a user) did

Authorization

Authorization involves the act of defining access-rights for subjects. An authorization policy specifies the operations that subjects are allowed to execute within a system.

Most modern operating systems implement authorization policies as formal sets of permissions that are variations or extensions of three basic types of access:

- Read (R): The subject can

  o Read file contents

  o List directory contents

- Write (W): The subject can change the contents of a file or directory with the following tasks:

  o Add

  o Update

  o Delete

  o Rename

- Execute (X): If the file is a program, the subject can cause the program to be run. (In Unix-style systems, the "execute" permission doubles as a "traverse directory" permission when granted for a directory.)

These rights and permissions are implemented differently in systems based on *discretionary access control (DAC)* and *mandatory access control (MAC)*.

Identification and Authentication (I&A)

Identification and Authentication (I&A) is the process of verifying that an identity is bound to the entity that makes an assertion or claim of identity. The I&A process assumes that there was an initial validation of the identity, commonly called identity proofing. Various methods of identity proofing are available, ranging from in-person validation using government issued identification, to anonymous methods that allow the claimant to remain anonymous, but known to the system if they return. The method used for identity proofing and validation should provide an assurance level commensurate with the intended use of the identity within the system. Subsequently, the entity asserts an identity together with an authenticator as a means for validation. The only requirements for the identifier is that it must be unique within its security domain.

Authenticators are commonly based on at least one of the following four factors:

- *Something you know*, such as a password or a personal identification number (PIN). This assumes that only the owner of the account knows the password or PIN needed to access the account.

- *Something you have*, such as a smart card or security token. This assumes that only the owner of the account has the necessary smart card or token needed to unlock the account.

- *Something you are*, such as fingerprint, voice, retina, or iris characteristics.

- *Where you are*, for example inside or outside a company firewall, or proximity of login location to a personal GPS device.

Access Approval

Access approval is the function that actually grants or rejects access during operations.

During access approval, the system compares the formal representation of the authorization policy with the access request, to determine whether the request shall be granted or rejected. Moreover, the access evaluation can be done online/ongoing.

Accountability

Accountability uses such system components as *audit trails* (records) and *logs,* to associate a subject with its actions. The information recorded should be sufficient to map the subject to a controlling user. Audit trails and logs are important for:

- Detecting security violations

- Re-creating security incidents

If no one is regularly reviewing your logs and they are not maintained in a secure and consistent manner, they may not be admissible as evidence.

Many systems can generate automated reports, based on certain predefined criteria or thresholds, known as clipping levels. *For example, a clipping level may be set to generate a report for the following:*

- More than three failed logon attempts in a given period

- Any attempt to use a disabled user account

These reports help a system administrator or security administrator to more easily identify possible break-in attempts.

Definition of clipping level: a disk's ability to maintain its magnetic properties and hold its content. A high-quality level range is 65–70%; low quality is below 55%.

Access Control Models

Access control models are sometimes categorized as either discretionary or non-discretionary. The three most widely recognized models are Discretionary Access Control (DAC), Mandatory Access Control (MAC), and Role Based Access Control (RBAC). MAC is non-discretionary.

Discretionary Access Control

Discretionary access control (DAC) is a policy determined by the owner of an object. The owner decides who is allowed to access the object, and what privileges they have.

Two important concepts in DAC are

- File and data ownership: Every object in the system has an *owner*. In most DAC systems, each object's initial owner is the subject that caused it to be created. The access policy for an object is determined by its owner.

- Access rights and permissions: These are the controls that an owner can assign to other subjects for specific resources.

Access controls may be discretionary in ACL-based or capability-based access control systems. (In capability-based systems, there is usually no explicit concept of 'owner', but the creator of an object has a similar degree of control over its access policy.)

Mandatory Access Control

Mandatory access control refers to allowing access to a resource if and only if rules exist that allow a given user to access the resource. It is difficult to manage, but its use is usually justified when used to protect highly sensitive information. Examples include certain government and military information. Management is often simplified (over what can be required) if the information can be protected using hierarchical access control, or by implementing sensitivity labels. What makes the method "mandatory" is the use of either rules or sensitivity labels.

- Sensitivity labels: In such a system subjects and objects must have labels assigned to them. A subject's sensitivity label specifies its level of trust. An object's sensitivity label specifies the level of trust required for access. In order to access a given object, the subject must have a sensitivity level equal to or higher than the requested object.

- Data import and export: Controlling the import of information from other systems and export to other systems (including printers) is a critical function of these systems, which must ensure that sensitivity labels are properly maintained and implemented so that sensitive information is appropriately protected at all times.

Two methods are commonly used for applying mandatory access control:

- Rule-based (or label-based) access control: This type of control further defines specific conditions for access to a requested object. A Mandatory Access Control system implements a simple form of rule-based access control to determine whether access should be granted or denied by matching:

  o An object's sensitivity label

  o A subject's sensitivity label

- Lattice-based access control: These can be used for complex access control decisions involving multiple objects and/or subjects. A lattice model is a mathematical structure that defines greatest lower-bound and least upper-bound values for a pair of elements, such as a subject and an object.

Few systems implement MAC; XTS-400 and SELinux are examples of systems that do.

Role-based Access Control

Role-based access control (RBAC) is an access policy determined by the system, not by the owner. RBAC is used in commercial applications and also in military systems, where multi-level security requirements may also exist. RBAC differs from DAC in that DAC allows users to control access to their resources, while in RBAC, access is controlled at the system level, outside of the user's control. Although RBAC is non-discretionary, it can be distinguished from MAC primarily in the way permissions are handled. MAC controls read and write permissions based on a user's clearance level and additional labels. RBAC controls collections of permissions that may include complex operations such as an e-commerce transaction, or may be as simple as read or write. A role in RBAC can be viewed as a set of permissions.

Three primary rules are defined for RBAC:

1. Role assignment: A subject can execute a transaction only if the subject has selected or been assigned a suitable role.

2. Role authorization: A subject's active role must be authorized for the subject. With rule 1 above, this rule ensures that users can take on only roles for which they are authorized.

3. Transaction authorization: A subject can execute a transaction only if the transaction is authorized for the subject's active role. With rules 1 and 2, this rule ensures that users can execute only transactions for which they are authorized.

Additional constraints may be applied as well, and roles can be combined in a hierarchy where higher-level roles subsume permissions owned by lower-level sub-roles.

Most IT vendors offer RBAC in one or more products.

Intent-based Access Control (IBAC)

Intent-based Access Control (IBAC), a novel access control model first proposed by Abdulaziz Almehmadi, is an access control system that detects the intention of the user requesting access answering the question "Why?" access is being requested as opposed to current access control systems that asks "Who?" is requesting access. IBAC is designed to prevent the insider threat as opposed to the current access control systems that are designed to prevent the outsider threat. IBAC is a risk-based access control that assesses risk of access based on the detected intent and the motivation level towards executing that intent. IBAC takes advantage of the robustness of P300-based Concealed Information Test to detect an intent of access and uses the brain signals to detect the motivation level. The access control system has been used on 30 participants with 100% detected intentions of access and all mal-intent users being rejected access before they commit their mal-intended action.

Emotion-based Access Control (EBAC)

Emotion-based Access Control (EBAC), a novel access control model first proposed by Abdulaziz Almehmadi, is an access control system that detects the emotion of the user requesting access in order to form an access decision. This form of access control adds the sensibility aspect to access control systems to further analyze the risk of granting an authorized user access. A user who has a high level of anger and might cause damage if granted access. As well as denying a malicious authorized user access can be useful, granting a non-authorized user who have good intentions of access can be useful as well (e.g. granting firefighters access to a facility in order to suppress damage).

In some cases, we would wish to deny access to authorized personals in the case that they request access to cause damage. On the other hand, we would wish to grant access to unauthorized individuals who may suppress damage or prevent catastrophic incidents.

EBAC uses emotion detection technology to supplement the access control systems by detecting the emotion of the person requesting access and using it as an additional authentication factor along with the recognized identity of the user as needed. The novelty of the approach is that access is granted based on the actual feelings of the users with regards to the requested resources. The approach is based on the detection of emotion based on the involuntary brain signals that are extremely hard to control or circumvent, and on using the detected emotion in the context of access control.

The EBAC system flow starts with the EEG signal acquisition. The EEG signals are sent via the Emotiv EPOC headset to a listener in the EBAC application. Signals are then analyzed and the emotion is detected with correspondence to the emotion level. The emotion and its rate are then categorized to be either positive or negative. Then data is sent to the decision maker to deny or grant access to the entity.

Attribute-based Access Control

In attribute-based access control (ABAC), access is granted not based on the rights of the subject associated with a user after authentication, but based on attributes of the user. The user has to prove so-called claims about his attributes to the access control engine. An attribute-based access control policy specifies which claims need to be satisfied in order to grant access to an object. For instance the claim could be "older than 18". Any user that can prove this claim is granted access. Users can be anonymous when authentication and identification are not strictly required. One does, however, require means for proving claims anonymously. This can for instance be achieved using anonymous credentials. XACML (extensible access control markup language) is a standard for attribute-based access control. XACML 3.0 was standardized in January 2013.

Break-Glass Access Control Models

Traditionally, access has the purpose of restricting access, thus most access control models follow the "default deny principle", i.e. if a specific access request is not explicitly allowed, it will be denied. This behavior might conflict with the regular operations of a system. In certain situations, humans are willing to take the risk that might be involved in violating an access control policy, if the potential benefit that can be achieved outweighs this risk. This need is especially visible in the health-care domain, where a denied access to patient records can cause the death of a patient. Break-Glass (also called break-the-glass) try to mitigate this by allowing users to override access control decision. Break-Glass can either be implemented in an access control specific manner (e.g. into RBAC), or generic (i.e., independent from the underlying access control model).

Access Control based on the Responsibility

In Aligning Access Rights to Governance Needs with the Responsibility MetaModel (ReMMo) in the Frame of Enterprise Architecture an expressive Responsibility meta-model has been defined and allows representing the existing responsibilities at the business layer and, thereby, allows engineering the access rights required to perform these responsibilities, at the application layer. A method has been proposed to define the access rights more accurately, considering the alignment of the responsibility and RBAC.

Host-based Access Control (HBAC)

The initialism HBAC stands for "host-based access control".

Attribute-based Access Control

Attribute-based access control (ABAC) defines an access control paradigm whereby access rights are granted to users through the use of policies which combine attributes together. The policies can use any type of attributes (user attributes, resource attributes, object, environment attributes etc.). This model supports Boolean logic, in which rules contain "IF, THEN" statements about who is making the request, the resource, and the action. For example: IF the requestor is a manager, THEN allow read/write access to sensitive data.

Unlike role-based access control (RBAC), which employs pre-defined roles that carry a specific set of privileges associated with them and to which subjects are assigned, the key difference with ABAC is the concept of policies that express a complex Boolean rule set that can evaluate many different attributes. Attribute values can be set-valued or atomic-valued. Set-valued attributes contain more than one atomic value. Examples are *role* and *project*. Atomic-valued attributes contain only one atomic value. Examples are clearance and sensitivity. Attributes can be compared to static values or to one another, thus enabling relation-based access control.

Although the concept itself existed for many years, ABAC is considered "next generation" authorization model because it provides dynamic, context-aware and risk-intelligent access control to resources allowing access control policies that include specific attributes from many different information systems to be defined to resolve an authorization and achieve an efficient regulatory compliance, allowing enterprises flexibility in their implementations based on their existing infrastructures.

Attribute-based access control is sometimes referred to as policy-based access control (PBAC) or claims-based access control (CBAC), which is a Microsoft-specific term.

Dimensions of Attribute-based Access Control

ABAC can be seen as:

- Externalized Authorization Management

- Dynamic Authorization Management

- Policy Based Access Control

- Fine-Grained Authorization

Components

Architecture

ABAC comes with a recommended architecture which is as follows:

1. The PEP or Policy Enforcement Point: it is responsible for protecting the apps & data you want to apply ABAC to. The PEP inspects the request and generates an authorization request from it which it sends to the PDP.

2. The PDP or Policy Decision Point is the brain of the architecture. This is the piece which evaluates incoming requests against policies it has been configured with. The PDP returns a Permit / Deny decision. The PDP may also use PIPs to retrieve missing metadata.

3. The PIP or Policy Information Point bridges the PDP to external sources of attributes e.g. LDAP or databases.

Attributes

Attributes can be about anything and anyone. They tend to fall into 4 different categories or functions (as in grammatical function):

1. Subject attributes: attributes that describe the user attempting the access e.g. age, clearance, department, role, job title...

2. Action attributes: attributes that describe the action being attempted e.g. read, delete, view, approve...

3. Resource (or object) attributes: attributes that describe the object being accessed e.g. the object type (medical record, bank account...), the department, the classification or sensitivity, the location...

4. Contextual (environment) attributes: attributes that deal with time, location or dynamic aspects of the access control scenario.

Policies

Policies are statements that bring together attributes to express what can happen and is not allowed. Policies in ABAC can be granting or denying policies. Policies can also be local or global and can be written in a way that they override other policies. Examples include:

1. A user can view a document if the document is in the same department as the user

2. A user can edit a document if they are the owner and if the document is in draft mode

3. Deny access before 9am

With ABAC you can have as many policies as you like that cater to many different scenarios and technologies.

Other Models

Historically, access control models have included mandatory access control (MAC), discretionary access control (DAC), mandatory integrity control, and more recently role-based access control (RBAC). These access control models are user-centric and do not take into account additional parameters such as resource information, relationship between the user (the requesting entity) and the resource, and dynamic information e.g. time of the day or user IP. ABAC tries to address this by defining access control based on attributes which describe the requesting entity (the user), the targeted object or resource, the desired action (view, edit, delete...), and environmental or contextual information. This is why access control is said to be attribute-based.

Implementations

One standard that implements attribute- and policy-based access control is XACML, the eXtensible Access Control Markup Language. XACML defines an architecture, a policy language, and a request / response scheme. It does not handle attribute management (user attribute assignment, object attribute assignment, environment attribute assignment) which is left to traditional IAM tools, databases, and directories.

Applications

The concept of ABAC can be applied at any level of the technology stack and an enterprise infrastructure. For example, ABAC can be used at the firewall, server, application, database, and data layer. The use of attributes bring additional context to evaluate the legitimacy of any request for access and inform the decision to grant or deny access.

An important consideration when evaluating ABAC solutions is to understand its potential overhead on performance and its impact on the user experience. It is expected that the more granular the controls, the higher the overhead.

API and Micro Services Security

ABAC can be used to apply attribute-based, fine-grained authorization to the API methods or functions. For instance, a banking API may expose an approveTransaction(transId) method. ABAC can be used to secure the call. With ABAC, a policy author can write the following:

- Policy: managers can approve transactions up to their approval limit

- Attributes used: role, action ID, object type, amount, approval limit

The flow would be as follows:

1. The user, Alice, calls the API method approveTransaction(123).

2. The API receives the call and authenticates the user.

3. An interceptor in the API calls out to the authorization engine (typically called a Policy Decision Point or PDP) and asks: *Can Alice approve transaction 123?*

4. The PDP retrieves the ABAC policy and necessary attributes.

5. The PDP reaches a decision e.g. Permit or Deny and returns it to the API interceptor.

6. If the decision is Permit, the underlying API business logic is called. Otherwise the API returns an error or access denied.

Application Security

One of the key benefits to ABAC is that the authorization policies and attributes can be defined in a technology neutral way. This means policies defined for APIs or databases can be reused in the application space. Common applications that can benefit from ABAC are:

1. content management systems

2. ERPs

3. home-grown applications

4. web applications

The same process and flow as the one described in the API section applies here too.

Database Security

Security for databases has long been specific to the database vendors: Oracle VPD, IBM FGAC, and Microsoft RLS are all means to achieve fine-grained ABAC-like security.

Using ABAC, it is possible to define policies that apply across multiple databases. This is called dynamic data masking.

An example would be:

- Policy: managers can view transactions in their region

- Reworked policy in a data-centric way: users with role == manager can do the action == SELECT on table == TRANSACTIONS if user.region == transaction. region

Data Security

Data security typically goes one step further than database security and applies control directly to the data element. This is often referred to as Data-Centric Security. On traditional relational databases, ABAC policies can control access to data at the table, column, field, cell and sub-cell using logical controls with filtering conditions and masking based on attributes. Attributes can be data, user, session or tools based to deliver the greatest level of flexibility in dynamically granting/denying access to a specific data element. On big data, and distributed file systems such as Hadoop, ABAC applied at the data layer control access to folder, sub-folder, file, sub-file and other granular.

Big Data Security

Attribute-based access control can also be applied to Big Data systems like Hadoop. Policies similar to those used previously can be applied when retrieving data from data lakes.

File Server Security

As of Windows Server 2012, Microsoft has implemented an ABAC approach to controlling access to files and folders. This achieved through dynamic access control lists (DACL) and Security Descriptor Definition Language (SDDL). SDDL can be seen as an ABAC language as it uses metadata of the user (claims) and of the file / folder to control access.

Discretionary Access Control

In computer security, discretionary access control (DAC) is a type of access control defined by the Trusted Computer System Evaluation Criteria "as a means of restricting access to objects based on the identity of subjects and/or groups to which they belong. The controls are discretionary in the sense that a subject with a certain access permission is capable of passing that permission (perhaps indirectly) on to any other subject (unless restrained by mandatory access control)".

Discretionary access control is commonly discussed in contrast to mandatory access control (MAC, sometimes termed *non-discretionary access control*). Occasionally a system as a whole is said to have "discretionary" or "purely discretionary" access control as a way of saying that the system lacks mandatory access control. On the other hand, systems can be said to implement both MAC and DAC simultaneously, where DAC refers to one category of access controls that subjects can transfer among each other, and MAC refers to a second category of access controls that imposes constraints upon the first.

Implementations

The meaning of the term in practice is not as clear-cut as the definition given in the TCSEC standard, because TCSEC definition of DAC does not impose implementation concept. There are at least two implementations: with owner (as widespread example) and with capabilities.

with Owner

The term DAC is commonly used in contexts that assume that every object has an *owner* that controls the permissions to access the object, probably because many systems do implement DAC using the concept of an owner. But the TCSEC definition does not say anything about owners, so technically an access control system doesn't have to have a concept of owner to meet the TCSEC definition of DAC.

Users (owners) have under this DAC implementation the ability to make policy decisions and/or assign security attributes. A straightforward example is the Unix file mode which represent write, read, and execute in each of the 3 bits for each of User, Group and Others. (It is prepended by another bit that indicates additional characteristics).

with Capabilities

As another example, capability systems are sometimes described as providing discretionary controls because they permit subjects to transfer their access to other subjects, even though capability-based security is fundamentally not about restricting access "based on the identity of subjects" (capability systems do not, in general, allow permissions to be passed "to any other subject"; the subject wanting to pass its permissions must first have access to the receiving subject, and subjects do not generally have access to all subjects in the system).

Identity-based Security

Identity-based security is an approach to control access to a digital product or service based on the authenticated identity of an individual. This allows organizations to grant access to specific users to access a variety of digital services using the same credentials, ensuring the accurate match between what users are entitled to and what they actually receive, while also permitting other access constraints such as company, device, location and application type (attributes). Underpinning the identity-based security approach is the Identity-Based Access Control (IBAC), (or identity-based licensing) concept.

NIST defines identity-based security policies as policies "based on the identities and/or attributes of the object (system resource) being accessed and of the subject (user, group of users, process, or device) requesting access."

Some of the advantages of the identity-based security approach include the ability to exercise very fine-grained control over who is allowed to use which services and which functions those users can perform, and that it is device-agnostic, offering the possibility to enforce access control policy across a variety of devices, such as smartphones, tablets, and PCs.

Identity-based Security Models

Cyberoam's Approach

The identity-based security network security approach put forward by Cyberoam includes security components that provides visibility and control over user activity in a particular network. It offers a network security system which includes a user's human identity as a part of the firewall rule matching criteria.

The concept includes treating a user's identity as the 8th Layer (also known as the human layer) in the network protocol stack, thus attaching user identity to security while authenticating, authorizing and auditing the network. This takes a different step from conventional security appliances, which bind security to IP-addresses. Such an approach allows organisations to create security policies that align to users and groups rather than to IP addresses which ultimately gives them more precise control over who can access the network—and what they can access.

Identity-based security prevents systems against address spoofing attacks by combining the point of encryption, authentication, and access control into a single unit.

Mandatory Access Control

In computer security, mandatory access control (MAC) refers to a type of access control by which the operating system constrains the ability of a *subject* or *initiator* to access or generally perform some sort of operation on an *object* or *target*. In practice, a subject is usually a process or thread; objects are constructs such as files, directories, TCP/UDP ports, shared memory segments, IO devices, etc. Subjects and objects each have a set of security attributes. Whenever a subject attempts to access an object, an authorization rule enforced by the operating system kernel examines these security attributes and decides whether the access can take place. Any operation by any subject on any object is tested against the set of authorization rules (aka *policy*) to determine if the operation is allowed. A database management system, in its access control mechanism, can also apply mandatory access control; in this case, the objects are tables, views, procedures, etc.

With mandatory access control, this security policy is centrally controlled by a security policy administrator; users do not have the ability to override the policy and, for example, grant access to files that would otherwise be restricted. By contrast, discretionary access control (DAC), which also governs the ability of subjects to access objects, allows users the ability to make policy decisions and/or assign security attributes. (The traditional Unix system of users, groups, and read-write-execute permissions is an example of DAC.) MAC-enabled systems allow policy administrators to implement organization-wide security policies. Under MAC (and unlike DAC), users cannot override or modify this policy, either accidentally or intentionally. This allows security administrators to define a central policy that is guaranteed (in principle) to be enforced for all users.

Historically and traditionally, MAC has been closely associated with multi-level security (MLS) and specialized military systems. In this context, MAC implies a high degree of rigor to satisfy the constraints of MLS systems. More recently, however, MAC has evolved out of the MLS niche and has started to become more mainstream. The more recent MAC implementations, such as SELinux and AppArmor for Linux and Mandatory Integrity Control for Windows, allow administrators to focus on issues such as network attacks and malware without the rigor or constraints of MLS.

Degrees of MAC System Strength

In some systems, users have the authority to decide whether to grant access to any other user. To allow that, all users have clearances for all data. This is not necessarily true of a MLS system. If individuals or processes exist that may be denied access to any of the data in the system environment, then the system must be trusted to enforce MAC. Since there can be various levels of data classification and user clearances, this implies a quantified scale for robustness. For example, more robustness is indicated for system environments containing classified Top Secret information and uncleared users than for one with Secret information and users cleared to at least Confidential. To promote consistency and eliminate subjectivity in degrees of robustness, an extensive scientific analysis and risk assessment of the topic produced a landmark benchmark standardization quantifying security robustness capabilities of systems and mapping them to the degrees of trust warranted for various security environments. The result was documented in CSC-STD-004-85. Two relatively independent components of robustness were defined: Assurance Level and Functionality. Both were specified with a degree of precision that warranted significant confidence in certifications based on these criteria.

Evaluation of MAC System Strength

The Common Criteria is based on this science and it intended to preserve the Assurance Level as EAL levels and the functionality specifications as Protection Profiles. Of these two essential components of objective robustness benchmarks, only EAL levels were faithfully preserved. In one case, TCSEC level C2 (not a MAC capable category) was fairly faithfully preserved in the Common Criteria, as the Controlled Access Protection Profile (CAPP). Multilevel security (MLS) Protection Profiles (such as MLSOSPP similar to B2) is more general than B2. They are pursuant to MLS, but lack the detailed implementation requirements of their Orange Book predecessors, focusing more on objectives. This gives certifiers more subjective flexibility in deciding whether the evaluated product's technical features adequately achieve the objective, potentially eroding consistency of evaluated products and making it easier to attain certification for less trustworthy products. For these reasons, the importance of the technical details of the Protection Profile is critical to determining the suitability of a product.

Such an architecture prevents an authenticated user or process at a specific classification or trust-level from accessing information, processes, or devices in a different level. This provides a containment mechanism of users and processes, both known and unknown (an unknown program (for example) might comprise an untrusted application where the system should monitor and/or control accesses to devices and files).

Implementations

A few MAC implementations, such as Unisys' Blacker project, were certified robust enough to separate Top Secret from Unclassified late in the last millennium. Their underlying technology became obsolete and they were not refreshed. Today there are no current implementations certified by TCSEC to that level of robust implementation. However, some less robust products exist.

- Amon Ott's RSBAC (Rule Set Based Access Control) provides a framework for Linux kernels that allows several different security policy / decision modules. One of the models implemented is Mandatory Access Control model. A general goal of RSBAC design was to try to reach (obsolete) Orange Book (TCSEC) B1 level. The model of mandatory access control used in RSBAC is mostly the same as in Unix System V/MLS, Version 1.2.1 (developed in 1989 by the National Computer Security Center of the USA with classification B1/TCSEC). RSBAC requires a set of patches to the stock kernel, which are maintained quite well by the project owner.

- An NSA research project called SELinux added a Mandatory Access Control architecture to the Linux Kernel, which was merged into the mainline version of Linux in August 2003. It utilizes a Linux 2.6 kernel feature called LSM (Linux Security Modules interface). Red Hat Enterprise Linux version 4 (and later versions) come with an SELinux-enabled kernel. Although SELinux is capable of restricting all processes in the system, the default *targeted* policy in RHEL confines the most vulnerable programs from the *unconfined domain* in which all other programs run. RHEL 5 ships 2 other binary policy types: *strict*, which attempts to implement least privilege, and *MLS*, which is based on *strict* and adds MLS labels. RHEL 5 contains additional MLS enhancements and received 2 LSPP/RBACPP/CAPP/EAL4+ certifications in June 2007.

- TOMOYO Linux is a lightweight MAC implementation for Linux and Embedded Linux, developed by NTT Data Corporation. It has been merged in Linux Kernel mainline version 2.6.30 in June 2009. Differently from the *label-based* approach used by SELinux, TOMOYO Linux performs a *pathname-based* Mandatory Access Control, separating security domains according to process invocation history, which describes the system behavior. Policy are described in terms of pathnames. A security domain is simply defined by a process call chain, and represented as a string. There are 4 modes: disabled, *learning*, permissive, enforcing. Administrators can assign different modes for different domains. TOMOYO Linux introduced the "learning" mode, in which the accesses occurred in the kernel are automatically analyzed and stored to generate MAC policy: this mode can be used as first step of policy writing, making it easy to customize later.

- SUSE Linux (now supported by Novell) and Ubuntu 7.10 have added a MAC implementation called AppArmor. AppArmor utilizes a Linux 2.6 kernel feature called LSM (Linux Security Modules interface). LSM provides a kernel API that allows modules of kernel code to govern CL (DAC ACL, access control lists). AppArmor is not capable of restricting all programs and is optionally in the Linux kernel as of version 2.6.36.

- Linux and many other Unix distributions have MAC for CPU (multi-ring), disk, and memory; while OS software may not manage privileges well, Linux became famous during the 1990s as being more secure and far more stable than non-Unix alternatives. Linux distributors disable MAC to being at best DAC for some devices – although this is true for any consumer electronics available today.

- Grsecurity is a patch for the Linux kernel providing a MAC implementation (precisely, it is a RBAC implementation). Hardened Gentoo offers a pre-patched kernel with grsecurity. grsecurity is not implemented via the LSM API.

- Microsoft Starting with Windows Vista and Server 2008 Windows incorporates Mandatory Integrity Control, which adds *Integrity Levels* (IL) to processes running in a login session. MIC restricts the access permissions of applications that are running under the same user account and which may be less trustworthy. Five integrity levels are defined: Low, Medium, High, System, and Trusted Installer. Processes started by a regular user gain a Medium IL; elevated processes have High IL. While processes inherit the integrity level of the process that spawned it, the integrity level can be customized on a per-process basis: e.g. IE7 and downloaded executables run with Low IL. Windows controls access to objects based on ILs, as well as for defining the boundary for window messages via User Interface Privilege Isolation. Named objects, including files, registry keys or other processes and threads, have an entry in the ACL governing access to them that defines the minimum IL of the process that can use the object. MIC enforces that a process can write to or delete an object only when its IL is equal to or higher than the object's IL. Furthermore, to prevent access to sensitive data in memory, processes can't open processes with a higher IL for read access.

- FreeBSD supports *Mandatory Access Control*, implemented as part of the TrustedBSD project. It was introduced in FreeBSD 5.0. Since FreeBSD 7.2, MAC support is enabled by default. The framework is extensible; various MAC modules implement policies such as Biba and Multi-Level Security.

- Sun's Trusted Solaris uses a mandatory and system-enforced access control mechanism (MAC), where clearances and labels are used to enforce a security policy. However note that the capability to manage labels does not imply the kernel strength to operate in Multi-Level Security mode. Access to the labels and control mechanisms are not robustly protected from corruption in protected domain maintained by a kernel. The applications a user runs are combined with the security label at which the user works in the session. Access to information, programs and devices are only weakly controlled.

- Apple's Mac OS X MAC framework is an implementation of the TrustedBSD MAC framework. A limited high-level sandboxing interface is provided by the command-line function sandbox_init.

- Oracle Label Security is an implementation of mandatory access control in the Oracle DBMS.

- SE-PostgreSQL is a work in progress as of 2008-01-27, providing integration into SE-Linux. It aims for integration into version 8.4, together with row-level restrictions.

- Trusted RUBIX is a mandatory access control enforcing DBMS that fully integrates with SE-Linux to restrict access to all database objects.

- Astra Linux OS developed for Russian Army has its own mandatory access control.

- Smack (*Simplified Mandatory Access Control Kernel*) is a Linux kernel security module that protects data and process interaction from malicious manipulation using a set of custom mandatory access control rules, with simplicity as its main design goal. It has been officially merged since the Linux 2.6.25 release.

Organisation-based Access Control

In computer security, organization-based access control (OrBAC) is an access control model first presented in 2003. The current approaches of the access control rest on the three entities (*subject, action, object*) to control the access the policy specifies that some subject has the permission to realize some action on some object.

OrBAC allows the policy designer to define a security policy independently of the implementation. The chosen method to fulfill this goal is the introduction of an abstract level.

- Subjects are abstracted into roles. A role is a set of subjects to which the same security rule apply.

- Similarly, an activity is a set of actions to which the same security rule apply.

- And, a view is a set of objects to which the same security rule apply.

Permission of a role to realize an activity on a view

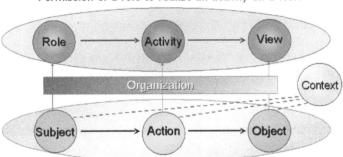

Permission of a subject to realize an action on an object

Each security policy is defined for and by an organization. Thus, the specification of the security policy is completely parameterized by the organization so that it is possible to handle simultaneously several security policies associated with different organizations. The model is not restricted to permissions, but also includes the possibility to specify prohibitions and obligations. From the three abstract entities (*roles, activities, views*), abstract privileges are defined. And from these abstract privileges, concrete privileges are derived.

OrBAC is context sensitive, so the policy could be expressed dynamically. Furthermore,

OrBAC owns concepts of hierarchy (*organization, role, activity, view, context*) and separation constraints. To design and implement security policies using the OrBAC model, the MotOrBAC tool has been developed. His simulation mode can be used to test a security policy. MotOrBAC also features a conflict detection function which helps the designer to find and solve conflicts.

Role-based Access Control

In computer systems security, role-based access control (RBAC) is an approach to restricting system access to authorized users. It is used by the majority of enterprises with more than 500 employees, and can implement mandatory access control (MAC) or discretionary access control (DAC). RBAC is sometimes referred to as role-based security.

Role-based-access-control (RBAC) is a policy neutral access control mechanism defined around roles and privileges. The components of RBAC such as role-permissions, user-role and role-role relationships make it simple to perform user assignments. A study by NIST has demonstrated that RBAC addresses many needs of commercial and government organizations. RBAC can be used to facilitate administration of security in large organizations with hundreds of users and thousands of permissions. Although RBAC is different from MAC and DAC access control frameworks, it can enforce these policies without any complication. Its popularity is evident from the fact that many products and businesses are using it directly or indirectly.

Design

Within an organization, roles are created for various job functions. The permissions to perform certain operations are assigned to specific roles. Members or staff (or other system users) are assigned particular roles, and through those role assignments acquire the computer permissions to perform particular computer-system functions. Since users are not assigned permissions directly, but only acquire them through their role (or roles), management of individual user rights becomes a matter of simply assigning appropriate roles to the user's account; this simplifies common operations, such as adding a user, or changing a user's department.

Three primary rules are defined for RBAC:

1. Role assignment: A subject can exercise a permission only if the subject has selected or been assigned a role.

2. Role authorization: A subject's active role must be authorized for the subject. With rule 1 above, this rule ensures that users can take on only roles for which they are authorized.

3. Permission authorization: A subject can exercise a permission only if the permission is authorized for the subject's active role. With rules 1 and 2, this rule ensures that users can exercise only permissions for which they are authorized.

Additional constraints may be applied as well, and roles can be combined in a hierarchy where higher-level roles subsume permissions owned by sub-roles.

With the concepts of role hierarchy and constraints, one can control RBAC to create or simulate lattice-based access control (LBAC). Thus RBAC can be considered to be a superset of LBAC.

When defining an RBAC model, the following conventions are useful:

- S = Subject = A person or automated agent

- R = Role = Job function or title which defines an authority level

- P = Permissions = An approval of a mode of access to a resource

- SE = Session = A mapping involving S, R and/or P

- SA = Subject Assignment

- PA = Permission Assignment

- RH = Partially ordered Role Hierarchy. RH can also be written: ≥ (The notation: x ≥ y means that x inherits the permissions of y.)

  o A subject can have multiple roles.

  o A role can have multiple subjects.

  o A role can have many permissions.

  o A permission can be assigned to many roles.

  o An operation can be assigned many permissions.

  o A permission can be assigned to many operations.

A constraint places a restrictive rule on the potential inheritance of permissions from opposing roles, thus it can be used to achieve appropriate separation of duties. For example, the same person should not be allowed to both create a login account and to authorize the account creation.

Thus, using set theory notation:

- $PA \subseteq P \times R$ and is a many to many permission to role assignment relation.

- $SA \subseteq S \times R$ and is a many to many subject to role assignment relation.

- $RH \subseteq R \times R$.

A subject may have *multiple* simultaneous sessions with/in different roles.

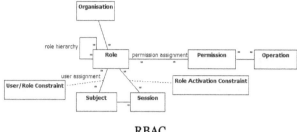

RBAC

Standardized Levels

The NIST/ANSI/INCITS RBAC standard (2004) recognizes three levels of RBAC:

1. core RBAC

2. hierarchical RBAC, which adds support for inheritance between roles

3. constrained RBAC, which adds separation of duties

Relation to other Models

RBAC is a flexible access control technology whose flexibility allows it to implement DAC or MAC. DAC with groups (e.g., as implemented in POSIX file systems) can emulate RBAC. MAC can simulate RBAC if the role graph is restricted to a tree rather than a partially ordered set.

Prior to the development of RBAC, the Bell-LaPadula (BLP) model was synonymous with MAC and file system permissions were synonymous with DAC. These were considered to be the only known models for access control: if a model was not BLP, it was considered to be a DAC model, and vice versa. Research in the late 1990s demonstrated that RBAC falls in neither category. Unlike context-based access control (CBAC), RBAC does not look at the message context (such as a connection's source). RBAC has also been criticized for leading to role explosion, a problem in large enterprise systems which require access control of finer granularity than what RBAC can provide as roles are inherently assigned to operations and data types. In resemblance to CBAC, an Entity-Relationship Based Access Control (ERBAC, although the same acronym is also used for modified RBAC systems, such as Extended Role-Based Access Control) system is able to secure instances of data by considering their association to the executing subject.

Comparing with ACL

RBAC differs from access control lists (ACLs), used in traditional discretionary access-control systems, in that it assigns permissions to specific operations with meaning in the organization, rather than to low level data objects. For example, an access control list could be used to grant or deny write access to a particular system file, but it would not dictate how that file could be changed. In an RBAC-based system, an operation might be to 'create a credit account' transaction in a financial application or to 'populate a blood sugar level test' record in a medical application. The assignment of permission to perform a particular operation is meaningful, because the operations are granular with meaning within the application. RBAC has been shown to be particularly well suited to separation of duties (SoD) requirements, which ensure that two or more people must be involved in authorizing critical operations. Necessary and sufficient conditions for safety of SoD in RBAC have been analyzed. An underlying principle of SoD is that no individual should be able to effect a breach of security through dual privilege. By extension, no person may hold a role that exercises audit, control or review authority over another, concurrently held role.

Then again, a "minimal RBAC Model", *RBACm*, can be compared with an ACL mechanism, *ACLg*, where only groups are permitted as entries in the ACL. Barkley (1997) showed that *RBACm* and *ACLg* are equivalent.

In modern SQL implementations, like ACL of the CakePHP framework, ACL also manage groups and inheritance in a hierarchy of groups. Under this aspect, specific "modern ACL" implementations can be compared with specific "modern RBAC" implementations, better than "old (file system) implementations".

For data interchange, and for "high level comparisons", ACL data can be translated to XACML.

Attribute based Access Control

Attribute-based access control or ABAC is a model which evolves from RBAC to consider additional attributes in addition to roles and groups. In ABAC, it is possible to use attributes of:

- the user e.g. citizenship, clearance,
- the resource e.g. classification, department, owner,
- the action, and
- the context e.g. time, location, IP.

ABAC is policy-based in the sense that it uses policies rather than static permissions to define what is allowed or what is not allowed.

Use and Availability

The use of RBAC to manage user privileges (computer permissions) within a single system or application is widely accepted as a best practice. A 2010 report prepared for NIST by the Research Triangle Institute analyzed the economic value of RBAC for enterprises, and estimated benefits per employee from reduced employee downtime, more efficient provisioning, and more efficient access control policy administration.

In an organization with a heterogeneous IT infrastructure and requirements that span dozens or hundreds of systems and applications, using RBAC to manage sufficient roles and assign adequate role memberships becomes extremely complex without hierarchical creation of roles and privilege assignments. Newer systems extend the older NIST RBAC model to address the limitations of RBAC for enterprise-wide deployments. The NIST model was adopted as a standard by INCITS as ANSI/INCITS 359-2004. A discussion of some of the design choices for the NIST model has also been published.

RBAC and Employees' Responsibilities Alignment

In Aligning Access Rights to Governance Needs with the Responsibility MetaModel (ReMMo) in the Frame of Enterprise Architecture an expressive Responsibility metamodel has been defined and allows representing the existing responsibilities at the business layer and, thereby, allows engineering the access rights required to perform these responsibilities, at the application layer. A method has been proposed to define the access rights more accurately, considering the alignment of the responsibility and RBAC.

References

- "What is identity-based licensing?". 10duke.com. 2016-02-02. Archived from the original on 2017-11-14. Retrieved 2017-11-14

- Abdulaziz Almehmadi and Khalil El-Khatib, "On the Possibility of Insider Threat Prevention Using Intent-Based Access Control (IBAC)", Systems Journal, IEEE , vol. PP, no. 99, pp. 1, 12, doi: 10.1109/JSYST.2015.2424677

- "Adobe Flash Media Rights Management Server 1.0 Overview for Microsoft Windows, Linux, and UNIX"(PDF). Workflows - Identity-based licensing. Adobe Systems. 2008-05-01. Archived (PDF) from the original on 2017-08-29. Retrieved 2017-11-14

- Ferreira, Ana; Chadwick, David; Farinha, Pedro; Correia, Ricardo; Zao, Gansen; Chiro, Rui; Antunes, Luis (2009). "How to Securely Break into RBAC: The BTG-RBAC Model". Computer Security Applications Conference (ACSAC). IEEE. pp. 23–31. doi:10.1109/ACSAC.2009.12

- Enrico, Sabbadin (2003-12-23). ".NET Identity and Principal Objects". informIT. Pearson Education. Archived from the original on 2017-11-14. Retrieved 2017-11-14

- Alberto Belussi; Barbara Catania; Eliseo Clementini; Elena Ferrari (2007). Spatial Data on the Web: Modeling and Management. Springer. p. 194. ISBN 978-3-540-69878-4

- "SP 800-162, Guide to Attribute Based Access Control (ABAC) Definition and Considerations" (PDF). NIST. 2014. Retrieved 2015-12-08

Fundamental Steps in Computer Security

3

A device can be protected from an attack, threat or vulnerability by adopting some countermeasures. This chapter is a compilation of topics that discuss different counter-measures such as security by design, vulnerability management, hardware protection mechanisms, etc. This chapter discusses in detail the theories and methodologies related to computer protection measures.

Security by Design

Secure by design, in software engineering, means that the software has been designed from the ground up to be secure. Malicious practices are taken for granted and care is taken to minimize impact when a security vulnerability is discovered or on invalid user input.

Generally, designs that work well do not rely on being secret. While not mandatory, proper security usually means that everyone is allowed to know and understand the design *because it is secure*. This has the advantage that many people are looking at the computer code, which improves the odds that any flaws will be found sooner. Attackers can also obtain the code, which makes it easier for them to find vulnerabilities as well.

Also, it is important that everything works with the least amount of privileges possible. For example, a Web server that runs as the administrative user ("root" or admin) can have the privilege to remove files and users that do not belong. A flaw in such a program could put the entire system at risk, whereas a Web server that runs inside an isolated environment and only has the privileges for required network and filesystem functions, cannot compromise the system it runs on unless the security around it is in itself also flawed.

Security by Design in Practice

Many things, especially input, should be distrusted by a secure design. A fault-tolerant program could even distrust its own internals.

Two examples of insecure design are allowing buffer overflows and format string vulnerabilities. The following C program demonstrates these flaws:

```c
#include <stdio.h>

int main()
{
    char a_chBuffer[100];

    printf("What is your name?\n");
    gets(a_chBuffer);
    printf("Hello, ");
    printf(a_chBuffer);
    printf("!\n");


    return 0;
}
```

Because the gets function in the C standard library does not stop writing bytes into buffer until it reads a newline character or EOF, typing more than 99 characters at the prompt constitutes a buffer overflow. Allocating 100 characters for buffer with the assumption that almost any given name from a user is no longer than 99 characters doesn't prevent the user from actually *typing* more than 99 characters. This can lead to arbitrary machine code execution.

The second flaw is that the program tries to print its input by passing it directly to the printf function. This function prints out its first argument, replacing conversion specifications (such as "%s", "%d", et cetera) sequentially with other arguments from its call stack as needed. Thus, if a malicious user entered "%d" instead of his name, the program would attempt to print out a non-existent integer value, and undefined behavior would occur.

A related mistake in Web programming is for an online script not to validate its parameters. For example, consider a script that fetches an article by taking a filename, which is then read by the script and parsed. Such a script might use the following hypothetical URL to retrieve an article about dog food:

```
http://www.example.net/cgi-bin/article.sh?name=dogfood.html
```

If the script has no input checking, instead trusting that the filename is always valid, a malicious user could forge a URL to retrieve configuration files from the webserver:

```
http://www.example.net/cgi-bin/article.sh?name=../../../../../etc/passwd
```

Depending on the script, this may expose the /etc/passwd file, which on Unix-like systems contains (among others) user IDs, their login names, home directory paths and shells.

Server/Client Architectures

In server/client architectures, the program at the other side may not be an authorised client and the client's server may not be an authorised server. Even when they are, a man-in-the-middle attack could compromise communications.

Often the easiest way to break the security of a client/server system is not to go head on to the security mechanisms, but instead to go around them. A man in the middle attack is a simple example of this, because you can use it to collect details to impersonate a user. Which is why it is important to consider encryption, hashing, and other security mechanisms in your design to ensure that information collected from a potential attacker won't allow access.

Another key feature to client-server security design is good coding practices. For example, following a known software design structure such as client and broker can help in designing a well-built structure with a solid foundation. Furthermore, if the software is to be modified in the future, it is even more important that it follows a logical foundation of separation between the client and server. This is because if a programmer comes in and cannot clearly understand the dynamics of the program they may end up adding or changing something that can add a security flaw. Even with the best design this is always a possibility, but the better standardized the design the less chance there is of this occurring.

Principle of Least Privilege

In information security, computer science, and other fields, the principle of least privilege (also known as the principle of minimal privilege or the principle of least authority) requires that in a particular abstraction layer of a computing environment, every module (such as a process, a user, or a program, depending on the subject) must be able to access only the information and resources that are necessary for its legitimate purpose.

Details

The principle means giving a user account only those privileges which are essential to perform its intended function. For example, a user account for the sole purpose of creating backups does not need to install software: hence, it has rights only to run backup and backup-related applications. Any other privileges, such as installing new software, are blocked. The principle applies also to a personal computer user who usually does work in a normal user account, and opens a privileged, password protected account (that is, a superuser) only when the situation absolutely demands it.

When applied to users, the terms *least user access* or *least-privileged user account* (LUA) are also used, referring to the concept that all user accounts at all times should run with as few privileges as possible, and also launch applications with as few privileges as possible.

The principle of least privilege is widely recognized as an important design consideration in enhancing the protection of data and functionality from faults (fault tolerance) and malicious behavior (computer security).

Benefits of the principle include:

- Better system stability. When code is limited in the scope of changes it can make to a system, it is easier to test its possible actions and interactions with other applications. In practice for example, applications running with restricted rights will not have access to perform operations that could crash a machine, or adversely affect other applications running on the same system.

- Better system security. When code is limited in the system-wide actions it may perform, vulnerabilities in one application cannot be used to exploit the rest of the machine. For example, Microsoft states "Running in standard user mode gives customers increased protection against inadvertent system-level damage caused by "shatter attacks" and malware, such as root kits, spyware, and undetectable viruses".

- Ease of deployment. In general, the fewer privileges an application requires the easier it is to deploy within a larger environment. This usually results from the first two benefits, applications that install device drivers or require elevated security privileges typically have additional steps involved in their deployment. For example, on Windows a solution with no device drivers can be run directly with no installation, while device drivers must be installed separately using the Windows installer service in order to grant the driver elevated privileges.

In practice, there exist multiple competing definitions of true least privilege. As program complexity increases at an exponential rate, so do the number of potential issues, rendering a predictive approach impractical. Examples include the values of variables it may process, addresses it will need, or the precise time such things will be required. Object capability systems allow, for instance, deferring granting a single-use privilege until the time when it will be used. Currently, the closest practical approach is to eliminate privileges that can be manually evaluated as unnecessary. The resulting set of privileges typically exceeds the true minimum required privileges for the process.

Another limitation is the granularity of control that the operating environment has over privileges for an individual process. In practice, it is rarely possible to control a process's access to memory, processing time, I/O device addresses or modes with the precision needed to facilitate only the precise set of privileges a process will require.

Implementation

The kernel always runs with maximum privileges since it is the operating system core and has hardware access. One of the principal responsibilities of an operating system, particularly a multi-user operating system, is management of the hardware's availability and requests to access it from running processes. When the kernel crashes, the mechanisms by which it maintains state also fail. Even if there is a way for the CPU to recover without a hard reset, the code that resumes execution is not always what it should be. Security continues to be enforced, but the operating system cannot respond to the failure properly because detection of the failure was not possible. This is because kernel execution either halted or the program counter resumed execution from somewhere in endless, and—usually—non-functional loop.

If execution picks up, after the crash, by loading and running trojan code, the author of the trojan code can usurp control of all processes. The principle of least privilege forces code to run with the lowest privilege/permission level possible so that, in the event this occurs—or even if code execution picks up from an unexpected location—what resumes the code execution would not have the ability to perform malicious or undesirable things. One method used to accomplish this can be implemented in the microprocessor hardware. In the Intel x86 architecture, the manufacturer designed four (ring 0 through ring 3) running "modes".

As implemented in some operating systems, processes execute with a potential privilege set and an active privilege set. Such privilege sets are inherited from the parent as determined by the semantics of *fork()*. An executable file that performs a privileged function—thereby technically constituting a component of the TCB, and concomitantly termed a trusted program or trusted process—may also be marked with a set of privileges, a logical extension of the notions of set user ID and set group ID. The inheritance of file privileges by a process are determined by the semantics of the *exec()* family of system calls. The precise manner in which potential process privileges, actual process privileges, and file privileges interact can become complex. In practice, least privilege is practiced by forcing a process to run with only those privileges required by the task. Adherence to this model is quite complex as well as error-prone.

Similar Principles

The Trusted Computer System Evaluation Criteria (TCSEC) concept of trusted computing base (TCB) minimization is a far more stringent requirement that is only applicable to the functionally strongest assurance classes, *viz.*, B3 and A1 (which are *evidentiarily* different but *functionally* identical).

Least privilege is often associated with privilege bracketing: that is, assuming necessary privileges at the last possible moment and dismissing them as soon as no longer strictly necessary, therefore ostensibly reducing fallout from erroneous code that unintentionally exploits more privilege than is merited. Least privilege has also been interpreted in the context of distribution of discretionary access control (DAC) permissions, for example asserting that giving user U read/write access to file F violates least privilege if U can complete his authorized tasks with only read permission.

Defense in Depth (Computing)

Defense in depth (also known as Castle Approach) is an information assurance (IA) concept in which multiple layers of security controls (defense) are placed throughout an information technology (IT) system. Its intent is to provide redundancy in the event a security control fails or a vulnerability is exploited that can cover aspects of *personnel, procedural, technical* and *physical* security for the duration of the system's life cycle.

Background

The idea behind the defense in depth approach is to defend a system against any particular attack using several independent methods. It is a layering tactic, conceived by the National Security Agency (NSA) as a comprehensive approach to information and electronic security.

Defense in depth is originally a military strategy that seeks to delay rather than prevent the advance of an attacker by yielding space to buy time. The placement of protection mechanisms, procedures and policies are intended to increase the dependability of an IT system, where multiple layers of defense prevent espionage and direct attacks against critical systems. In terms of computer network defense, defense in depth measures should not only prevent security breaches but also buy an organization time to detect and respond to an attack and so reduce and mitigate the consequences of a breach.

Controls

Defense in depth can be divided into three areas: Physical, Technical, and Administrative.

Physical Controls

Physical controls are anything that physically limits or prevents access to IT systems. Fences, guards, dogs, and CCTV systems and the like.

Technical Controls

Technical controls are hardware or software whose purpose is to protect systems and resources. Examples of technical controls would be disk encryption, fingerprint readers, and Windows Active Directory. Hardware technical controls differ from physical controls in that they prevent access to the contents of a system, but not the physical systems themselves.

Administrative Controls

Administrative controls are an organization's policies and procedures. Their purpose is to ensure that there is proper guidance available in regards to security and that regulations are met. They include things such as hiring practices, data handling procedures, and security requirements.

Full Disclosure (Computer Security)

In the field of computer security, independent researchers often discover flaws in software that can be abused to cause unintended behaviour, these flaws are called vulnerabilities. The process by which the analysis of these vulnerabilities is shared with third parties is the subject of much debate, and is referred to as the researcher's *disclosure policy*. Full disclosure is the practice of publishing analysis of software vulnerabilities as early as possible, making the data accessible to everyone without restriction. The primary purpose of widely disseminating information about vulnerabilities is so that potential victims are as knowledgeable as those who attack them.

In his essay on the topic, Bruce Schneier stated "Full disclosure -- the practice of making the details of security vulnerabilities public -- is a damned good idea. Public scrutiny is the only reliable way to improve security, while secrecy only makes us less secure". Leonard Rose, co-creator of an electronic mailing list that has superseded bugtraq to become the de facto forum for disseminating advisories, explains "We don't believe in security by obscurity, and as far as we know, full disclosure is the only way to ensure that everyone, not just the insiders, have access to the information we need."

The Vulnerability Disclosure Debate

The controversy around the public disclosure of sensitive information isn't new. The issue of full disclosure was first raised in the context of locksmithing, in a 19th-century controversy regarding whether weaknesses in lock systems should be kept secret in the locksmithing community, or revealed to the public. Today, there are three major disclosure policies under which most others can be categorized: Non Disclosure, Coordinated Disclosure, and Full Disclosure.

The major stakeholders in vulnerability research have their disclosure policies shaped by various motivations, it is not uncommon to observe campaigning, marketing or lobbying for their preferred policy to be adopted and chastising those who dissent. Many prominent security researchers favor full disclosure, whereas most vendors prefer coordinated disclosure. Non disclosure is generally favoured by commercial exploit vendors and blackhat hackers.

Coordinated Disclosure

Proponents of coordinated disclosure believe that software vendors have the right to control vulnerability information concerning their products. The primary tenet of coordinated disclosure is that nobody should be informed about a vulnerability until the software vendor gives their permission. While there are often exceptions or variations of this policy, distribution must initially be limited and vendors are given privileged access to nonpublic research. Advocates for coordinated disclosure often prefer the weighted but less-descriptive term "responsible disclosure" coined by Microsoft Security Manager Scott Culp in his essay "It's Time to End Information Anarchy" (referring to full disclosure). Microsoft later asked for the term to be phased out in favour of "coordinated disclosure".

Although the reasoning varies, many practitioners argue that end-users cannot benefit from access to vulnerability information without guidance or patches from the vendor, so the risks of sharing research with malicious actors is too great for too little benefit. As Microsoft explain, "[Coordinated disclosure] serves everyone's best interests by ensuring that customers receive comprehensive, high-quality updates for security vulnerabilities but are not exposed to malicious attacks while the update is being developed."

Full Disclosure

Full disclosure is the policy of publishing information on vulnerabilities without restriction as early as possible, making the information accessible to the general public without restriction. In general, proponents of full disclosure believe that the benefits of freely available vulnerability research outweigh the risks, whereas opponents prefer to limit the distribution.

The free availability of vulnerability information allows users and administrators to understand and react to vulnerabilities in their systems, and allows customers to pressure vendors to fix vulnerabilities that vendors may otherwise feel no incentive to solve. There are some fundamental problems with coordinated disclosure that full disclosure can resolve.

- If customers do not know about vulnerabilities, they cannot request patches, and vendors experience no economic incentive to correct vulnerabilities.

- Administrators cannot make informed decisions about the risks to their systems, as information on vulnerabilities is restricted.

- Malicious researchers who also know about the flaw, have a long period of time to continue exploiting the flaw.

Discovery of a specific flaw or vulnerability is not a mutually exclusive event, multiple researchers with differing motivations can and do discover the same flaws independently.

There is no standard way to make vulnerability information available to the public, researchers often use mailing lists dedicated to the topic, academic papers or industry conferences.

Non Disclosure

Non disclosure is the principle that no vulnerability information should be shared, or should only be shared under non-disclosure agreement (either contractually or informally).

Common proponents of non-disclosure include commercial exploit vendors, researchers who intend to exploit the flaws they find, and vendors who believe that any vulnerability information whatsoever assists attackers.

Debate

Arguments against Coordinated Disclosure

Researchers in favour of coordinated disclosure believe that users cannot make use of advanced knowledge of vulnerabilities without guidance from the vendor, and that the majority is best served by limiting distribution of vulnerability information. Advocates argue that low-skilled attackers can use this information to perform sophisticated attacks that would otherwise be beyond their ability, and the potential benefit does not outweigh the potential harm caused by malevolent actors. Only when the vendor has prepared guidance that even the most unsophisticated users can digest should the information be made public.

This argument presupposes that vulnerability discovery is a mutually exclusive event, that only one person can discover a vulnerability. There are many examples of vulnerabilities being discovered simultaneously, often being exploited in secrecy before discovery by other researchers. While there may exist users who cannot benefit from vulnerability information, full disclosure advocates believe this demonstrates a contempt for the intelligence of end users. While it's true that some users cannot benefit from vulnerability information, if they're concerned with the security of their networks they are in a position to hire an expert to assist them as you would hire a mechanic to help with a car.

Arguments against Non Disclosure

Non disclosure is typically used when a researcher intends to use knowledge of a vulnerability to attack computer systems operated by their enemies, or to trade knowledge of a vulnerability to a third party for profit, who will typically use it to attack their enemies.

Researchers practicing non disclosure are generally not concerned with improving security or protecting networks. However, some proponents argue that they simply do not want to assist vendors, and claim no intent to harm others.

While full and coordinated disclosure advocates declare similar goals and motivations, simply disagreeing on how best to achieve them, non disclosure is entirely incompatible.

Code Review

Code review is systematic examination (sometimes referred to as peer review) of computer source code. It is intended to find mistakes overlooked in software development, improving the overall quality of software. Reviews are done in various forms such as pair programming, informal walkthroughs, and formal inspections.

Introduction

Simple Definition

A code review is a process where two or more developers visually inspect a set of program code, typically, several times. The code can be a method, a class, or an entire program. The main code-review objectives are:

1. Best Practice ~ A more efficient, less error-prone, or more elegant way to accomplish a given task.

2. Error Detection ~ Discovering logical or transitional errors.

3. Vulnerability Exposure ~ Identifying and averting common vulnerabilities like Cross-Site Scripting [XSS], Injection, Buffer Overflow, Excessive Disclosure, etc. Although many controls are inapplicable and can be ignored, a STIG [e.g., Application Security STIG 4.3] provides an excellent vulnerability checklist.

4. Malware Discovery ~ This often-overlooked and very special code-review objective looks for segments of code that appear extraneous, questionable, or flat-out weird. The intent is to discover back doors, Trojans, and time bombs. In today's world malevolent code is a very real threat and should not be overlooked, especially by Government agencies.

Artifacts

The most important byproduct of a properly conducted code review is a written record describing:

- Who ~ Names of those involved in the Review.

- When ~ Date and time the Review was conducted.

- Why ~ Best-Practice, Error Detection, Vulnerability Exposure, Malware Discovery or a combination.

- Where ~ Office number or other location identifier.

- What ~ Name of the class, method, or program, plus line ranges and other particulars specific to the reviewed code.

- Result ~ What was disclosed during the course of the Review.

Details

Code reviews can often find and remove common vulnerabilities such as format string exploits, race conditions, memory leaks and buffer overflows, thereby improving software security. Online software repositories based on Subversion (with Redmine or Trac), Mercurial, Git or others allow groups of individuals to collaboratively review code. Additionally, specific tools for collaborative code review can facilitate the code review process.

Automated code reviewing software lessens the task of reviewing large chunks of code on the developer by systematically checking source code for known vulnerabilities. A 2012 study by VDC Research reports that 17.6% of the embedded software engineers surveyed currently use automated tools for peer code review and 23.7% expect to use them within 2 years.

Capers Jones' ongoing analysis of over 12,000 software development projects showed that the latent defect discovery rate of formal inspection is in the 60-65% range. For informal inspection, the figure is less than 50%. The latent defect discovery rate for most forms of testing is about 30%.

Code review rates should be between 200 and 400 lines of code per hour. Inspecting and reviewing more than a few hundred lines of code per hour for critical software (such as safety critical embedded software) may be too fast to find errors. Industry data indicates that code reviews can accomplish at most an 85% defect removal rate with an average rate of about 65%.

The types of defects detected in code reviews have also been studied. Empirical studies provided evidence that up to 75% of code review defects affect software evolvability rather than functionality, making code reviews an excellent tool for software companies with long product or system life cycles.

Types

Code review practices fall into two main categories: formal code review and lightweight code review.

Formal code review, such as a Fagan inspection, involves a careful and detailed process with multiple participants and multiple phases. Formal code reviews are the traditional method of review, in which software developers attend a series of meetings and review code line by line, usually using printed copies of the material. Formal inspections are extremely thorough and have been proven effective at finding defects in the code under review.

Lightweight code review typically requires less overhead than formal code inspections. Lightweight reviews are often conducted as part of the normal development process:

- Over-the-shoulder – one developer looks over the author's shoulder as the latter walks through the code.

- Email pass-around – source code management system emails code to reviewers automatically after checkin is made.

- Pair programming – two authors develop code together at the same workstation, as is common in Extreme Programming.

- Tool-assisted code review – authors and reviewers use software tools, informal ones such as pastebins and IRC, or specialized tools designed for peer code review.

Some of these are also known as walkthrough (informal) or "critique" (fast and informal) code review types.

Many teams that eschew traditional, formal code review use one of the above forms of lightweight review as part of their normal development process. A code review case study published in the book *Best Kept Secrets of Peer Code Review* found that lightweight reviews uncovered as many bugs as formal reviews, but were faster and more cost-effective in contradiction to the study done by Capers Jones.

Criticism

Historically, formal code reviews have required a considerable investment in preparation for the review event and execution time. Use of code analysis tools can support this activity. Especially tools that work in the IDE as they provide direct feedback to developers of coding standard compliance.

Unit Testing

In computer programming, unit testing is a software testing method by which individual units of source code, sets of one or more computer program modules together with associated control data, usage procedures, and operating procedures, are tested to determine whether they are fit for use.

Description

Intuitively, one can view a unit as the smallest testable part of an application. In procedural programming, a unit could be an entire module, but it is more commonly an individual function or procedure. In object-oriented programming, a unit is often an entire interface, such as a class, but could be an individual method. Unit tests are short code fragments created by programmers or occasionally by white box testers during the development process. It forms the basis for component testing.

Ideally, each test case is independent from the others. Substitutes such as method stubs, mock objects, fakes, and test harnesses can be used to assist testing a module in isolation. Unit tests are typically written and run by software developers to ensure that code meets its design and behaves as intended.

Because some classes may have references to other classes, testing a class can frequently spill over into testing another class. A common example of this is classes that depend on a database: in order to test the class, the tester often writes code that interacts with the database. This is a mistake, because a unit test should usually not go outside of its own class boundary, and especially should not cross such process/ network boundaries because this can introduce unacceptable performance problems to the unit test-suite. Crossing such unit boundaries turns unit tests into integration tests, and when such test cases fail, it may be unclear which component is causing the failure. Instead, the software developer should create an abstract interface around the database queries, and then implement that interface with their own mock object. By abstracting this necessary attachment from the code (temporarily reducing the net effective coupling), the independent unit can be more thoroughly tested than may have been previously achieved. This results in a higher-quality unit that is also more maintainable.

Techniques

Unit testing is commonly automated, but may still be performed manually. The IEEE does not favor one over the other. The objective in unit testing is to isolate a unit and validate its correctness. A manual approach to unit testing may employ a step-by-step instructional document. However, automation is efficient for achieving this, and enables the many benefits listed in this topic. Conversely, if not planned carefully, a careless manual unit test case may execute as an integration test case that involves many software components, and thus preclude the achievement of most if not all of the goals established for unit testing.

To fully realize the effect of isolation while using an automated approach, the unit or code body under test is executed within a framework outside of its natural environment. In other words, it is executed outside of the product or calling context for which it was originally created. Testing in such an isolated manner reveals unnecessary dependencies between the code being tested and other units or data spaces in the product. These dependencies can then be eliminated.

Using an automation framework, the developer codes criteria, or a test oracle or result that is known to be good, into the test to verify the unit's correctness. During test case execution, the framework logs tests that fail any criterion. Many frameworks will also automatically flag these failed test cases and report them in a summary. Depending upon the severity of a failure, the framework may halt subsequent testing.

As a consequence, unit testing is traditionally a motivator for programmers to create decoupled and cohesive code bodies. This practice promotes healthy habits in software development. Design patterns, unit testing, and refactoring often work together so that the best solution may emerge.

Parameterized Unit Testing

Parameterized unit tests (PUTs) are tests that take parameters. Unlike traditional unit tests, which are usually closed methods, PUTs take any set of parameters. PUTs have been supported by TestNG, JUnit and various .NET test frameworks. Suitable parameters for the unit tests may be supplied manually or in some cases are automatically generated by the test framework. Testing tools like QuickCheck exist to generate test inputs for PUTs.

Advantages

The goal of unit testing is to isolate each part of the program and show that the individual parts are correct. A unit test provides a strict, written contract that the piece of code must satisfy. As a result, it affords several benefits.

Find Problems Early

Unit testing finds problems early in the development cycle. This includes both bugs in the programmer's implementation and flaws or missing parts of the specification for the unit. The process of writing a thorough set of tests forces the author to think through inputs, outputs, and error conditions, and thus more crisply define the unit's desired behavior. The cost of finding a bug before coding begins or when the code is first written is considerably lower than the cost of detecting, identifying, and correcting the bug later; bugs may also cause problems for the end-users of the software. Code can be impossible or difficult to test if poorly written, thus unit testing can force developers to structure functions and objects in better ways.

In test-driven development (TDD), which is frequently used in both extreme programming and scrum, unit tests are created before the code itself is written. When the tests pass, that code is considered complete. The same unit tests are run against that function frequently as the larger code base is developed either as the code is changed or via an automated process with the build. If the unit tests fail, it is considered to be a bug either in the changed code or the tests themselves. The unit tests then allow the location of the fault or failure to be easily traced. Since the unit tests alert the development team of the problem before handing the code off to testers or clients, it is still early in the development process.

Facilitates Change

Unit testing allows the programmer to refactor code or upgrade system libraries at a later date, and make sure the module still works correctly (e.g., in regression testing). The procedure is to write test cases for all functions and methods so that whenever a change causes a fault, it can be quickly identified. Unit tests detect changes which may break a design contract.

Simplifies Integration

Unit testing may reduce uncertainty in the units themselves and can be used in a bottom-up testing style approach. By testing the parts of a program first and then testing the sum of its parts, integration testing becomes much easier.

Documentation

Unit testing provides a sort of living documentation of the system. Developers looking to learn what functionality is provided by a unit, and how to use it, can look at the unit tests to gain a basic understanding of the unit's interface (API).

Unit test cases embody characteristics that are critical to the success of the unit. These characteristics can indicate appropriate/inappropriate use of a unit as well as negative behaviors that are to be trapped by the unit. A unit test case, in and of itself, documents these critical characteristics, although many software development environments do not rely solely upon code to document the product in development.

Design

When software is developed using a test-driven approach, the combination of writing the unit test to specify the interface plus the refactoring activities performed after the test is passing, may take the place of formal design. Each unit test can be seen as a design element specifying classes, methods, and observable behaviour.

Disadvantages

Decision Problem

Testing will not catch every error in the program, because it cannot evaluate every execution path in any but the most trivial programs. This problem is a superset of the halting problem, which is undecidable. The same is true for unit testing. Additionally, unit testing by definition only tests the functionality of the units themselves. Therefore, it will not catch integration errors or broader system-level errors (such as functions performed across multiple units, or non-functional test areas such as performance). Unit testing should be done in conjunction with other software testing activities, as they can only show the presence or absence of particular errors; they cannot prove a complete absence of errors. To guarantee correct behavior for every execution path and every possible input, and ensure the absence of errors, other techniques are required, namely the application of formal methods to proving that a software component has no unexpected behavior.

Not Integration Testing

An elaborate hierarchy of unit tests does not equal integration testing. Integration with peripheral units should be included in integration tests, but not in unit tests. Integration testing typically still relies heavily on humans testing manually; high-level or global-scope testing can be difficult to automate, such that manual testing often appears faster and cheaper.

Combinatorial Problem

Software testing is a combinatorial problem. For example, every Boolean decision statement requires at least two tests: one with an outcome of "true" and one with an outcome of "false". As a result, for every line of code written, programmers often need 3 to 5 lines of test code. This obviously takes time and its investment may not be worth the effort. There are also many problems that cannot easily be tested at all – for example those that are nondeterministic or involve multiple threads. In addition, code for a unit test is likely to be at least as buggy as the code it is testing. Fred Brooks in *The Mythical Man-Month* quotes: "Never go to sea with two chronometers; take one or three." Meaning, if two chronometers contradict, how do you know which one is correct?

Realism

Another challenge related to writing the unit tests is the difficulty of setting up realistic and useful tests. It is necessary to create relevant initial conditions so the part of the application being tested behaves like part of the complete system. If these initial conditions are not set correctly, the test will not be exercising the code in a realistic context, which diminishes the value and accuracy of unit test results.

Record Keeping

To obtain the intended benefits from unit testing, rigorous discipline is needed throughout the software development process. It is essential to keep careful records not only of the tests that have been performed, but also of all changes that have been made to the source code of this or any other unit in the software. Use of a version control system is essential. If a later version of the unit fails a particular test that it had previously passed, the version-control software can provide a list of the source code changes (if any) that have been applied to the unit since that time.

Sustainability Challenges

It is also essential to implement a sustainable process for ensuring that test case failures are reviewed regularly and addressed immediately. If such a process is not implemented and ingrained into the team's workflow, the application will evolve out of sync with the unit test suite, increasing false positives and reducing the effectiveness of the test suite.

Platform Differences

Unit testing embedded system software presents a unique challenge: Because the software is being developed on a different platform than the one it will eventually run on, you cannot readily run a test program in the actual deployment environment, as is possible with desktop programs.

External Work

Unit tests tend to be easiest when a method has input parameters and some output. It is not as easy to create unit tests when a major function of the method is to interact with something external to the application. For example, a method that will work with a database might require a mock up of database interactions to be created, which probably won't be as comprehensive as the real database interactions.

Example

Here is a set of test cases that specify a number of elements of the implementation. First, that there must be an interface called Adder, and an implementing class with a zero-argument constructor called AdderImpl. It goes on to assert that the Adder interface should have a method called add, with two integer parameters, which returns another integer. It also specifies the behaviour of this method for a small range of values over a number of test methods.

```
import static org.junit.Assert.*;


import org.junit.Test;


public class TestAdder {


    @Test
```

```
public void testSumPositiveNumbersOneAndOne() {

    Adder adder = new AdderImpl();

    assert(adder.add(1, 1) == 2);

}


// can it add the positive numbers 1 and 2?
@Test
public void testSumPositiveNumbersOneAndTwo() {

    Adder adder = new AdderImpl();

    assert(adder.add(1, 2) == 3);

}


// can it add the positive numbers 2 and 2?
@Test
public void testSumPositiveNumbersTwoAndTwo() {

    Adder adder = new AdderImpl();

    assert(adder.add(2, 2) == 4);

}


// is zero neutral?
@Test
public void testSumZeroNeutral() {

    Adder adder = new AdderImpl();

    assert(adder.add(0, 0) == 0);

}


// can it add the negative numbers -1 and -2?
@Test
public void testSumNegativeNumbers() {

    Adder adder = new AdderImpl();

    assert(adder.add(-1, -2) == -3);

}
```

```
    // can it add a positive and a negative?
    @Test
    public void testSumPositiveAndNegative() {
        Adder adder = new AdderImpl();
        assert(adder.add(-1, 1) == 0);
    }


    // how about larger numbers?
    @Test
    public void testSumLargeNumbers() {
        Adder adder = new AdderImpl();
        assert(adder.add(1234, 988) == 2222);
    }


}
```

In this case the unit tests, having been written first, act as a design document specifying the form and behaviour of a desired solution, but not the implementation details, which are left for the programmer. Following the "do the simplest thing that could possibly work" practice, the easiest solution that will make the test pass is shown below.

```
interface Adder {
    int add(int a, int b);
}
class AdderImpl implements Adder {
    public int add(int a, int b) {
        return a + b;
    }
}
```

As Executable Specifications

Using unit-tests as a design specification has one significant advantage over other design methods: The design document (the unit-tests themselves) can itself be used to verify the implementation. The tests will never pass unless the developer implements a solution according to the design.

Unit testing lacks some of the accessibility of a diagrammatic specification such as a

UML diagram, but they may be generated from the unit test using automated tools. Most modern languages have free tools (usually available as extensions to IDEs). Free tools, like those based on the xUnit framework, outsource to another system the graphical rendering of a view for human consumption.

Applications

Extreme Programming

Unit testing is the cornerstone of extreme programming, which relies on an automated unit testing framework. This automated unit testing framework can be either third party, e.g., xUnit, or created within the development group.

Extreme programming uses the creation of unit tests for test-driven development. The developer writes a unit test that exposes either a software requirement or a defect. This test will fail because either the requirement isn't implemented yet, or because it intentionally exposes a defect in the existing code. Then, the developer writes the simplest code to make the test, along with other tests, pass.

Most code in a system is unit tested, but not necessarily all paths through the code. Extreme programming mandates a "test everything that can possibly break" strategy, over the traditional "test every execution path" method. This leads developers to develop fewer tests than classical methods, but this isn't really a problem, more a restatement of fact, as classical methods have rarely ever been followed methodically enough for all execution paths to have been thoroughly tested. Extreme programming simply recognizes that testing is rarely exhaustive (because it is often too expensive and time-consuming to be economically viable) and provides guidance on how to effectively focus limited resources.

Crucially, the test code is considered a first class project artifact in that it is maintained at the same quality as the implementation code, with all duplication removed. Developers release unit testing code to the code repository in conjunction with the code it tests. Extreme programming's thorough unit testing allows the benefits mentioned above, such as simpler and more confident code development and refactoring, simplified code integration, accurate documentation, and more modular designs. These unit tests are also constantly run as a form of regression test.

Unit testing is also critical to the concept of Emergent Design. As emergent design is heavily dependent upon refactoring, unit tests are an integral component.

Unit Testing Frameworks

Unit testing frameworks are most often third-party products that are not distributed as part of the compiler suite. They help simplify the process of unit testing, having been developed for a wide variety of languages. Examples of testing frameworks include open source solutions such as the various code-driven testing frameworks known collectively as xUnit, and proprietary/commercial solutions such as Cantata for C/C++Typemock Isolator.NET/Isolator++, TBrun, JustMock, Parasoft Development Testing (Jtest, Parasoft C/C++test, dotTEST), Testwell CTA++ and VectorCAST/C++.

It is generally possible to perform unit testing without the support of a specific framework by writing client code that exercises the units under test and uses assertions, exception handling, or other control flow mechanisms to signal failure. Unit testing without a framework is valuable in that there is a barrier to entry for the adoption of unit testing; having scant unit tests is hardly better than having none at all, whereas once a framework is in place, adding unit tests becomes relatively easy. In some frameworks many advanced unit test features are missing or must be hand-coded.

Language-level Unit Testing Support

Some programming languages directly support unit testing. Their grammar allows the direct declaration of unit tests without importing a library (whether third party or standard). Additionally, the boolean conditions of the unit tests can be expressed in the same syntax as boolean expressions used in non-unit test code, such as what is used for if and while statements.

Languages with built-in unit testing support include:

- Apex
- Cobra
- Crystal
- D
- Go
- LabVIEW
- MATLAB
- Python
- Ruby
- Rust

Some languages without built-in unit-testing support have very good unit testing libraries/frameworks. Those languages include:

- ABAP
- C#
- Clojure
- Elixir
- Java
- JavaScript
- Obix
- Objective-C
- PHP
- PowerShell
- Racket
- Scala
- tcl
- Visual Basic .NET

Capability-based Security

Capability-based security is a concept in the design of secure computing systems, one of the existing security models. A capability (known in some systems as a key) is a communicable, unforgeable token of authority. It refers to a value that references an object along with an associated set of access rights. A user program on a capability-based operating system must use a capability to access an object. Capability-based security refers to the principle of designing user programs such that they directly share capabilities with each other according to the principle of least privilege, and to the operating system infrastructure necessary to make such transactions efficient and secure. Capability-based security is to be contrasted with an approach that uses hierarchical protection domains.

Although most operating systems implement a facility which resembles capabilities, they typically do not provide enough support to allow for the exchange of capabilities among possibly mutually untrusting entities to be the primary means of granting and distributing access rights throughout the system. A capability-based system, in contrast, is designed with that goal in mind.

Capabilities as discussed in this topic should not be confused with POSIX 1e/2c "Capabilities". The latter are coarse-grained privileges that cannot be transferred between processes.

Introduction

Capabilities achieve their objective of improving system security by being used in place of forgeable references. A forgeable reference (for example, a path name) identifies an object, but does not specify which access rights are appropriate for that object and the user program which holds that reference. Consequently, any attempt to access the referenced object must be validated by the operating system, based on the ambient authority of the requesting program, typically via the use of an access control list (ACL). Instead, in a system with capabilities, the mere fact that a user program possesses that capability entitles it to use the referenced object in accordance with the rights that are specified by that capability. In theory, a system with capabilities removes the need for any access control list or similar mechanism by giving all entities all and only the capabilities they will actually need.

A capability is typically implemented as a privileged data structure that consists of a section that specifies access rights, and a section that uniquely identifies the object to be accessed. The user does not access the data structure or object directly, but instead via a handle. In practice, it is used much like a file descriptor in a traditional operating system (a traditional handle), but to access every object on the system. Capabilities are typically stored by the operating system in a list, with some mechanism in place to prevent the program from directly modifying the contents of the capability (so as to forge access rights or change the object it points to). Some systems have also been based on capability-based addressing (hardware support for capabilities), such as Plessey System 250.

Programs possessing capabilities can perform functions on them, such as passing them on to other programs, converting them to a less-privileged version, or deleting them. The operating system must ensure that only specific operations can occur to the capabilities in the system, in order to maintain the integrity of the security policy.

Examples

A capability is defined to be a protected object reference which, by virtue of its possession by a user process, grants that process the capability (hence the name) to interact with an object in certain ways. Those ways might include reading data associated with an object, modifying the object, executing the data in the object as a process, and other conceivable access rights. The capability logically consists of a reference that uniquely identifies a particular object and a set of one or more of these rights.

Suppose that, in a user process's memory space, there exists the following string:

```
/etc/passwd
```

Although this identifies a unique object on the system, it does not specify access rights and hence is not a capability. Suppose there is instead the following two values:

```
/etc/passwd
```

```
O_RDWR
```

This identifies an object along with a set of access rights. It, however, is still not a capability because the user process's *possession* of these values says nothing about whether that access would actually be legitimate.

Now suppose that the user program successfully executes the following statement:

```
int fd = open("/etc/passwd", O_RDWR);
```

The variable fd now contains the index of a file descriptor in the process's file descriptor table. This file descriptor *is* a capability. Its existence in the process's file descriptor table is sufficient to know that the process does indeed have legitimate access to the object. A key feature of this arrangement is that the file descriptor table is in kernel memory and cannot be directly manipulated by the user program.

Sharing between Processes

In traditional operating systems, programs often communicate with each other and with storage using references like those in the first two examples. Path names are often passed as command-line parameters, sent via sockets, and stored on disk. These references are not capabilities, and must be validated before they can be used. In these systems, a central question is "on whose *authority* is a given reference to be evaluated?" This becomes a critical issue especially for processes which must act on behalf of two different authority-bearing entities. They become susceptible to a programming error known as the confused deputy problem, very frequently resulting in a security hole.

In a capability-based system, the capabilities themselves are passed between processes and storage using a mechanism that is known by the operating system to maintain the integrity of those capabilities.

One novel approach to solving this problem involves the use of an orthogonally persistent operating system. (This was realised in the Flex machine.). In such a system, there is no need for entities to be discarded and their capabilities be invalidated, and hence require an ACL-like mechanism to restore those capabilities at a later time. The operating system maintains the integrity and security of the capabilities contained within all storage, both volatile and nonvolatile, at all times; in part by performing all serialization tasks by itself, rather than requiring user programs to do so, as is the case in most operating systems. Because user programs are relieved of this responsibility, there is no need to trust them to reproduce only legal capabilities, nor to validate requests for access using an access control mechanism.

POSIX Capabilities

POSIX draft 1003.1e specifies a concept of permissions called "capabilities". However, POSIX capabilities differ from capabilities in this topic—POSIX capability is not associated with any object; a process having CAP_NET_BIND_SERVICE capability can listen on any TCP port under 1024. In contrast, Capsicum capabilities on FreeBSD and Linux hybridize a true capability-system model with the UNIX design and POSIX API. Capsicum capabilities are a refined form of file descriptor, a delegable right between processes and additional object types beyond classic POSIX, such as processes, can be referenced via capabilities. In Capsicum capability mode, processes are unable to utilize global namespaces (such as the filesystem namespace) to look up objects, and must instead inherit or be delegated them.

Implementations

Research and commercial systems employing capability-based security include the following:

- Tahoe-LAFS - open-source capability-based filesystem

- GNOSIS

  o KeyKOS

- ▪ EROS - The Extremely Reliable Operating System - KeyKOS successor
  - ◆ CapROS - EROS successor, project to further develop EROS code base for commercial use
  - ◆ Coyotos - EROS successor, for research
- Cambridge CAP computer
- Carnegie Mellon University C.mmp with Hydra (operating system)
- Carnegie Mellon University CM* with StarOS
- IBM System/38 and AS/400
- Intel iAPX 432
- Plessey System 250
- Flex
- L4 microkernel - Open Kernel Labs - OKL4 and NICTA - seL4, TU-Dresden - Fiasco.OC
- Amoeba distributed operating system
- FreeBSD Capsicum framework
- Google Fuchsia

Vulnerability Management

Vulnerability Scanner

A vulnerability scanner is a computer program designed to assess computers, computer systems, networks or applications for known weaknesses. In plain words, these scanners are used to discover the weak points or poorly constructed parts. It's utilized for the identification and detection of vulnerabilities relating to mis-configured assets or flawed software that resides on a network-based asset such as a firewall, router, web server, application server, etc. Modern vulnerability scanners will allow for both authenticated and unauthenticated scans to occur. Modern scanners are typically available as SaaS (Software as a Service) by providers over the internet as a web application and the amount of host information is vast. The modern vulnerability scanner has the capabilities to customize vulnerability reports, installed software, open ports, certificates and much other host information that can be queried by users to increase network security.

- Authenticated Scans allow for the scanner to directly access network based assets using remote administrative protocols such as secure shell (SSH) or remote desktop protocol (RDP) and authenticate using provided system credentials. This allows the vulnerability scanner to access low-level data, such as specific services and configuration details of the host operating system. It's then able to provide detailed and accurate information about the operating system and installed software, including configuration issues and missing security patches.

- Unauthenticated Scans is a method that can result in a high number of false positives and is unable to provide detailed information about the assets operating system and installed software. This method is typically used by threat actors or security analyst trying determine the security posture of externally accessible assets.

Types

- Port scanner (e.g. Nmap)

- Network vulnerability scanner (e.g. Nessus, SAINT, OpenVAS, INFRA Security Scanner, Nexpose)

- Web application security scanner (e.g. Nikto, Acunetix, Burp Suite, OWASP ZAP, w3af)

- Database security scanner

- Host based vulnerability scanner (Lynis)

- ERP security scanner

- Single vulnerability tests

Penetration Test

A penetration test, colloquially known as a pen test, is an authorized simulated attack on a computer system, performed to evaluate the security of the system. The test is performed to identify both weaknesses (also referred to as vulnerabilities), including the potential for unauthorized parties to gain access to the system's features and data, as well as strengths, enabling a full risk assessment to be completed.

The process typically identifies the target systems and a particular goal—then reviews available information and undertakes various means to attain the goal. A penetration test target may be a white box (which provides background and system information) or black box (which provides only basic or no information except the company name). A penetration test can help determine whether a system is vulnerable to attack, if the defenses were sufficient, and which defenses (if any) the test defeated.

Security issues that the penetration test uncovers should be reported to the system owner. Penetration test reports may also assess potential impacts to the organization and suggest countermeasures to reduce risk.

The goals of a penetration test vary depending on the type of approved activity for any given engagement with the primary goal focused on finding vulnerabilities that could be exploited by a nefarious actor, and informing the client of those vulnerabilities along with recommended mitigation strategies.

Penetration tests are a component of a full security audit. For example, the Payment Card Industry Data Security Standard requires penetration testing on a regular schedule, and after system changes.

Flaw hypothesis methodology is a systems analysis and penetration prediction technique where a list of hypothesized flaws in a software system are compiled through analysis of the specifications and documentation for the system. The list of hypothesized flaws is then prioritized on the basis of the estimated probability that a flaw actually exists, and on the ease of exploiting it to the extent of control or compromise. The prioritized list is used to direct the actual testing of the system.

Tools

A wide variety of security assessment tools are available to assist with penetration testing, including free-of-charge, free software, and commercial software.

Specialized OS Distributions

Several operating system distributions are geared towards penetration testing. Such distributions typically contain a pre-packaged and pre-configured set of tools. The penetration tester does not have to hunt down each individual tool, which might increase the risk complications—such as compile errors, dependencies issues, configuration errors. Also, acquiring additional tools may not be practical in the tester's context.

Popular penetration testing OS examples include:

- Kali Linux (replaced BackTrack December 2012) based on Debian

- Parrot Security OS based on Debian

- BlackArch based on ArchLinux

- BackBox based on Ubuntu

- Pentoo based on Gentoo

- WHAX based on Slackware

Many other specialized operating systems facilitate penetration testing—each more or less dedicated to a specific field of penetration testing.

A number of Linux distributions include known OS and Application vulnerabilities, and can be deployed as *targets*. Such systems help new security professionals try the latest security tools in a lab environment. Examples include Damn Vulnerable Linux (DVL), the OWASP Web Testing Environment (WTW), and Metasploitable.

Software Frameworks

- Burp Suite

- Metasploit Project

- Nmap

- OWASP ZAP

- W3af

Automated Testing Tools

The process of penetration testing may be simplified as two parts:

1. Discover vulnerabilities—combinations of legal operations that let the tester execute an illegal operation

2. Exploit the vulnerabilities—specify the illegal operation

Once the attacker has exploited one vulnerability they may gain access to other machines so the process repeats i.e. look for new vulnerabilities and attempt to exploit them. This process is referred to as pivoting.

Vulnerabilities

Legal operations that let the tester execute an illegal operation include unescaped SQL commands, unchanged salts in source-visible projects, human relationships, and old hash or crypto functions. A single flaw may not be enough to enable a critically serious exploit. Leveraging multiple known flaws and shaping the payload in a way that appears as a valid operation is almost always required. Metasploit provides a ruby library for common tasks, and maintains a database of known exploits.

Under budget and time constraints, fuzzing is a common technique that discovers vulnerabilities. It aims to get an un-handled error through random input. The tester uses random input to access less often used code paths. Well-trodden code paths are usually free of errors. Errors are useful because they either expose more information, such as HTTP server crashes with full info trace-backs—or are directly usable, such as buffer overflows.

Imagine a website has 100 text input boxes. A few are vulnerable to SQL injections on certain strings. Submitting random strings to those boxes for a while hopefully hits the bugged code path. The error shows itself as a broken HTML page half rendered because of an SQL error. In this case, only text boxes are treated as input streams. However, software systems have many possible input streams, such as cookie and session data, the uploaded file stream, RPC channels, or memory. Errors can happen in any of these input streams. The test goal is to first get an un-handled error, and then understand the flaw based on the failed test case. Testers write an automated tool to test their understanding of the flaw until it is correct. After that, it may become obvious how to package the payload so that the target system triggers its execution. If this is not viable, one can hope that another error produced by the fuzzer yields more fruit. The use of a fuzzer saves time by not checking adequate code paths where exploits are unlikely.

Payload

The illegal operation, or payload in Metasploit terminology, can include functions for logging keystrokes, taking screenshots, installing adware, stealing credentials, or altering data. Some companies maintain large databases of known exploits and provide products that automatically test target systems for vulnerabilities:

- Metasploit

- Nessus

- Nmap

- OpenVAS

- W3af

Reducing Vulnerabilities

Formal Verification

In the context of hardware and software systems, formal verification is the act of proving or disproving the correctness of intended algorithms underlying a system with respect to a certain formal specification or property, using formal methods of mathematics.

Formal verification can be helpful in proving the correctness of systems such as: cryptographic protocols, combinational circuits, digital circuits with internal memory, and software expressed as source code.

The verification of these systems is done by providing a formal proof on an abstract mathematical model of the system, the correspondence between the mathematical model and the nature of the system being otherwise known by construction. Examples of mathematical objects often used to model systems are: finite state machines, labelled transition systems, Petri nets, vector addition systems, timed automata, hybrid automata, process algebra, formal semantics of programming languages such as operational semantics, denotational semantics, axiomatic semantics and Hoare logic.

Approaches

One approach and formation is model checking, which consists of a systematically exhaustive exploration of the mathematical model (this is possible for finite models, but also for some infinite models where infinite sets of states can be effectively represented finitely by using abstraction or taking advantage of symmetry). Usually this consists of exploring all states and transitions in the model, by using smart and domain-specific abstraction techniques to consider whole groups of states in a single operation and reduce computing time. Implementation techniques include state space enumeration, symbolic state space enumeration, abstract interpretation, symbolic simulation, abstraction refinement. The properties to be verified are often described in temporal logics, such as linear temporal logic (LTL), Property Specification Language (PSL), SystemVerilog Assertions (SVA), or computational tree logic (CTL). The great advantage of model checking is that it is often fully automatic; its primary disadvantage is that it does not in general scale to large systems; symbolic models are typically limited to a few hundred bits of state, while explicit state enumeration requires the state space being explored to be relatively small.

Another approach is deductive verification. It consists of generating from the system and its specifications (and possibly other annotations) a collection of mathematical *proof obligations*, the truth of which imply conformance of the system to its specification, and discharging these obligations using either interactive theorem provers (such as HOL, ACL2, Isabelle, Coq or PVS), automatic theorem provers, or satisfiability modulo theories (SMT) solvers. This approach has the disadvantage that it typically requires the user to understand in detail why the system works correctly, and to convey this information to the verification system, either in the form of a sequence of theorems to be proved or in the form of specifications of system components (e.g. functions or procedures) and perhaps subcomponents (such as loops or data structures).

Software

Formal verification of software programs involves proving that a program satisfies a formal specification of its behavior. Subareas of formal verification include deductive verification, abstract interpretation, automated theorem proving, type systems, and lightweight formal methods. A promising type-based verification approach is dependently typed programming, in which the types of functions include (at least part of) those functions' specifications, and type-checking the code establishes its correctness against those specifications. Fully featured dependently typed languages support deductive verification as a special case.

Another complementary approach is program derivation, in which efficient code is produced from functional specifications by a series of correctness-preserving steps. An example of this approach is the Bird-Meertens Formalism, and this approach can be seen as another form of correctness by construction.

These techniques can be *sound*, meaning that the verified properties can be logically deduced from the semantics, or *unsound*, meaning that there is no such guarantee. A sound technique yields a result only once it has searched the entire space of possibilities. An example of an unsound technique is one that searches only a subset of the possibilities, for instance only integers up to a certain number, and give a "good-enough" result. Techniques can also be *decidable*, meaning that their algorithmic implementations are guaranteed to terminate with an answer, or undecidable, meaning that they may never terminate. Because they are bounded, unsound techniques are often more likely to be decidable than sound ones.

Verification and Validation

Verification is one aspect of testing a product's fitness for purpose. Validation is the complementary aspect. Often one refers to the overall checking process as V & V.

- Validation: "Are we trying to make the right thing?", i.e., is the product specified to the user's actual needs?

- Verification: "Have we made what we were trying to make?", i.e., does the product conform to the specifications?

The verification process consists of static/structural and dynamic/behavioral aspects. E.g., for a software product one can inspect the source code (static) and run against specific test cases (dynamic). Validation usually can be done only dynamically, i.e., the product is tested by putting it through typical and atypical usages ("Does it satisfactorily meet all use cases?").

Automated Program Repair

Automated program repair involves repairing software bugs, with very limited or no human intervention. Program repair is performed with respect to an oracle, encompassing the desired functionality of the program which is used for validation of the generated fix. A simple example is a test-suite—the input/output pairs specify the functionality of the program. A variety of techniques are employed, most notably using satisfiability modulo theories (SMT) solvers, and genetic programming, using evolutionary computing to generate and evaluate possible candidates for fixes. The former method is deterministic, while the latter is randomized.

Program repair combines techniques from formal verification and program synthesis. Fault-localization techniques in formal verification are used to compute program points which might be possible bug-locations, which can be targeted by the synthesis modules. Repair systems often focus on a small pre-defined class of bugs in order to reduce the search space. Industrial use is limited owing to the computational cost of existing techniques.

Industry use

The growth in complexity of designs increases the importance of formal verification techniques in the hardware industry. At present, formal verification is used by most or all leading hardware companies, but its use in the software industry is still languishing. This could be attributed to the greater need in the hardware industry, where errors have greater commercial significance. Because of the potential subtle interactions between components, it is increasingly difficult to exercise a realistic set of possibilities by simulation. Important aspects of hardware design are amenable to automated proof methods, making formal verification easier to introduce and more productive.

As of 2011, several operating systems have been formally verified: NICTA's Secure Embedded L4 microkernel, sold commercially as seL4 by OK Labs; OSEK/VDX based real-time operating system ORIENTAIS by East China Normal University; Green Hills Software's Integrity operating system; and SYSGO's PikeOS.

As of 2017, formal verification has been applied to the design of large computer networks through a mathematical model of the network, and as part of a new network technology category, intent-based networking. Network software vendors that offer formal verification solutions include Cisco Forward Networks and Veriflow Systems.

The CompCert C compiler is a formally verified C compiler implementing the majority of ISO C.

Multi-factor Authentication

Multi-factor authentication (MFA) is a method of confirming a user's claimed identity in which a user is granted access only after successfully presenting 2 or more pieces of evidence (or factors) to an authentication mechanism: knowledge (something they and only they know), possession (something they and only they have), and inherence (something they and only they are).

Two-factor authentication (also known as 2FA) is a type (subset) of multi-factor authentication. It is a method of confirming a user's claimed identity by utilizing a combination of *two* different factors: 1) something they know, 2) something they have, or 3) something they are.

A good example of two-factor authentication is the withdrawing of money from a ATM; only the correct combination of a bank card (something that the user possesses) and a PIN (personal identification number, something that the user knows) allows the transaction to be carried out.

Two-step verification or two-step authentication is a method of confirming a user's claimed identity by utilizing something they know (password) and a second factor other than something they have or something they are. An example of a second step is the user repeating back something that was sent to them through an out-of-band mechanism. Or the second step might be a 6 digit number generated by an app that is common to the user and the authentication system.

Authentication Factors

The use of multiple authentication factors to prove one's identity is based on the premise that an unauthorized actor is unlikely to be able to supply the factors required for access. If, in an authentication attempt, at least one of the components is missing or supplied incorrectly, the user's identity is not established with sufficient certainty and access to the asset (e.g., a building, or data) being protected by multi-factor authentication then remains blocked. The authentication factors of a multi-factor authentication scheme may include:

- some physical object in the possession of the user, such as a USB stick with a secret token, a bank card, a key, etc.

- some secret known to the user, such as a password, PIN, TAN, etc.

- some physical characteristic of the user (biometrics), such as a fingerprint, eye iris, voice, typing speed, pattern in key press intervals, etc.

Knowledge Factors

Knowledge factors are the most commonly used form of authentication. In this form, the user is required to prove knowledge of a secret in order to authenticate.

A password is a secret word or string of characters that is used for user authentication. This is the most commonly used mechanism of authentication. Many multi-factor authentication techniques rely on password as one factor of authentication. Variations include both longer ones formed from multiple words (a passphrase) and the shorter, purely numeric, personal identification number (PIN) commonly used for ATM access. Traditionally, passwords are expected to be memorized.

Many secret questions such as "Where were you born?" are poor examples of a knowledge factor because they may be known to a wide group of people, or be able to be researched.

Possession Factors

Possession factors ("something the user and only the user has") have been used for authentication for centuries, in the form of a key to a lock. The basic principle is that the key embodies a secret which is shared between the lock and the key, and the same principle underlies possession factor authentication in computer systems. A security token is an example of a possession factor.

Disconnected Tokens

RSA SecurID token, an example of a disconnected token generator.

Disconnected tokens have no connections to the client computer. They typically use a built-in screen to display the generated authentication data, which is manually typed in by the user.

Connected Tokens

Connected tokens are devices that are *physically* connected to the computer to be used. Those devices transmit data automatically. There are a number of different types, including card readers, wireless tags and USB tokens.

Inherence Factors

These are factors associated with the user, and are usually bio-metric methods, including fingerprint readers, retina scanners or voice recognition.

Mobile Phone Two-step Authentication

Mobile phone's apps, SMS, direct push notifications, etc. are not considered 'something you have' and thus are not considered in the multi-factor/two-factor equation. Mobile phone two-step authentication is more secure than single factor password protection but suffers some security concerns. Phones can be cloned and apps can be running on several phones, SMS can be read by cell phone maintenance personnel. Not least, cell phones can be compromised in general, meaning the phone is no longer something you and only you have.

The major drawback of authentication performed including something that the user possesses is that the physical token (the USB stick, the bank card, the key or similar) must be carried around by the user, practically at all times. Loss and theft are a risk. Many organizations forbid USB and electronic devices being carried in or out owing to malware and data theft risks, and most important machines do not have USB ports for the same reason. Physical tokens usually do not scale, typically requiring a new token for each new account and system. There are also costs involved in procuring and subsequently replacing tokens of this kind. In addition, there are inherent conflicts and unavoidable trade-offs between usability and security.

Mobile phone two-step authentication, where devices such as mobile phones and smartphones, was developed to provide an alternative method that would avoid such issues. To authenticate themselves, people can use their personal access codes to the device (i.e. something that only the individual user knows) plus a one-time-valid, dynamic passcode, typically consisting of 4 to 6 digits. The passcode can be sent to their mobile device by SMS or push notification or can be generated by a one-time-passcode-generator (app). In all three cases, the advantage of using a mobile phone is that there is no need for an additional dedicated token as users tend to carry their mobile devices around at all times.

SMS is the most broadly adopted multi-factor authentication method to date for consumer-facing accounts, though in 2016 and 2017 respectively, both Google and Apple have started offering user two-step authentication with push notification as an alternative method, although this method is not Out-of-band. Despite its popularity, SMS verification has been condemned as a form of authentication by the NIST and has been publicly criticized by many security advocates. As such, SMS verification is no longer considered verification.

Security of the mobile-delivered security tokens fully depends on the mobile operator's operational security and can be easily breached by wiretapping or SIM cloning by national security agencies.

Advantages of Mobile Phone two-step Authentication

- No additional tokens are necessary because it uses mobile devices that are (usually) carried all the time.

- As they are constantly changed, dynamically generated passcodes are safer to use than fixed (static) log-in information.

- Depending on the solution, passcodes that have been used are automatically replaced in order to ensure that a valid code is always available; acute transmission/reception problems do not therefore prevent logins.

- The option to specify a maximum permitted number of incorrect entries reduces the risk of attacks by unauthorized persons.

- It is user friendly.

Disadvantages of Mobile Phone Two-step Authentication

- The mobile phone must be carried by the user, charged, and kept in range of a cellular network whenever authentication might be necessary. If the phone is unable to display messages, such as if it becomes damaged or shuts down for an update or due to temperature extremes (e.g. winter exposure), access is often impossible without backup plans.

- The user must share their personal mobile number with the provider, reducing personal privacy and potentially allowing spam.

- The user may be charged by their mobile carrier for messaging fees.

- Text messages to mobile phones using SMS are insecure and can be intercepted. The token can thus be stolen and used by third parties.

- Text messages may not be delivered instantly, adding additional delays to the authentication process.

- Account recovery typically bypasses mobile phone two-factor authentication.

- Modern smart phones are used both for browsing email and for receiving SMS. Email is usually always logged in. So if the phone is lost or stolen, all accounts for which the email is the key can be hacked as the phone can receive the second factor. So smart phones combine the two factors into one factor.

- Mobile phones can be stolen, potentially allowing the thief to gain access into the user's accounts.

- SIM cloning gives hackers access to mobile phone connections. Social engineering attacks against mobile operator companies resulted in handing over duplicate SIM cards to criminals.

Advances in Mobile Two-factor Authentication

Advances in research of two-factor authentication for mobile devices consider different methods in which a second factor can be implemented while not posing a hindrance to the user. With the continued use and improvements in the accuracy of mobile hardware such as GPS, microphone, and gyro/acceleromoter, the ability to use them as a second factor of authentication is becoming more trustworthy. For example, by recording the ambient noise of the user's location from a mobile device and comparing it with the recording of the ambient noise from the computer in the same room on which the user is trying to authenticate, one is able to have an effective second factor of authentication. This also reduces the amount of time and effort needed to complete the process.

Legislation and Regulation

The Payment Card Industry (PCI) Data Security Standard, requirement 8.3, requires the use of MFA for all remote network access that originates from outside the network to a Card Data Environment (CDE). Beginning with PCI-DSS version 3.2, the use of

MFA is required for all administrative access to the CDE, even if the user is within a trusted network.

United States

Details for authentication in the USA are defined with the Homeland Security Presidential Directive 12 (HSPD-12).

Existing authentication methodologies involve the explained three types of basic "factors". Authentication methods that depend on more than one factor are more difficult to compromise than single-factor methods.

IT regulatory standards for access to Federal Government systems require the use of multi-factor authentication to access sensitive IT resources, for example when logging on to network devices to perform administrative tasks and when accessing any computer using a privileged login.

NIST Special Publication 800-63-3 discusses various forms of two-factor authentication and provides guidance on using them in business processes requiring different levels of assurance.

In 2005, the United States' Federal Financial Institutions Examination Council issued guidance for financial institutions recommending financial institutions conduct risk-based assessments, evaluate customer awareness programs, and develop security measures to reliably authenticate customers remotely accessing online financial services, officially recommending the use of authentication methods that depend on more than one factor (specifically, what a user knows, has, and is) to determine the user's identity. In response to the publication, numerous authentication vendors began improperly promoting challenge-questions, secret images, and other knowledge-based methods as "multi-factor" authentication. Due to the resulting confusion and widespread adoption of such methods, on August 15, 2006, the FFIEC published supplemental guidelines—which states that by definition, a "true" multi-factor authentication system must use distinct instances of the three factors of authentication it had defined, and not just use multiple instances of a single factor.

Security

According to proponents, multi-factor authentication could drastically reduce the incidence of online identity theft and other online fraud, because the victim's password would no longer be enough to give a thief permanent access to their information. However, many multi-factor authentication approaches remain vulnerable to phishing, man-in-the-browser, and man-in-the-middle attacks.

Multi-factor authentication may be ineffective against modern threats, like ATM skimming, phishing, and malware.

In May 2017 O2 Telefónica, a German mobile service provider, confirmed that cyber-criminals had exploited SS7 vulnerabilities to bypass SMS based two-step authentication to do unauthorized withdrawals from users bank accounts. The criminals first infected the account holder's computers in an attempt to steal their bank account credentials and phone numbers. Then the attackers purchased access to a fake telecom provider and set-up a redirect for the victim's phone number to a handset controlled by them. Finally the attackers logged into victims' online bank accounts and requested for the money on the accounts to be withdrawn to accounts owned by the criminals. SMS passcodes were routed to phone numbers controlled by the attackers and the criminals transferred the money out.

Implementation Considerations

Many multi-factor authentication products require users to deploy client software to make multi-factor authentication systems work. Some vendors have created separate installation packages for network login, Web access credentials and VPN connection credentials. For such products, there may be four or five different software packages to push down to the client PC in order to make use of the token or smart card. This translates to four or five packages on which version control has to be performed, and four or five packages to check for conflicts with business applications. If access can be operated using web pages, it is possible to limit the overheads outlined above to a single application. With other multi-factor authentication solutions, such as "virtual" tokens and some hardware token products, no software must be installed by end users.

There are drawbacks to multi-factor authentication that are keeping many approaches from becoming widespread. Some consumers have difficulty keeping track of a hardware token or USB plug. Many consumers do not have the technical skills needed to install a client-side software certificate by themselves. Generally, multi-factor solutions require additional investment for implementation and costs for maintenance. Most hardware token-based systems are proprietary and some vendors charge an annual fee per user. Deployment of hardware tokens is logistically challenging. Hardware tokens may get damaged or lost and issuance of tokens in large industries such as banking or even within large enterprises needs to be managed. In addition to deployment costs, multi-factor authentication often carries significant additional support costs. A 2008 survey of over 120 U.S. credit unions by the *Credit Union Journal* reported on the support costs associated with two-factor authentication. In their report, software certificates and software toolbar approaches were reported to have the highest support costs.

Examples

Several popular web services employ multi-factor authentication, usually as an optional feature that is deactivated by default.

- Two-factor authentication

- Many Internet services (among them: Google, Amazon AWS) use open Time-based One-time Password Algorithm (TOTP) to support two-step authentication.

Hardware Protection Mechanisms

Computer Security Compromised by Hardware Failure

Computer security compromised by hardware failure is a branch of computer security applied to hardware. The objective of computer security includes protection of information and property from theft, corruption, or natural disaster, while allowing the information and property to remain accessible and productive to its intended users. Such secret information could be retrieved by different ways. This topic focus on the retrieval of data thanks to misused hardware or hardware failure. Hardware could be misused or exploited to get secret data. This topic collects main types of attack that can be lead in a data thief.

Computer security can be comprised by devices, such as keyboards, monitors or printers (thanks to electromagnetic or acoustic emanation for example) or by components of the computer, such as the memory, the network card or the processor (thanks to time or temperature analysis for example).

Devices

Monitor

The monitor is the main device used to access data on a computer. It has been shown that monitors radiate or reflect data on their environment, potentially giving attackers access to information displayed on the monitor.

Electromagnetic Emanations

Video display units radiate:

- narrowband harmonics of the digital clock signals;

- broadband harmonics of the various 'random' digital signals such as the video signal.

Known as compromising emanations or TEMPEST radiation, a code word for a U.S. government programme aimed at attacking the problem, the electromagnetic broadcast of data has been a significant concern in sensitive computer applications. Eavesdroppers can reconstruct video screen content from radio frequency emanations. Each (radiated) harmonic of the video signal shows a remarkable resemblance to a broadcast TV signal. It is therefore possible to reconstruct the picture displayed on the video display unit from the radiated emission by means of a normal television receiver. If no preventive measures are taken, eavesdropping on a video display unit is possible at distances up to several hundreds of meters, using only a normal black-and-white TV receiver, a directional antenna and an antenna amplifier. It is even possible to pick up information from some types of video display units at a distance of over 1 kilometer. If more sophisticated receiving and decoding equipment is used, the maximum distance can be much greater.

Compromising Reflections

What is displayed by the monitor is reflected on the environment. The time-varying diffuse reflections of the light emitted by a CRT monitor can be exploited to recover the original monitor image. This is an eavesdropping technique for spying at a distance on data that is displayed on an arbitrary computer screen, including the currently prevalent LCD monitors.

The technique exploits reflections of the screen's optical emanations in various objects that one commonly finds in close proximity to the screen and uses those reflections to recover the original screen content. Such objects include eyeglasses, tea pots, spoons, plastic bottles, and even the eye of the user. This attack can be successfully mounted to spy on even small fonts using inexpensive, off-the-shelf equipment (less than 1500 dollars) from a distance of up to 10 meters. Relying on more expensive equipment allowed to conduct this attack from over 30 meters away, demonstrating that similar attacks are feasible from the other side of the street or from a close-by building.

Many objects that may be found at a usual workplace can be exploited to retrieve information on a computer's display by an outsider. Particularly good results were obtained from reflections in a user's eyeglasses or a tea pot located on the desk next to the screen. Reflections that stem from the eye of the user also provide good results. However, eyes are harder to spy on at a distance because they are fast-moving objects and require high exposure times. Using more expensive equipment with lower exposure times helps to remedy this problem.

The reflections gathered from curved surfaces on close-by objects indeed pose a substantial threat to the confidentiality of data displayed on the screen. Fully invalidating this threat without at the same time hiding the screen from the legitimate user seems difficult, without using curtains on the windows or similar forms of strong optical shielding. Most users, however, will not be aware of this risk and may not be willing to close the curtains on a nice day. The reflection of an object, a computer display, in a curved mirror creates a virtual image that is located behind the reflecting surface. For a flat mirror this virtual image has the same size and is located behind the mirror at the same distance as the original object. For curved mirrors, however, the situation is more complex.

Keyboard

Electromagnetic Emanations

Computer keyboards are often used to transmit confidential data such as passwords. Since they contain electronic components, keyboards emit electromagnetic waves. These emanations could reveal sensitive information such as keystrokes. Electromagnetic emanations have turned out to constitute a security threat to computer equipment. The figure below presents how a keystroke is retrieved and what material is necessary.

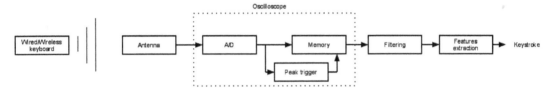

Diagram presenting all material necessary to detect keystrokes

The approach is to acquire the raw signal directly from the antenna and to process the entire captured electromagnetic spectrum. Thanks to this method, four different kinds of compromising electromagnetic emanations have been detected, generated by wired and wireless keyboards. These emissions lead to a full or a partial recovery of the keystrokes. The best practical attack fully recovered 95% of the keystrokes of a PS/2 keyboard at a distance up to 20 meters, even through walls. Because each keyboard has a specific fingerprint based on the clock frequency inconsistencies, it can determine the source keyboard of a compromising emanation, even if multiple keyboards from the same model are used at the same time.

The four different kinds way of compromising electromagnetic emanations are described below.

The Falling Edge Transition Technique

When a key is pressed, released or held down, the keyboard sends a packet of information known as a scan code to the computer. The protocol used to transmit these scan codes is a bidirectional serial communication, based on four wires: Vcc (5 volts), ground, data and clock. Clock and data signals are identically generated. Hence, the compromising emanation detected is the combination of both signals. However, the edges of the data and the clock lines are not superposed. Thus, they can be easily separated to obtain independent signals.

The Generalized Transition Technique

The Falling Edge Transition attack is limited to a partial recovery of the keystrokes. This is a significant limitation. The GTT is a falling edge transition attack improved, which recover almost all keystrokes. Indeed, between two traces, there is exactly one data rising edge. If attackers are able to detect this transition, they can fully recover the keystrokes.

The Modulation Technique

Harmonics compromising electromagnetic emissions come from unintentional emanations such as radiations emitted by the clock, non-linear elements, crosstalk, ground pollution, etc. Determining theoretically the reasons of these compromising radiations is a very complex task. These harmonics correspond to a carrier of approximately 4 MHz which is very likely the internal clock of the micro-controller inside the keyboard. These harmonics are correlated with both clock and data signals, which describe modulated signals (in amplitude and frequency) and the full state of both clock and data signals. This means that the scan code can be completely recovered from these harmonics.

The Matrix Scan Technique

Keyboard manufacturers arrange the keys in a matrix. The keyboard controller, often an 8-bit processor, parses columns one-by-one and recovers the state of 8 keys at once. This matrix scan process can be described as 192 keys (some keys may not be used, for instance modern keyboards use 104/105 keys) arranged in 24 columns and 8 rows. These columns are continuously pulsed one-by-one for at least 3µs. Thus, these leads may act as an antenna and generate electromagnetic emanations. If an attacker is able to capture these emanations, he can easily recover the column of the pressed key. Even if this signal does not fully describe the pressed key, it still gives partial information on the transmitted scan code, i.e. the column number.

Note that the matrix scan routine loops continuously. When no key is pressed, we still have a signal composed of multiple equidistant peaks. These emanations may be used to remotely detect the presence of powered computers. Concerning wireless keyboards, the wireless data burst transmission can be used as an electromagnetic trigger to detect exactly when a key is pressed, while the matrix scan emanations are used to determine the column it belongs to.

Summary

Some techniques can only target some keyboards. This table sums up which technique could be used to find keystroke for different kind of keyboard.

Technique name	Wired Keyboard	Laptop Keyboard	Wireless Keyboard
Falling Edge Transition Technique	Yes	Yes	
Generalized Transition Technique	Yes	Yes	
Modulation Technique	Yes	Yes	
Matrix Scan Technique	Yes	Yes	Yes

In their paper called "Compromising Electromagnetic Emanations of Wired and Wireless Keyboards", Martin Vuagnoux and Sylvain Pasini tested 12 different keyboard models, with PS/2, USB connectors and wireless communication in different setups: a semi-anechoic chamber, a small office, an adjacent office and a flat in a building. The table below presents their results.

Type of keyboard	Number of tested keyboard	FETT	GTT	MT	MST
PS/2	7	7/7	6/7	4/7	5/7
USB	2	0/2	0/2	0/2	2/2
Laptop	2	1/2	1/2	0/2	2/2
Wireless	1	0/1	0/1	0/1	1/1

Acoustic Emanations

Attacks against emanations caused by human typing have attracted interest in recent years. In particular, works showed that keyboard acoustic emanations do leak information that can be exploited to reconstruct the typed text.

PC keyboards, notebook keyboards are vulnerable to attacks based on differentiating the sound emanated by different keys. This attack takes as input an audio signal containing a recording of a single word typed by a single person on a keyboard, and a dictionary of words. It is assumed that the typed word is present in the dictionary. The aim of the attack is to reconstruct the original word from the signal. This attack, taking as input a 10-minute sound recording of a user typing English text using a keyboard, and then recovering up to 96% of typed characters. This attack is inexpensive because the other hardware required is a parabolic microphone and non-invasive because it does not require physical intrusion into the system. The attack employs a neural network to recognize the key being pressed. It combines signal processing and efficient data structures and algorithms, to successfully reconstruct single words of 7-13 characters from a recording of the clicks made when typing them on a keyboard. The sound of clicks can differ slightly from key to key, because the keys are positioned at different positions on the keyboard plate, although the clicks of different keys sound similar to the human ear.

On average, there were only 0.5 incorrect recognitions per 20 clicks, which shows the exposure of keyboard to the eavesdropping using this attack. The attack is very efficient, taking under 20 seconds per word on a standard PC. A 90% or better success rate of finding the correct word for words of 10 or more characters, and a success rate of 73% over all the words tested. In practice, a human attacker can typically determine if text is random. An attacker can also identify occasions when the user types user names and passwords. Short audio signals containing a single word, with seven or more characters long was considered. This means that the signal is only a few seconds long. Such short words are often chosen as a password. The dominant factors affecting the attack's success are the word length, and more importantly, the number of repeated characters within the word.

This is a procedure that makes it possible to efficiently uncover a word out of audio recordings of keyboard click sounds. More recently, extracting information out of an other type of emanations was demonstrated: acoustic emanations from mechanical devices such as dot-matrix printers.

Video Eavesdropping on Keyboard

While extracting private information by watching somebody typing on a keyboard might seem to be an easy task, it becomes extremely challenging if it has to be automated. However, an automated tool is needed in the case of long-lasting surveillance procedures or long user activity, as a human being is able to reconstruct only a few characters per minute. The paper "ClearShot: Eavesdropping on Keyboard Input from Video" presents a novel approach to automatically recovering the text being typed on a keyboard, based solely on a video of the user typing.

Automatically recognizing the keys being pressed by a user is a hard problem that requires sophisticated motion analysis. Experiments show that, for a human, reconstructing a few sentences requires lengthy hours of slow-motion analysis of the video. The attacker might install a surveillance device in the room of the victim, might take control of an existing camera by exploiting a vulnerability in the camera's control software, or might simply point a mobile phone with an integrated camera at the laptop's keyboard when the victim is working in a public space.

Balzarotti's analysis is divided into two main phases (figure below). The first phase analyzes the video recorded by the camera using computer vision techniques. For each frame of the video, the computer vision analysis computes the set of keys that were likely pressed, the set of keys that were certainly not pressed, and the position of space characters. Because the results of this phase of the analysis are noisy, a second phase, called the text analysis, is required. The goal of this phase is to remove errors using both language and context-sensitive techniques. The result of this phase is the reconstructed text, where each word is represented by a list of possible candidates, ranked by likelihood.

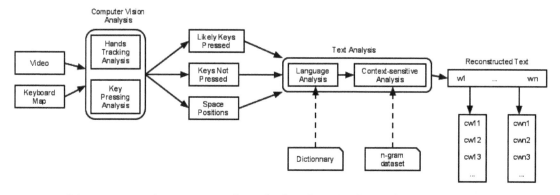

Diagram presenting steps to go through when detecting keystroke with video input

Printer

Acoustic Emanations

With acoustic emanations, an attack that recovers what a dot-matrix printer process-ing English text is printing is possible. It is based on a record of the sound the printer makes, if the microphone is close enough to it. This attack recovers up to 72% of print-ed words, and up to 95% if knowledge about the text are done, with a microphone at a distance of 10 cm from the printer.

After an upfront training phase ("a" in the picture below), the attack ("b" in the picture below) is fully automated and uses a combination of machine learning, audio process-ing, and speech recognition techniques, including spectrum features, Hidden Markov Models and linear classification. The fundamental reason why the reconstruction of the printed text works is that, the emitted sound becomes louder if more needles strike the paper at a given time. There is a correlation between the number of needles and the intensity of the acoustic emanation.

A training phase was conducted where words from a dictionary are printed and char-acteristic sound features of these words are extracted and stored in a database. The trained characteristic features was used to recognize the printed English text. But, this task is not trivial. Major challenges include :

1. Identifying and extracting sound features that suitably capture the acoustic em-anation of dot-matrix printers;

2. Compensating for the blurred and overlapping features that are induced by the substantial decay time of the emanations;

3. Identifying and eliminating wrongly recognized words to increase the overall percentage of correctly identified words (recognition rate).

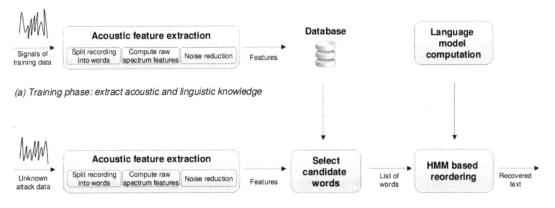

(a) Training phase: extract acoustic and linguistic knowledge

(b) Recognition phase: recognize printed text using acoustic and linguistic features

Diagram presenting phases when retrieving data from a printer

Computer Components

Timing Attack

Timing attacks enable an attacker to extract secrets maintained in a security system by observing the time it takes the system to respond to various queries.

SSH is designed to provide a secure channel between two hosts. Despite the encryption and authentication mechanisms it uses, SSH has weaknesses. In interactive mode, every individual keystroke that a user types is sent to the remote machine in a separate IP packet immediately after the key is pressed, which leaks the inter-keystroke timing information of users' typing. Below, the picture represents the command *su* processed through a SSH connection.

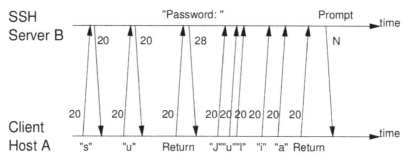

Network messages sent between the host and the client for
the command 'su' – numbers are size of network packet in byte

A very simple statistical techniques suffice to reveal sensitive information such as the length of users' passwords or even root passwords. By using advanced statistical techniques on timing information collected from the network, the eavesdropper can learn significant information about what users type in SSH sessions. Because the time it takes the operating system to send out the packet after the keypress is in general negligible comparing to the interkeystroke timing, this also enables an eavesdropper to learn the precise interkeystroke timings of users' typing from the arrival times of packets.

Memory

Physical Chemistry

Data remanence problems not only affect obvious areas such as RAM and non-volatile memory cells but can also occur in other areas of the device through hot-carrier effects (which change the characteristics of the semiconductors in the device) and various other effects which are examined alongside the more obvious memory-cell remanence problems. It is possible to analyse and recover data from these cells and from semiconductor devices in general long after it should (in theory) have vanished.

Electromigration, which means to physically move the atom to new locations (to physically alter the device itself) is another type of attack. It involves the relocation of metal atoms due to high current densities, a phenomenon in which atoms are carried along by an "electron wind" in the opposite direction to the conventional current, producing voids at the negative electrode and hillocks and whiskers at the positive electrode. Void formation leads to a local increase in current density and Joule heating (the interaction of electrons and metal ions to produce thermal energy), producing further electromigration effects. When the external stress is removed, the disturbed system tends to relax back to its original equilibrium state, resulting in a backflow which heals some of the electromigration damage. In the long term though, this can cause device failure, but in less extreme cases it simply serves to alter a device's operating characteristics in noticeable ways.

For example, the excavations of voids leads to increased wiring resistance and the growth of whiskers leads to contact formation and current leakage. An example of a conductor which exhibits whisker growth due to electromigration is shown in the figure below:

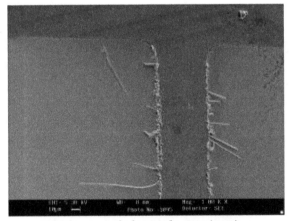

Whisker growth due to electromigration

One example which exhibits void formation (in this case severe enough to have led to complete failure) is shown in this figure:

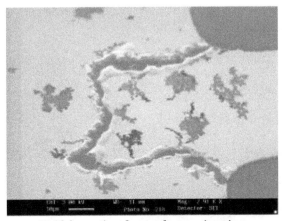

Void formation due to electromigration

Temperature

Contrary to popular assumption, DRAMs used in most modern computers retain their contents for several seconds after power is lost, even at room temperature and even if removed from a motherboard.

Many products do cryptographic and other security-related computations using secret keys or other variables that the equipment's operator must not be able to read out or alter. The usual solution is for the secret data to be kept in volatile memory inside a tamper-sensing enclosure. Security processors typically store secret key material in static RAM, from which power is removed if the device is tampered with. At temperatures below −20 °C, the contents of SRAM can be 'frozen'. It is interesting to know the period of time for which a static RAM device will retain data once the power has been removed. Low temperatures can increase the data retention time of SRAM to many seconds or even minutes.

Read/Write Exploits Thanks to FireWire

Maximillian Dornseif presented a technique in these slides, which let him take the control of an Apple computer thanks to an iPod. The attacks needed a first generic phase where the iPod software was modified so that it behaves as master on the FireWire bus. Then the iPod had full read/write access on the Apple Computer when the iPod was plugged into a FireWire port. FireWire is used by : audio devices, printers, scanners, cameras, gps, etc. Generally, a device connected by FireWire has full access (read/write). Indeed, OHCI Standard (FireWire standard) reads :

> Physical requests, including physical read, physical write and lock requests to some CSR registers (section 5.5), are handled directly by the Host Controller without assistance by system software.
>
> — OHCI Standard

So, any device connected by FireWire can read and write data on the computer memory. For example, a device can :

- Grab the screen contents ;

- Just search the memory for strings such as login, passwords ;

- Scan for possible key material ;

- Search cryptographic keys stored in RAM ;

- Parse the whole physical memory to understand logical memory layout.

or

- Mess up the memory ;

- Change screen content ;

- Change UID/GID of a certain process ;

- Inject code into a process ;

- Inject an additional process.

Processor

Cache Attack

To increase the computational power, processors are generally equipped with a cache memory which decreases the memory access latency. Below, the figure shows the hierarchy between the processor and the memory. First the processor looks for data in the cache L1, then L2, then in the memory.

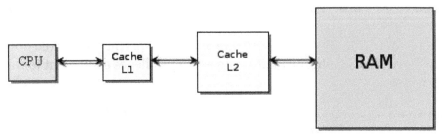

Processor cache hierarchy

When the data is not where the processor is looking for, it is called a cache-miss. Below, pictures show how the processor fetch data when there are two cache levels.

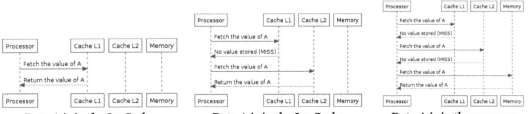

Data A is in the L1-Cache   Data A is in the L2-Cache   Data A is in the memory

Unfortunately caches contain only a small portion of the application data and can introduce additional latency to the memory transaction in the case of a miss. This involves also additional power consumption which is due to the activation of memory devices down in the memory hierarchy. The miss penalty has been already used to attack symmetric encryption algorithms, like DES. The basic idea proposed in this paper is to force a cache miss while the processor is executing the AES encryption algorithm on a known plain text. The attacks allow an unprivileged process to attack other process running in parallel on the same processor, despite partitioning methods such as memory protection, sandboxing and virtualization.

Timing Attack

By carefully measuring the amount of time required to perform private key operations, attackers may be able to find fixed Diffie-Hellman exponents, factor RSA keys, and break other cryptosystems. Against a vulnerable system, the attack is computationally inexpensive and often requires only known ciphertext. The attack can be treated as a signal detection problem. The signal consists of the timing variation due to the target exponent bit, and noise results from measurement inaccuracies and timing variations due to unknown exponent bits. The properties of the signal and noise determine the number of timing measurements required to for the attack. Timing attacks can potentially be used against other cryptosystems, including symmetric functions.

Privilege Escalation

A simple and generic processor backdoor can be used by attackers as a means to privilege escalation to get to privileges equivalent to those of any given running operating system. Also, a non-privileged process of one of the non-privileged invited domain running on top of a virtual machine monitor can get to privileges equivalent to those of the virtual machine monitor.

Loïc Duflot studied Intel processors in the paper "CPU bugs, CPU backdoors and consequences on security" ; he explains that the processor defines four different privilege rings numbered from 0 (most privileged) to 3 (least privileged). Kernel code is usually running in ring 0, whereas user-space code is generally running in ring 3. The use of some security-critical assembly language instructions is restricted to ring 0 code. In order to escalate privilege through the backdoor, the attacker must :

1. activate the backdoor by placing the CPU in the desired state ;

2. inject code and run it in ring 0 ;

3. get back to ring 3 in order to return the system to a stable state. Indeed, when code is running in ring 0, system calls do not work : Leaving the system in ring 0 and running a random system call (exit() typically) is likely to crash the system.

The backdoors Loïc Duflot presents are simple as they only modify the behavior of three assembly language instructions and have very simple and specific activation conditions, so that they are very unlikely to be accidentally activated. Recent inventions have begun to target these types of processor-based escalation attacks.

Trusted Platform Module

Trusted Platform Module (TPM, also known as ISO/IEC 11889) is an international standard for a secure cryptoprocessor, a dedicated microcontroller designed to secure hardware through integrated cryptographic keys.

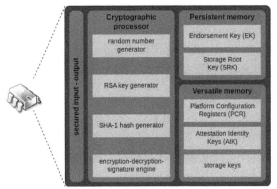

Components of a Trusted Platform Module complying with the TPM version 1.2 standard

Overview

Trusted Platform Module provides

- A random number generator.

- Facilities for the secure generation of cryptographic keys for limited uses.

- Remote attestation: Creates a nearly unforgeable hash key summary of the hardware and software configuration. The software in charge of hashing the configuration data determines the extent of the summary. This allows a third party to verify that the software has not been changed.

- Binding: Encrypts data using the TPM bind key, a unique RSA key descended from a storage key.

- Sealing: Similar to binding, but in addition, specifies the TPM state for the data to be decrypted (unsealed).

Computer programs can use a TPM to authenticate hardware devices, since each TPM chip has a unique and secret RSA key burned in as it is produced. Pushing the security down to the hardware level provides more protection than a software-only solution.

Uses

The United States Department of Defense (DoD) specifies that "new computer assets (e.g., server, desktop, laptop, thin client, tablet, smartphone, personal digital assistant, mobile phone) procured to support DoD will include a TPM version 1.2 or higher where required by DISA STIGs and where such technology is available." DoD anticipates that TPM is to be used for device identification, authentication, encryption, and device integrity verification.

Platform Integrity

The primary scope of TPM is to assure the integrity of a platform. In this context, "integrity" means "behave as intended", and a "platform" is any computer device regardless of its operating system. It is to ensure that the boot process starts from a trusted combination of hardware and software, and continues until the operating system has fully booted and applications are running.

The responsibility of assuring said integrity using TPM is with the firmware and the operating system. For example, Unified Extensible Firmware Interface (UEFI) can use TPM to form a root of trust: The TPM contains several Platform Configuration Registers (PCRs) that allow secure storage and reporting of security relevant metrics. These metrics can be used to detect changes to previous configurations and decide how to proceed. Good examples can be found in Linux Unified Key Setup (LUKS), BitLocker and PrivateCore vCage memory encryption.

An example of TPM use for platform integrity is the Trusted Execution Technology (TXT), which creates a chain of trust. It could remotely attest that a computer is using the specified hardware and software.

Disk Encryption

Full disk encryption utilities, such as dm-crypt and BitLocker, can use this technology to protect the keys used to encrypt the computer's storage devices and provide integrity authentication for a trusted boot pathway that includes firmware and boot sector.

Password Protection

Operating systems often require authentication (involving a password or other means) to protect keys, data or systems. If the authentication mechanism is implemented in software only, the access is prone to dictionary attacks. Since TPM is implemented in a dedicated hardware module, a dictionary attack prevention mechanism was built in, which effectively protects against guessing or automated dictionary attacks, while still allowing the user a sufficient and reasonable number of tries. Without this level of protection, only passwords with high complexity would provide sufficient protection.

Other uses and Concerns

Any application can use a TPM chip for:

- Digital rights management

- Protection and enforcement of software licenses

- Prevention of cheating in online games

Other uses exist, some of which give rise to privacy concerns. The "physical presence" feature of TPM addresses some of these concerns by requiring BIOS-level confirmation for operations such as activating, deactivating, clearing or changing ownership of TPM by someone who is physically present at the console of the machine.

TPM Implementations

Trusted Platform Module installed on a motherboard

Starting in 2006, many new laptops have been sold with a built-in TPM chip. In the future, this concept could be co-located on an existing motherboard chip in computers, or any other device where the TPM facilities could be employed, such as a cellphone. On a PC, either the LPC bus or the SPI bus is used to connect to the TPM chip.

TCG has certified TPM chips manufactured by Infineon Technologies, Nuvoton, and STMicroelectronics, having assigned TPM vendor IDs to Advanced Micro Devices, Atmel, Broadcom, IBM, Infineon, Intel, Lenovo, National Semiconductor, Nationz Technologies, Nuvoton, Qualcomm, Rockchip, Standard Microsystems Corporation, STMicroelectronics, Samsung, Sinosun, Texas Instruments, and Winbond.

There are five different types of TPM 2.0 implementations:

- Discrete TPMs are dedicated chips that implement TPM functionality in their own tamper resistant semiconductor package. They are the most secure type of TPM.

- Integrated TPMs are part of another chip. While they use hardware that resists software bugs, they are not required to implement tamper resistance. Intel has integrated TPMs in some of its chipsets.

- Firmware TPMs are software-only solutions that run in a CPU's trusted execution environment. Since these TPMs are entirely software solutions, these TPMs are vulnerable to software bugs within themselves. AMD and Qualcomm have implemented firmware TPMs.

- Software TPMs are software emulators of TPMs that run with no more protection than a regular program gets within an operating system. They depend entirely on the environment that they run in, so they provide no more security than what can be provided by the normal execution environment, and they are vulnerable to their own software bugs. They are useful for development purposes.

- Virtual TPMs are provided by a hypervisor. Therefore, they rely on the hypervisor to provide them with an isolated execution environment beyond that provided to the software running inside the virtual machine. For the virtual machine running inside the hypervisor, they are as good as discrete TPMs.

TPM 1.2 vs TPM 2.0

While TPM 2.0 addresses many of the same use cases and has similar features, the details are different. TPM 2.0 is not backward compatible to TPM 1.2.

Specification	TPM 1.2	TPM 2.0
Architecture	The one-size-fits-all specification consists of three parts.	A complete specification consists of a platform-specific specification which references a common four-part TPM 2.0 library. Platform-specific specifications define what parts of the library are mandatory, optional, or banned for that platform; and detail other requirements for that platform. Platform-specific specifications include PC Client, mobile, and Automotive-Thin.
Algorithms	SHA-1 and RSA are required. AES is optional. Triple DES was once an optional algorithm in earlier versions of TPM 1.2, but has been banned in TPM 1.2 version 94. The MGF1 hash-based mask generation function that is defined in PKCS#1 is required.	The PC Client Platform TPM Profile (PTP) Specification requires SHA-1 and SHA-256 for hashes; RSA, ECC using the Barreto-Naehrig 256-bit curve, and ECC using the NIST P-256 curve for public-key cryptography and asymmetric digital signature generation and verification; HMAC for symmetric digital signature generation and verification; 128-bit AES for symmetric-key algorithm; and the MGF1 hash-based mask generation function that is defined in PKCS#1 are required by the TCG PC Client Platform TPM Profile (PTP) Specification. Many other algorithms are also defined but are optional.
Crypto Primitives	A random number generator, a public-key cryptographic algorithm, a cryptographic hash function, a mask generation function, digital signature generation and verification, and Direct Anonymous Attestation are required. Symmetric-key algorithms and exclusive or are optional. Key generation is also required.	A random number generator, public-key cryptographic algorithms, cryptographic hash functions, symmetric-key algorithms, digital signature generation and verification, mask generation functions, exclusive or, and ECC-based Direct Anonymous Attestation using the Barreto-Naehrig 256-bit curve are required by the TCG PC Client Platform TPM Profile (PTP) Specification. The TPM 2.0 common library specification also requires key generation and key derivation functions.
Hierarchy	One (storage)	Three (platform, storage and endorsement)
Root Keys	One (SRK RSA-2048)	Multiple keys and algorithms per hierarchy

Authorization	HMAC, PCR, locality, physical presence	Password, HMAC, and policy (which covers HMAC, PCR, locality, and physical presence).
NV RAM	Unstructured data	Unstructured data, Counter, Bitmap, Extend

The TPM 2.0 policy authorization includes the 1.2 HMAC, locality, physical presence, and PCR. It adds authorization based on an asymmetric digital signature, indirection to another authorization secret, counters and time limits, NVRAM values, a particular command or command parameters, and physical presence. It permits the ANDing and ORing of these authorization primitives to construct complex authorization policies.

Criticism

TCG has faced resistance to the deployment of this technology in some areas, where some authors see possible uses not specifically related to Trusted Computing, which may raise privacy concerns. The concerns include the abuse of remote validation of software (where the manufacturer—and not the user who owns the computer system—decides what software is allowed to run) and possible ways to follow actions taken by the user being recorded in a database, in a manner that is completely undetectable to the user.

The VeraCrypt disk encryption utility does not support TPM. An FAQ from the developer alleges that the attacker who has physical or administrative access to a computer can circumvent TPM, e.g., by installing a hardware keystroke logger to capture passwords (or other sensitive information), by resetting TPM, or by capturing memory contents and retrieving TPM-issued keys. The problem with this allegation is that it is true in the absence of TPM as well; TPM at least stops some physical tampering. Furthermore, there is no remedy for it. It is a security principle that "If a bad guy has unrestricted physical access to your computer, it's not your computer anymore."

The private endorsement key is fundamental to the security of the TPM circuit, and is never made available to the end-user. This private key must be known to the hardware chip manufacturer at manufacture time, otherwise they would not be able to burn the key into the circuit. There are no guarantees that this private key is not kept by the manufacturer or shared with government agencies. Anyone with access to the private endorsement key would be able to forge the chips identity and break some of the security that the chip provides. Thus, the security of the TPM relies entirely on the manufacturer and the authorities in the country where the hardware is produced.

Attacks

In 2010, Christopher Tarnovsky presented an attack against TPMs at Black Hat, where he claimed to be able to extract TPM secrets. He was able to do this after 6 months of work by inserting a probe and spying on an internal bus for the Infineon SLE 66 CL PC.

In 2015, as part of the Snowden revelations, it was revealed that in 2010 a US CIA team claimed at an internal conference to have carried out a differential power analysis attack against TPMs that was able to extract secrets.

In October 2017, it was reported that a code library developed by Infineon, which had been in widespread use in its TPMs, allowed RSA private keys to be inferred from public keys. As a result, all systems depending upon the privacy of such keys were vulnerable to compromise, such as identity theft or spoofing.

Cryptosystems that store encryption keys directly in the TPM without blinding could be at particular risk to these types of attacks, as passwords and other factors would be meaningless if the attacks can extract encryption secrets.

Availability

Currently TPM is used by nearly all PC and notebook manufacturers, primarily offered on professional product lines.

TPM is implemented by several vendors:

- Advantech provides TPM on many of its products, especially its Gaming boards and Energy Automation Computers.

- In 2006, with the introduction of first Macintosh models with Intel processors, Apple started to ship Macs with TPM. Apple never provided an official driver, but there was a port under GPL available. Apple has not shipped a computer with TPM since 2006.

- Atmel manufactures TPM devices that it claims to be compliant to the Trusted Platform Module specification version 1.2 revision 116 and offered with several interfaces (LPC, SPI, and I2C), modes (FIPS 140-2 certified and standard mode), temperature grades (commercial and industrial), and packages (TSSOP and QFN). Atmel's TPMs support PCs and embedded devices. Atmel also provides TPM development kits to support integration of its TPM devices into various embedded designs.

- Google includes TPMs in Chromebooks as part of their security model.

- Infineon provides both TPM chips and TPM software, which is delivered as OEM versions with new computers, as well as separately by Infineon for products with TPM technology which complies to TCG standards. For example, Infineon licensed TPM management software to Broadcom Corp. in 2004.

- Microsoft operating systems Windows Vista and later use the chip in conjunction with the included disk encryption component named BitLocker. Microsoft had announced that from January 1, 2015 all computers will have to be equipped with a TPM 2.0 module in order to pass Windows 8.1 hardware certification. However, in a December 2014 review of the Windows Certification Program this was instead made an option requirement. However, TPM 2.0 is required for connected standby systems. Virtual machines running on Hyper-V can have their own virtual TPM module starting with Windows 10 1511 and Windows Server 2016.

- In 2011, Taiwanese manufacturer MSI launched its Windpad 110W tablet featuring an AMD CPU and Infineon Security Platform TPM, which ships with controlling software version 3.7. The chip is disabled by default but can be enabled with the included, pre-installed software.

- Nuvoton provides TPM devices implementing Trusted Computing Group (TCG) version 1.2 and 2.0 specifications for PC applications. Nuvoton also provides TPM devices implementing these specifications for embedded systems and IoT (Internet of Things) applications via I2C and SPI host interfaces. Nuvoton's TPM complies with Common Criteria (CC) with assurance level EAL 4 augmented, FIPS 140-2 level 1 and TCG Compliance requirements, all supported within a single device.

- Oracle ships TPMs in their recent X- and T-Series Systems such as T3 or T4 series of servers. Support is included in Solaris 11.

- PrivateCore vCage uses TPM chips in conjunction with Intel Trusted Execution Technology (TXT) to validate systems on bootup.

- In mobile devices security, there are some alternatives to TPM; for example, TrustKernel's T6 secure operating system simulates the functionality of TPM in mobile devices using the ARM TrustZone technology.

- VMware ESXi hypervisor has supported TPM since 4.x, and from 5.0 it is enabled by default.

- Xen hypervisor has support of virtualized TPMs. Each guest gets its own unique, emulated, software TPM.

- KVM, combined with QEMU, has support for virtualized TPMs. As of 2012, it supports passing through the physical TPM chip to a single dedicated guest, while it is planned to also provide emulated TPMs to guests.

There are also hybrid types; for example, TPM can be integrated into an Ethernet controller, thus eliminating the need for a separate motherboard component.

Secure Coding

Securing coding is the practice of developing computer software in a way that guards against the accidental introduction of security vulnerabilities. Defects, bugs and logic flaws are consistently the primary cause of commonly exploited software vulnerabilities. Through the analysis of thousands of reported vulnerabilities, security professionals have discovered that most vulnerabilities stem from a relatively small number of common software programming errors. By identifying the insecure coding practices that lead to these errors and educating developers on secure alternatives, organizations can take proactive steps to help significantly reduce or eliminate vulnerabilities in software before deployment.

Buffer Overflow Prevention

Buffer overflows, a common software security vulnerability, happen when a process tries to store data beyond a fixed-length buffer. For example, if there are 8 slots to store items in, there will be a problem if there is an attempt to store 9 items. In computer memory the overflowed data may overwrite data in the next location which can result in a security vulnerability (stack smashing) or program termination (segmentation fault).

An example of a C program prone to a buffer overflow is

```
int vulnerable_function(char * large_user_input) {

        char dst[SMALL];

        strcpy(dst, large_user_input);

}
```

If the user input is larger than the destination buffer, a buffer overflow will occur. To fix this unsafe program, use strncpy to prevent a possible buffer overflow.

```
int secure_function(char * user_input) {

        char dst[BUF_SIZE];

    //copy a maximum of BUF_SIZE bytes

        strncpy(dst, user_input,BUF_SIZE);

}
```

Another secure alternative is to dynamically allocate memory on the heap using malloc.

```
char * secure_copy(char * src) {

        int len = strlen(src);

        char * dst = (char *) malloc(len + 1);

        if(dst != NULL){

                strncpy(dst, src, len);

                //append null terminator

            dst[len] = '\0';

        }

        return dst;

}
```

In the above code snippet, the program attempts to copy the contents of *src* into *dst,* while also checking the return value of malloc to ensure that enough memory was able to be allocated for the destination buffer.

Format String Attack Prevention

A Format String Attack is when a malicious user supplies specific inputs that will eventually be entered as an argument to a function that performs formatting, such as printf(). The attack involves the adversary reading from or writing to the stack.

The C printf function writes output to stdout. If the parameter of the printf function is not properly formatted, several security bugs can be introduced. Below is a program that is vulnerable to a format string attack.

```
int vulnerable_print(char * malicious_input) {

        printf(malicious_input);

}
```

A malicious argument passed to the program could be "%s%s%s%s%s%s%s", which can crash the program from improper memory reads.

Integer Overflow Prevention

Integer overflow occurs when an arithmetic operation results in an integer too large to be represented within the available space. A program which does not properly check for integer overflow introduces potential software bugs and exploits.

Below is a program which checks for overflow by confirming the sum is greater than or equal to x and y. If the sum did overflow, the sum would be less than x or less than y.

```
bool isValid(unsigned int x, unsigned int y) {

        unsigned int sum = x + y;

        return sum < MAX;

}
```

If the sum of x and y are less than the defined MAX, the program will return true, otherwise isValid will return false. The problem with the code is it does not check for integer overflow on the addition operation. If the sum of x and y is greater than the available space to store the integer, the integer will overflow and "roll over" to a value less than MAX.

Below is a program which checks for overflow by confirming the sum is greater than or equal to x and y. If the sum did overflow, the sum would be less than x or less than y.

```
bool isValid(unsigned int x, unsigned int y) {

        unsigned int sum = x + y;

        return sum >= x && sum >= y && sum < MAX;

}
```

References

- Heiser, Jay (January 2001). "Exposing Infosecurity Hype". Information Security Mag. TechTarget. Archived from the original on 28 March 2006. Retrieved 29 April 2013

- Moore, Robert (2005). Cybercrime: Investigating High Technology Computer Crime. Matthew Bender & Company. p. 258. ISBN 1-59345-303-5

- Bisant, David B. (October 1989). "A Two-Person Inspection Method to Improve Programming Productivity". IEEE Transactions on Software Engineering. 15 (10): 1294–1304. doi:10.1109/TSE.1989.559782. Retrieved 9 October 2015

- Jones, Capers (June 2008). "Measuring Defect Potentials and Defect Removal Efficiency" (PDF). Crosstalk, The Journal of Defense Software Engineering. Retrieved 2010-10-05

- Scahill, Jeremy ScahillJosh BegleyJeremy; Begley2015-03-10T07:35:43+00:00, Josh. "The CIA Campaign to Steal Apple's Secrets". The Intercept. Retrieved 2017-08-10

- Viega, John; Gary McGraw (2001). Building Secure Software: How to Avoid Security Problems the Right Way. MAddison-Wesley Professional. p. 528. ISBN 978-0201721522

- "Replacing Vulnerable Software with Secure Hardware: The Trusted Platform Module (TPM) and How to Use It in the Enterprise" (PDF). Trusted computing group. 2008. Retrieved 2014-06-07

Network and Internet Security

Network and internet security are important aspects of computer security. In order to completely understand computer security, it is necessary to understand the processes related to network and internet security. The following chapter elucidates the varied processes and mechanisms associated with these areas of study.

Network Security

Network security consists of the policies and practices adopted to prevent and monitor unauthorized access, misuse, modification, or denial of a computer network and network-accessible resources. Only network security can remove trojan horse viruses if it is activated. Network security involves the authorization of access to data in a network, which is controlled by the network administrator. Users choose or are assigned an ID and password or other authenticating information that allows them access to information and programs within their authority. Network security covers a variety of computer networks, both public and private, that are used in everyday jobs; conducting transactions and communications among businesses, government agencies and individuals. Networks can be private, such as within a company, and others which might be open to public access. Network security is involved in organizations, enterprises, and other types of institutions. It does as its title explains: It secures the network, as well as protecting and overseeing operations being done. The most common and simple way of protecting a network resource is by assigning it a unique name and a corresponding password.

Network Security Concept

Network security starts with Authentication, commonly with a username and a password. Since this requires just one detail authenticating the user name—i.e., the password—this is sometimes termed one-factor authentication. With two-factor authentication, something the user 'has' is also used (e.g., a security token or 'dongle', an ATM card, or a mobile phone); and with three-factor authentication, something the user 'is' is also used (e.g., a fingerprint or retinal scan).

Once authenticated, a firewall enforces access policies such as what services are allowed to be accessed by the network users. Though effective to prevent unauthorized access, this component may fail to check potentially harmful content such as computer worms or Trojans being transmitted over the network. Anti-virus software or an intrusion prevention system (IPS) help detect and inhibit the action of such malware. An anomaly-based intrusion detection system may also monitor the network like wireshark traffic and may be logged for audit purposes and for later high-level analysis. Newer systems combining unsupervised machine learning with full network traffic analysis can detect active network attackers from malicious insiders or targeted external attackers that have compromised a user machine or account.

Communication between two hosts using a network may be encrypted to maintain privacy.

Honeypots, essentially decoy network-accessible resources, may be deployed in a network as surveillance and early-warning tools, as the honeypots are not normally accessed for legitimate purposes. Techniques used by the attackers that attempt to compromise these decoy resources are studied during and after an attack to keep an eye on new exploitation techniques. Such analysis may be used to further tighten security of the actual network being protected by the honeypot. A honeypot can also direct an attacker's attention away from legitimate servers. A honeypot encourages attackers to spend their time and energy on the decoy server while distracting their attention from the data on the real server. Similar to a honeypot, a honeynet is a network set up with intentional vulnerabilities. Its purpose is also to invite attacks so that the attacker's methods can be studied and that information can be used to increase network security. A honeynet typically contains one or more honeypots.

Firewall

In computing, a firewall is a network security system that monitors and controls incoming and outgoing network traffic based on predetermined security rules. A firewall typically establishes a barrier between a trusted internal network and untrusted external network, such as the Internet.

Firewalls are often categorized as either network firewalls or host-based firewalls. Network firewalls filter traffic between two or more networks and run on network hardware. Host-based firewalls run on host computers and control network traffic in and out of those machines.

Types

Firewalls are generally categorized as network-based or host-based. Network-based firewalls are positioned on the gateway computers of LANs, WANs and intranets. They are either software appliances running on general-purpose hardware, or hardware-based firewall computer appliances. Firewall appliances may also offer other functionality to the internal network they protect, such as acting as a DHCP or VPN server for that network. Host-based firewalls are positioned on the network node itself and control network traffic in and out of those machines.. The host-based firewall may be a daemon or service as a part of the operating system or an agent application such as endpoint security or protection. Each has advantages and disadvantages. However, each has a role in layered security.

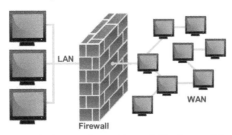

An illustration of where a firewall would be located in a network

Firewalls also vary in type depending on where communication originates, where it is intercepted, and the state of communication being traced.

Network Layer or Packet Filters

Network layer firewalls, also called packet filters, operate at a relatively low level of the TCP/IP protocol stack, not allowing packets to pass through the firewall unless they match the established rule set. The firewall administrator may define the rules; or default rules may apply. The term "packet filter" originated in the context of BSD operating systems.

Network layer firewalls generally fall into two sub-categories, stateful and stateless.

Stateful firewalls maintain context about active sessions, and use that "state information" to speed packet processing. Any existing network connection can be described by several properties, including source and destination IP address, UDP or TCP ports, and the current stage of the connection's lifetime (including session initiation, handshaking, data transfer, or completion connection). If a packet does not match an existing connection, it will be evaluated according to the ruleset for new connections. If a packet matches an existing connection based on comparison with the firewall's state table, it will be allowed to pass without further processing.

Stateless firewalls require less memory, and can be faster for simple filters that require less time to filter than to look up a session. They may also be necessary for filtering stateless network protocols that have no concept of a session. However, they cannot make more complex decisions based on what stage communications between hosts have reached.

Newer firewalls can filter traffic based on many packet attributes like source IP address, source port, destination IP address or port, destination service like HTTP or FTP. They can filter based on protocols, TTL values, network block of the originator, of the source, and many other attributes.

Commonly used packet filters on various versions of Unix are *ipfw* (FreeBSD, Mac OS X (< 10.7)), *NPF* (NetBSD), *PF* (Mac OS X (> 10.4), OpenBSD, and some other BSDs), *iptables/ipchains* (Linux) and *IPFilter*.

Application-layer

Application-layer firewalls work on the application level of the TCP/IP stack (i.e., all browser traffic, or all telnet or FTP traffic), and may intercept all packets traveling to or from an application. They block other packets (usually dropping them without acknowledgment to the sender).

On inspecting all packets for improper content, firewalls can restrict or prevent outright the spread of networked computer worms and Trojans. The additional inspection criteria can add extra latency to the forwarding of packets to their destination.

Application firewalls function by determining whether a process should accept any given connection. Application firewalls accomplish their function by hooking into socket calls to filter the connections between the application layer and the lower layers of the OSI model. Application firewalls that hook into socket calls are also referred to as socket filters. Application firewalls work much like a packet filter but application filters apply filtering rules (allow/block) on a per process basis instead of filtering connections on a per port basis. Generally, prompts are used to define rules for processes that have not yet received a connection. It is rare to find application firewalls not combined or used in conjunction with a packet filter.

Also, application firewalls further filter connections by examining the process ID of data packets against a rule set for the local process involved in the data transmission. The extent of the filtering that occurs is defined by the provided rule set. Given the variety of software that exists, application firewalls only have more complex rule sets for the standard services, such as sharing services. These per-process rule sets have limited efficacy in filtering every possible association that may occur with other processes. Also, these per-process rule sets cannot defend against modification of the process via exploitation, such as memory corruption exploits. Because of these limitations, application firewalls are beginning to be supplanted by a new generation of application firewalls that rely on mandatory access control (MAC), also referred to as sandboxing, to protect vulnerable services.

Proxies

A proxy server (running either on dedicated hardware or as software on a general-purpose machine) may act as a firewall by responding to input packets (connection requests, for example) in the manner of an application, while blocking other packets. A proxy server is a gateway from one network to another for a specific network application, in the sense that it functions as a proxy on behalf of the network user.

Proxies make tampering with an internal system from the external network more difficult, so that misuse of one internal system would not necessarily cause a security breach exploitable from outside the firewall (as long as the application proxy remains intact and properly configured). Conversely, intruders may hijack a publicly reachable system and use it as a proxy for their own purposes; the proxy then masquerades as that system to other internal machines. While use of internal address spaces enhances security, crackers may still employ methods such as IP spoofing to attempt to pass packets to a target network.

Network Address Translation

Firewalls often have network address translation (NAT) functionality, and the hosts protected behind a firewall commonly have addresses in the "private address range", as defined in RFC 1918. Firewalls often have such functionality to hide the true address of computer which is connected to the network. Originally, the NAT function was developed to address the limited number of IPv4 routable addresses that could be used or assigned to companies or individuals as well as reduce both the amount and therefore cost of obtaining enough public addresses for every computer in an organization. Although NAT on its own is not considered a security feature, hiding the addresses of protected devices has become an often used defense against network reconnaissance.

Intrusion Detection System

An intrusion detection system (IDS) is a device or software application that monitors a network or systems for malicious activity or policy violations. Any detected activity or violation is typically reported either to an administrator or collected centrally using a security information and event management (SIEM) system. A SIEM system combines outputs from multiple sources, and uses alarm filtering techniques to distinguish malicious activity from false alarms.

There is a wide spectrum of IDS, varying from antivirus software to hierarchical systems that monitor the traffic of an entire backbone network. The most common classifications are network intrusion detection systems (NIDS) and host-based intrusion detection systems (HIDS). A system that monitors important operating system files is an example of a HIDS, while a system that analyzes incoming network traffic is an example of a NIDS. It is also possible to classify IDS by detection approach: the most well-known variants are signature-based detection (recognizing bad patterns, such as malware) and anomaly-based detection (detecting deviations from a model of "good" traffic, which often relies on machine learning). Some IDS have the ability to respond to detected intrusions. Systems with response capabilities are typically referred to as an intrusion prevention system.

Comparison with Firewalls

Though they both relate to network security, an IDS differs from a firewall in that a firewall looks outwardly for intrusions in order to stop them from happening. Firewalls limit access between networks to prevent intrusion and do not signal an attack from inside the network. An IDS describes a suspected intrusion once it has taken place and signals an alarm. An IDS also watches for attacks that originate from within a system. This is traditionally achieved by examining network communications, identifying heuristics and patterns (often known as signatures) of common computer attacks, and taking action to alert operators. A system that terminates connections is called an intrusion prevention system, and is another form of an application layer firewall.

Intrusion Detection

IDS can be classified by where detection takes place (network or host) and the detection method that is employed.

Analyzed Activity

Network Intrusion Detection Systems

Network intrusion detection systems (NIDS) are placed at a strategic point or points within the network to monitor traffic to and from all devices on the network. It performs an analysis of passing traffic on the entire subnet, and matches the traffic that is passed on the subnets to the library of known attacks. Once an attack is identified, or abnormal behavior is sensed, the alert can be sent to the administrator. An example of an NIDS would be installing it on the subnet where firewalls are located in order to see if someone is trying to break into the firewall. Ideally one would scan all inbound and outbound traffic, however doing so might create a bottleneck that would impair the overall speed of the network. OPNET and NetSim are commonly used tools for simulating network intrusion detection systems. NID Systems are also capable of comparing signatures for similar packets to link and drop harmful detected packets which have a signature matching the records in the NIDS. When we classify the design of the NIDS according to the system interactivity property, there are two types: on-line and off-line NIDS, often referred to as inline and tap mode, respectively. On-line NIDS deals with the network in real time. It analyses the Ethernet packets and applies some rules, to decide if it is an attack or not. Off-line NIDS deals with stored data and passes it through some processes to decide if it is an attack or not.

Host Intrusion Detection Systems

Host intrusion detection systems (HIDS) run on individual hosts or devices on the network. A HIDS monitors the inbound and outbound packets from the device only and will alert the user or administrator if suspicious activity is detected. It takes a snapshot of existing system files and matches it to the previous snapshot. If the critical system files were modified or deleted, an alert is sent to the administrator to investigate. An example of HIDS usage can be seen on mission critical machines, which are not expected to change their configurations.

Intrusion detection systems can also be system-specific using custom tools and honeypots.

Detection Method

Signature-based

Signature-based IDS refers to the detection of attacks by looking for specific patterns, such as byte sequences in network traffic, or known malicious instruction sequences used by malware. This terminology originates from anti-virus software, which refers to these detected patterns as signatures. Although signature-based IDS can easily detect known attacks, it is impossible to detect new attacks, for which no pattern is available.

Anomaly-based

Anomaly-based intrusion detection systems were primarily introduced to detect unknown attacks, in part due to the rapid development of malware. The basic approach is to use machine learning to create a model of trustworthy activity, and then compare new behavior against this model. Although this approach enables the detection of previously unknown attacks, it may suffer from false positives: previously unknown legitimate activity may also be classified as malicious.

New types of what could be called anomaly-based intrusion detection systems are being viewed by Gartner as User and Entity Behavior Analytics (UEBA) (an evolution of the user behavior analytics category) and network traffic analysis (NTA). In particular, NTA deals with malicious insiders as well as targeted external attacks that have compromised a user machine or account. Gartner has noted that some organizations have opted for NTA over more traditional IDS.

Intrusion Prevention

Some systems may attempt to stop an intrusion attempt but this is neither required nor expected of a monitoring system. Intrusion detection and prevention systems (IDPS) are primarily focused on identifying possible incidents, logging information about them, and reporting attempts. In addition, organizations use IDPS for other purposes, such as identifying problems with security policies, documenting existing threats and deterring individuals from violating security policies. IDPS have become a necessary addition to the security infrastructure of nearly every organization.

IDPS typically record information related to observed events, notify security administrators of important observed events and produce reports. Many IDPS can also respond to a detected threat by attempting to prevent it from succeeding. They use several response techniques, which involve the IDPS stopping the attack itself, changing the security environment (e.g. reconfiguring a firewall) or changing the attack's content.

Intrusion prevention systems (IPS), also known as intrusion detection and prevention systems (IDPS), are network security appliances that monitor network or system activities for malicious activity. The main functions of intrusion prevention systems are to identify malicious activity, log information about this activity, report it and attempt to block or stop it.

Intrusion prevention systems are considered extensions of intrusion detection systems because they both monitor network traffic and/or system activities for malicious activity. The main differences are, unlike intrusion detection systems, intrusion prevention systems are placed in-line and are able to actively prevent or block intrusions that are detected. IPS can take such actions as sending an alarm, dropping detected malicious packets, resetting a connection or blocking traffic from the offending IP address. An IPS also can correct cyclic redundancy check (CRC) errors, defragment packet streams, mitigate TCP sequencing issues, and clean up unwanted transport and network layer options.

Classification

Intrusion prevention systems can be classified into four different types:

1. Network-based intrusion prevention system (NIPS): monitors the entire network for suspicious traffic by analyzing protocol activity.

2. Wireless intrusion prevention system (WIPS): monitor a wireless network for suspicious traffic by analyzing wireless networking protocols.

3. Network behavior analysis (NBA): examines network traffic to identify threats that generate unusual traffic flows, such as distributed denial of service (DDoS) attacks, certain forms of malware and policy violations.

4. Host-based intrusion prevention system (HIPS): an installed software package which monitors a single host for suspicious activity by analyzing events occurring within that host.

Detection Methods

The majority of intrusion prevention systems utilize one of three detection methods: signature-based, statistical anomaly-based, and stateful protocol analysis.

1. Signature-based detection: Signature-based IDS monitors packets in the

Network and compares with pre-configured and pre-determined attack patterns known as signatures.

2. Statistical anomaly-based detection: An IDS which is anomaly-based will monitor network traffic and compare it against an established baseline. The baseline will identify what is "normal" for that network – what sort of bandwidth is generally used and what protocols are used. It may however, raise a False Positive alarm for legitimate use of bandwidth if the baselines are not intelligently configured.

3. Stateful protocol analysis detection: This method identifies deviations of protocol states by comparing observed events with "pre-determined profiles of generally accepted definitions of benign activity".

Limitations

*   Noise can severely limit an intrusion detection system's effectiveness. Bad packets generated from software bugs, corrupt DNS data, and local packets that escaped can create a significantly high false-alarm rate.

*   It is not uncommon for the number of real attacks to be far below the number of false-alarms. Number of real attacks is often so far below the number of false-alarms that the real attacks are often missed and ignored.

*   Many attacks are geared for specific versions of software that are usually outdated. A constantly changing library of signatures is needed to mitigate threats. Outdated signature databases can leave the IDS vulnerable to newer strategies.

*   For signature-based IDS, there will be lag between a new threat discovery and its signature being applied to the IDS. During this lag time, the IDS will be unable to identify the threat.

*   It cannot compensate for weak identification and authentication mechanisms or for weaknesses in network protocols. When an attacker gains access due to weak authentication mechanisms then IDS cannot prevent the adversary from any malpractice.

*   Encrypted packets are not processed by most intrusion detection devices. Therefore, the encrypted packet can allow an intrusion to the network that is undiscovered until more significant network intrusions have occurred.

*   Intrusion detection software provides information based on the network address that is associated with the IP packet that is sent into the network. This is beneficial if the network address contained in the IP packet is accurate. However, the address that is contained in the IP packet could be faked or scrambled.

- Due to the nature of NIDS systems, and the need for them to analyse protocols as they are captured, NIDS systems can be susceptible to the same protocol-based attacks to which network hosts may be vulnerable. Invalid data and TCP/IP stack attacks may cause an NIDS to crash.

Evasion Techniques

There are a number of techniques which attackers are using, the following are considered 'simple' measures which can be taken to evade IDS:

- Fragmentation: by sending fragmented packets, the attacker will be under the radar and can easily bypass the detection system's ability to detect the attack signature.

- Avoiding defaults: The TCP port utilised by a protocol does not always provide an indication to the protocol which is being transported. For example, an IDS may expect to detect a trojan on port 12345. If an attacker had reconfigured it to use a different port, the IDS may not be able to detect the presence of the trojan.

- Coordinated, low-bandwidth attacks: coordinating a scan among numerous attackers (or agents) and allocating different ports or hosts to different attackers makes it difficult for the IDS to correlate the captured packets and deduce that a network scan is in progress.

- Address spoofing/proxying: attackers can increase the difficulty of the ability of Security Administrators to determine the source of the attack by using poorly secured or incorrectly configured proxy servers to bounce an attack. If the source is spoofed and bounced by a server, it makes it very difficult for IDS to detect the origin of the attack.

- Pattern change evasion: IDS generally rely on 'pattern matching' to detect an attack. By changing the data used in the attack slightly, it may be possible to evade detection. For example, an Internet Message Access Protocol (IMAP) server may be vulnerable to a buffer overflow, and an IDS is able to detect the attack signature of 10 common attack tools. By modifying the payload sent by the tool, so that it does not resemble the data that the IDS expects, it may be possible to evade detection.

Development

The earliest preliminary IDS concept was delineated in 1980 by James Anderson at the National Security Agency and consisted of a set of tools intended to help administrators review audit trails. User access logs, file access logs, and system event logs are examples of audit trails.

Fred Cohen noted in 1987 that it is impossible to detect an intrusion in every case, and that the resources needed to detect intrusions grow with the amount of usage.

Dorothy E. Denning, assisted by Peter G. Neumann, published a model of an IDS in 1986 that formed the basis for many systems today. Her model used statistics for anomaly detection, and resulted in an early IDS at SRI International named the Intrusion Detection Expert System (IDES), which ran on Sun workstations and could consider both user and network level data. IDES had a dual approach with a rule-based Expert System to detect known types of intrusions plus a statistical anomaly detection component based on profiles of users, host systems, and target systems. Lunt proposed adding an Artificial neural network as a third component. She said all three components could then report to a resolver. SRI followed IDES in 1993 with the Next-generation Intrusion Detection Expert System (NIDES).

The Multics intrusion detection and alerting system (MIDAS), an expert system using P-BEST and Lisp, was developed in 1988 based on the work of Denning and Neumann. Haystack was also developed in that year using statistics to reduce audit trails.

In 1986 the National Security Agency started an IDS research transfer program under Rebecca Bace. Bace later published the seminal text on the subject, *Intrusion Detection*, in 2000.

Wisdom & Sense (W&S) was a statistics-based anomaly detector developed in 1989 at the Los Alamos National Laboratory. W&S created rules based on statistical analysis, and then used those rules for anomaly detection.

In 1990, the Time-based Inductive Machine (TIM) did anomaly detection using inductive learning of sequential user patterns in Common Lisp on a VAX 3500 computer. The Network Security Monitor (NSM) performed masking on access matrices for anomaly detection on a Sun-3/50 workstation. The Information Security Officer's Assistant (ISOA) was a 1990 prototype that considered a variety of strategies including statistics, a profile checker, and an expert system. ComputerWatch at AT&T Bell Labs used statistics and rules for audit data reduction and intrusion detection.

Then, in 1991, researchers at the University of California, Davis created a prototype Distributed Intrusion Detection System (DIDS), which was also an expert system. The Network Anomaly Detection and Intrusion Reporter (NADIR), also in 1991, was a prototype IDS developed at the Los Alamos National Laboratory's Integrated Computing Network (ICN), and was heavily influenced by the work of Denning and Lunt. NADIR used a statistics-based anomaly detector and an expert system.

The Lawrence Berkeley National Laboratory announced Bro in 1998, which used its own rule language for packet analysis from libpcap data. Network Flight Recorder (NFR) in 1999 also used libpcap.

APE was developed as a packet sniffer, also using libpcap, in November, 1998, and was renamed Snort one month later. Snort has since become the world's largest used IDS/IPS system with over 300,000 active users. It can monitor both local systems, and remote capture points using the TZSP protocol.

The Audit Data Analysis and Mining (ADAM) IDS in 2001 used tcpdump to build profiles of rules for classifications. In 2003, Yongguang Zhang and Wenke Lee argue for the importance of IDS in networks with mobile nodes.

In 2015, Viegas and his colleagues proposed an anomaly-based intrusion detection engine, aiming System-on-Chip (SoC) for applications in Internet of Things (IoT), for instance. The proposal applies machine learning for anomaly detection, providing energy-efficiency to a Decision Tree, Naive-Bayes, and k-Nearest Neighbors classifiers implementation in an Atom CPU and its hardware-friendly implementation in a FPGA. In the literature, this was the first work that implement each classifier equivalently in software and hardware and measures its energy consumption on both. Additionally, it was the first time that was measured the energy consumption for extracting each features used to make the network packet classification, implemented in software and hardware.

Anomaly-based Intrusion Detection System

An anomaly-based intrusion detection system, is an intrusion detection system for detecting both network and computer intrusions and misuse by monitoring system activity and classifying it as either *normal* or *anomalous*. The classification is based on heuristics or rules, rather than patterns or signatures, and attempts to detect any type of misuse that falls out of normal system operation. This is as opposed to signature-based systems, which can only detect attacks for which a signature has previously been created.

In order to positively identify attack traffic, the system must be taught to recognize normal system activity. The two phases of a majority of anomaly detection systems consist of the training phase (where a profile of normal behaviors is built) and testing phase (where current traffic is compared with the profile created in the training phase). Anomalies are detected in several ways, most often with artificial intelligence type techniques. Systems using artificial neural networks have been used to great effect. Another method is to define what normal usage of the system comprises using a strict mathematical model, and flag any deviation from this as an attack. This is known as strict anomaly detection. Other techniques used to detect anomalies include data mining methods, grammar based methods, and Artificial Immune System.

Network-based anomalous intrusion detection systems often provide a second line of defense to detect anomalous traffic at the physical and network layers after it has passed through a firewall or other security appliance on the border of a network. Host-based anomalous intrusion detection systems are one of the last layers of defense and reside on computer end points. They allow for fine-tuned, granular protection of end points at the application level.

Anomaly-based Intrusion Detection at both the network and host levels have a few shortcomings; namely a high false-positive rate and the ability to be fooled by a correctly delivered attack. Attempts have been made to address these issues through techniques used by PAYL and MCPAD.

Honeypot

In computer terminology, a honeypot is a computer security mechanism set to detect, deflect, or, in some manner, counteract attempts at unauthorized use of information systems. Generally, a honeypot consists of data (for example, in a network site) that appears to be a legitimate part of the site, but is actually isolated and monitored, and that seems to contain information or a resource of value to attackers, who are then blocked. This is similar to police sting operations, colloquially known as "baiting," a suspect.

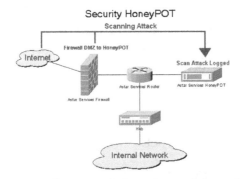

Honeypot diagram to help understand the topic

Types

Honeypots can be classified based on their deployment (use/action) and based on their level of involvement. Based on deployment, honeypots may be classified as

- production honeypots
- research honeypots

Production honeypots are easy to use, capture only limited information, and are used primarily by corporations. Production honeypots are placed inside the production network with other production servers by an organization to improve their overall state of security. Normally, production honeypots are low-interaction honeypots, which are easier to deploy. They give less information about the attacks or attackers than research honeypots.

Research honeypots are run to gather information about the motives and tactics of the black hat community targeting different networks. These honeypots do not add direct value to a specific organization; instead, they are used to research the threats that organizations face and to learn how to better protect against those threats. Research honeypots are complex to deploy and maintain, capture extensive information, and are used primarily by research, military, or government organizations.

Based on design criteria, honeypots can be classified as:

- pure honeypots

- high-interaction honeypots

- low-interaction honeypots

Pure honeypots are full-fledged production systems. The activities of the attacker are monitored by using a bug tap that has been installed on the honeypot's link to the network. No other software needs to be installed. Even though a pure honeypot is useful, stealthiness of the defense mechanisms can be ensured by a more controlled mechanism.

High-interaction honeypots imitate the activities of the production systems that host a variety of services and, therefore, an attacker may be allowed a lot of services to waste his time. By employing virtual machines, multiple honeypots can be hosted on a single physical machine. Therefore, even if the honeypot is compromised, it can be restored more quickly. In general, high-interaction honeypots provide more security by being difficult to detect, but they are expensive to maintain. If virtual machines are not available, one physical computer must be maintained for each honeypot, which can be exorbitantly expensive. Example: Honeynet.

Low-interaction honeypots simulate only the services frequently requested by attackers. Since they consume relatively few resources, multiple virtual machines can easily be hosted on one physical system, the virtual systems have a short response time, and less code is required, reducing the complexity of the virtual system's security. Example: Honeyd.

Deception Technology

Recently, a new market segment called deception technology has emerged using basic honeypot technology with the addition of advanced automation for scale. Deception technology addresses the automated deployment of honeypot resources over a large commercial enterprise or government institution.

Malware Honeypots

Malware honeypots are used to detect malware by exploiting the known replication and attack vectors of malware. Replication vectors such as USB flash drives can easily be verified for evidence of modifications, either through manual means or utilizing special-purpose honeypots that emulate drives. Malware increasingly is used to search for and steal cryptocurrencies, which provides opportunities for services such as Bitcoin Vigil to create and monitor honeypots by using small amount of money to provide early warning alerts of malware infection.

Spam Versions

Spammers abuse vulnerable resources such as open mail relays and open proxies. Some system administrators have created honeypot programs that masquerade as these abusable resources to discover spammer activity. There are several capabilities such honeypots provide to these administrators and the existence of such fake abusable systems makes abuse more difficult or risky. Honeypots can be a powerful countermeasure to abuse from those who rely on very high volume abuse (e.g., spammers).

These honeypots can reveal the abuser's IP address and provide bulk spam capture (which enables operators to determine spammers' URLs and response mechanisms). For open relay honeypots, it is possible to determine the e-mail addresses ("dropboxes") spammers use as targets for their test messages, which are the tool they use to detect open relays. It is then simple to deceive the spammer: transmit any illicit relay e-mail received addressed to that dropbox e-mail address. That tells the spammer the honeypot is a genuine abusable open relay, and they often respond by sending large quantities of relay spam to that honeypot, which stops it. The apparent source may be another abused system—spammers and other abusers may use a chain of abused systems to make detection of the original starting point of the abuse traffic difficult.

This in itself is indicative of the power of honeypots as anti-spam tools. In the early days of anti-spam honeypots, spammers, with little concern for hiding their location, felt safe testing for vulnerabilities and sending spam directly from their own systems. Honeypots made the abuse riskier and more difficult.

Spam still flows through open relays, but the volume is much smaller than in 2001 to 2002. While most spam originates in the U.S., spammers hop through open relays across political boundaries to mask their origin. Honeypot operators may use intercepted relay tests to recognize and thwart attempts to relay spam through their honeypots. "Thwart" may mean "accept the relay spam but decline to deliver it." Honeypot operators may discover other details concerning the spam and the spammer by examining the captured spam messages.

Open relay honeypots include Jackpot, written in Java by Jack Cleaver; *smtpot.py*, written in Python by Karl A. Krueger; and *spamhole (honeypot)|spamhole*, written in C. The *Bubblegum Proxypot* is an open source honeypot (or "proxypot").

Email Trap

An email address that is not used for any other purpose than to receive spam can also be considered a spam honeypot. Compared with the term "spamtrap", the term "honeypot" might be more suitable for systems and techniques that are used to detect or counterattacks and probes. With a spamtrap, spam arrives at its destination "legitimately"—exactly as non-spam email would arrive.

An amalgam of these techniques is Project Honey Pot, a distributed, open source project that uses honeypot pages installed on websites around the world. These honeypot pages disseminate uniquely tagged spamtrap email addresses and spammers can then be tracked—the corresponding spam mail is subsequently sent to these spamtrap e-mail addresses.

Database Honeypot

Databases often get attacked by intruders using SQL injection. As such activities are not recognized by basic firewalls, companies often use database firewalls for protection. Some of the available SQL database firewalls provide/support honeypot architectures so that the intruder runs against a trap database while the web application remains functional.

Detection

Just as honeypots are weapons against spammers, honeypot detection systems are spammer-employed counter-weapons. As detection systems would likely use unique characteristics of specific honeypots to identify them, a great deal of honeypots in use makes the set of unique characteristics larger and more daunting to those seeking to detect and thereby identify them. This is an unusual circumstance in software: a situation in which "versionitis" (a large number of versions of the same software, all differing slightly from each other) can be beneficial. There's also an advantage in having some easy-to-detect honeypots deployed. Fred Cohen, the inventor of the Deception Toolkit, even argues that every system running his honeypot should have a deception port that adversaries can use to detect the honeypot. Cohen believes that this might deter adversaries.

Honey Nets

"A 'honey net' is a network of high interaction honeypots that simulates a production network and configured such that all activity is monitored, recorded and in a degree, discreetly regulated."

-Lance Spitzner,
Honeynet Project

Two or more honeypots on a network form a *honey net*. Typically, a honey net is used for monitoring a larger and/or more diverse network in which one honeypot may not be sufficient. Honey nets and honeypots are usually implemented as parts of larger network intrusion detection systems. A *honey farm* is a centralized collection of honeypots and analysis tools.

The concept of the honey net first began in 1999 when Lance Spitzner, founder of the Honeynet Project, published the paper "To Build a Honeypot".

Metaphor

The metaphor of a bear being attracted to and stealing honey is common in many traditions, including Germanic and Slavic. A common Germanic kenning for the bear was "honey eater". The tradition of bears stealing honey has been passed down through stories and folklore, especially the well known Winnie the Pooh.

Internet Security

Example of Webtitan Web Filter by TitanHQ blocking a restricted site.

Internet security is a branch of computer security specifically related to the Internet, often involving browser security but also network security on a more general level, as it applies to other applications or operating systems as a whole. Its objective is to establish rules and measures to use against attacks over the Internet. The Internet represents an insecure channel for exchanging information leading to a high risk of intrusion or fraud, such as phishing, online viruses, trojans, worms and more.

Many methods are used to protect the transfer of data, including encryption and from-the-ground-up engineering. The current focus is on prevention as much as on real time protection against well known and new threats.

Threats

Malicious Software

A computer user can be tricked or forced into downloading software onto a computer that is of malicious intent. Such software comes in many forms, such as viruses, Trojan horses, spyware, and worms.

- Malware, short for malicious software, is any software used to disrupt computer operation, gather sensitive information, or gain access to private computer systems. Malware is defined by its malicious intent, acting against the requirements of the computer user, and does not include software that causes unintentional harm due to some deficiency. The term badware is sometimes used, and applied to both true (malicious) malware and unintentionally harmful software.

- A botnet is a network of zombie computers that have been taken over by a robot or bot that performs large-scale malicious acts for the creator of the botnet.

- Computer Viruses are programs that can replicate their structures or effects by infecting other files or structures on a computer. The common use of a virus is to take over a computer to steal data.

- Computer worms are programs that can replicate themselves throughout a computer network, performing malicious tasks throughout.

- Ransomware is a type of malware which restricts access to the computer system that it infects, and demands a ransom paid to the creator(s) of the malware in order for the restriction to be removed.

- Scareware is scam software with malicious payloads, usually of limited or no benefit, that are sold to consumers via certain unethical marketing practices. The selling approach uses social engineering to cause shock, anxiety, or the perception of a threat, generally directed at an unsuspecting user.

- Spyware refers to programs that surreptitiously monitor activity on a computer system and report that information to others without the user's consent.

- A Trojan horse, commonly known as a *Trojan*, is a general term for malicious software that pretends to be harmless, so that a user willingly allows it to be downloaded onto the computer.

- KeyLogger, Keystroke logging, often referred to as keylogging or keyboard capturing, is the action of recording (logging) the keys struck on a keyboard.

Denial-of-service Attacks

A denial-of-service attack (DoS attack) or distributed denial-of-service attack (DDoS attack) is an attempt to make a computer resource unavailable to its intended users. Another way of understanding DDoS is seeing it as attacks in cloud computing environment that are growing due to the essential characteristics of cloud computing. Although the means to carry out, motives for, and targets of a DoS attack may vary, it generally consists of the concerted efforts to prevent an Internet site or service from functioning efficiently or at all, temporarily or indefinitely. According to businesses who participated in an international business security survey, 25% of respondents experienced a DoS attack in 2007 and 16.8% experienced one in 2010.

Phishing

Phishing is an attack which targets online users for extraction of their sensitive information such as username, password and credit card information. Phishing occurs when the attacker pretends to be a trustworthy entity, either via email or web page. Victims are directed to fake web pages, which are dressed to look legitimate, via spoof emails, instant messenger/social media or other avenues. Often tactics such as email spoofing are used to make emails appear to be from legitimate senders, or long complex subdomains hide the real website host. Insurance group RSA said that phishing accounted for worldwide losses of $1.5 billion in 2012.

Application Vulnerabilities

Applications used to access Internet resources may contain security vulnerabilities such as memory safety bugs or flawed authentication checks. The most severe of these bugs can give network attackers full control over the computer. Most security applications and suites are incapable of adequate defense against these kinds of attacks.

Remedies

Network Layer Security

TCP/IP protocols may be secured with cryptographic methods and security protocols. These protocols include Secure Sockets Layer (SSL), succeeded by Transport Layer Security (TLS) for web traffic, Pretty Good Privacy (PGP) for email, and IPsec for the network layer security.

Internet Protocol Security (IPsec)

IPsec is designed to protect TCP/IP communication in a secure manner. It is a set of security extensions developed by the Internet Task Force (IETF). It provides security and authentication at the IP layer by transforming data using encryption. Two main types of transformation that form the basis of IPsec: the Authentication Header (AH) and ESP. These two protocols provide data integrity, data origin authentication, and anti-replay service. These protocols can be used alone or in combination to provide the desired set of security services for the Internet Protocol (IP) layer.

The basic components of the IPsec security architecture are described in terms of the following functionalities:

- Security protocols for AH and ESP

- Security association for policy management and traffic processing

- Manual and automatic key management for the Internet key exchange (IKE)

- Algorithms for authentication and encryption

The set of security services provided at the IP layer includes access control, data origin integrity, protection against replays, and confidentiality. The algorithm allows these sets to work independently without affecting other parts of the implementation. The IPsec implementation is operated in a host or security gateway environment giving protection to IP traffic.

Multi-factor Authentication

Multi-factor authentication (MFA) is a method of computer access control in which a user is granted access only after successfully presenting several separate pieces of evidence to an authentication mechanism – typically at least two of the following categories: knowledge (something they know), possession (something they have), and inherence (something they are). Internet resources, such as websites and email, may be secured using multi-factor authentication.

Security Token

Some online sites offer customers the ability to use a six-digit code which randomly changes every 30–60 seconds on a security token. The keys on the security token have built in mathematical computations and manipulate numbers based on the current time built into the device. This means that every thirty seconds there is only a certain array of numbers possible which would be correct to validate access to the online account. The website that the user is logging into would be made aware of that device's serial number and would know the computation and correct time built into the device to verify that the number given is indeed one of the handful of six-digit numbers that works in that given 30-60 second cycle. After 30–60 seconds the device will present a new random six-digit number which can log into the website.

Electronic Mail Security

Background

Email messages are composed, delivered, and stored in a multiple step process, which starts with the message's composition. When the user finishes composing the message and sends it, the message is transformed into a standard format: an RFC 2822 formatted message. Afterwards, the message can be transmitted. Using a network connection, the mail client, referred to as a mail user agent (MUA), connects to a mail transfer agent (MTA) operating on the mail server. The mail client then provides the sender's identity to the server. Next, using the mail server commands, the client sends the recipient list to the mail server. The client then supplies the message. Once the mail server receives and processes the message, several events occur: recipient server identification, connection establishment, and message transmission. Using Domain Name System (DNS) services, the sender's mail server determines the mail server(s) for the recipient(s). Then, the server opens up a connection(s) to the recipient mail server(s) and sends the message employing a process similar to that used by the originating client, delivering the message to the recipient(s).

Pretty Good Privacy (PGP)

Pretty Good Privacy provides confidentiality by encrypting messages to be transmitted or data files to be stored using an encryption algorithm such as Triple DES or CAST-128. Email messages can be protected by using cryptography in various ways, such as the following:

- Signing an email message to ensure its integrity and confirm the identity of its sender.

- Encrypting the body of an email message to ensure its confidentiality.

- Encrypting the communications between mail servers to protect the confidentiality of both message body and message header.

The first two methods, message signing and message body encryption, are often used together; however, encrypting the transmissions between mail servers is typically used only when two organizations want to protect emails regularly sent between each other. For example, the organizations could establish a virtual private network (VPN) to encrypt the communications between their mail servers over the Internet. Unlike methods that can only encrypt a message body, a VPN can encrypt entire messages, including email header information such as senders, recipients, and subjects. In some cases, organizations may need to protect header information. However, a VPN solution alone cannot provide a message signing mechanism, nor can it provide protection for email messages along the entire route from sender to recipient.

Multipurpose Internet Mail Extensions (MIME)

MIME transforms non-ASCII data at the sender's site to Network Virtual Terminal (NVT) ASCII data and delivers it to client's Simple Mail Transfer Protocol (SMTP) to be sent through the Internet. The server SMTP at the receiver's side receives the NVT ASCII data and delivers it to MIME to be transformed back to the original non-ASCII data.

Message Authentication Code

A Message authentication code (MAC) is a cryptography method that uses a secret key to encrypt a message. This method outputs a MAC value that can be decrypted by the receiver, using the same secret key used by the sender. The Message Authentication Code protects both a message's data integrity as well as its authenticity.

Firewalls

A computer firewall controls access between networks. It generally consists of gateways and filters which vary from one firewall to another. Firewalls also screen network traffic and are able to block traffic that is dangerous. Firewalls act as the intermediate server between SMTP and Hypertext Transfer Protocol (HTTP) connections.

Role of Firewalls in Web Security

Firewalls impose restrictions on incoming and outgoing Network packets to and from private networks. Incoming or outgoing traffic must pass through the firewall; only authorized traffic is allowed to pass through it. Firewalls create checkpoints between an internal private network and the public Internet, also known as *choke points* (borrowed from the identical military term of a combat limiting geographical feature). Firewalls can create choke points based on IP source and TCP port number. They can also serve as the platform for IPsec. Using tunnel mode capability, firewall can be used to implement VPNs. Firewalls can also limit network exposure by hiding the internal network system and information from the public Internet.

Types of Firewall

Packet Filter

A packet filter is a first generation firewall that processes network traffic on a packet-by-packet basis. Its main job is to filter traffic from a remote IP host, so a router is needed to connect the internal network to the Internet. The router is known as a screening router, which screens packets leaving and entering the network.

Stateful Packet Inspection

In a stateful firewall the circuit-level gateway is a proxy server that operates at the network level of an Open Systems Interconnection (OSI) model and statically defines what traffic will be allowed. Circuit proxies will forward Network packets (formatted unit of data) containing a given port number, if the port is permitted by the algorithm. The main advantage of a proxy server is its ability to provide Network Address Translation (NAT), which can hide the user's IP address from the Internet, effectively protecting all internal information from the Internet.

Application-level Gateway

An application-level firewall is a third generation firewall where a proxy server operates at the very top of the OSI model, the IP suite application level. A network packet is forwarded only if a connection is established using a known protocol. Application-level gateways are notable for analyzing entire messages rather than individual packets of data when the data are being sent or received.

Browser Choice

Web browser statistics tend to affect the amount a Web browser is exploited. For example, Internet Explorer 6, which used to own a majority of the Web browser market share, is considered extremely insecure because vulnerabilities were exploited due to its former popularity. Since browser choice is now more evenly distributed (Internet Explorer at 28.5%, Firefox at 18.4%, Google Chrome at 40.8%, and so on), vulnerabilities are exploited in many different browsers.

Internet Security Products

Antivirus

Antivirus software and Internet security programs can protect a programmable device from attack by detecting and eliminating viruses; Antivirus software was mainly shareware in the early years of the Internet, but there are now several free security applications on the Internet to choose from for all platforms.

Password Managers

A password manager is a software application that helps a user store and organize passwords. Password managers usually store passwords encrypted, requiring the user to create a master password; a single, ideally very strong password which grants the user access to their entire password database from top to bottom.

Security Suites

So called *security suites* were first offered for sale in 2003 (McAfee) and contain a suite of firewalls, anti-virus, anti-spyware and more. They also offer theft protection, portable storage device safety check, private Internet browsing, cloud anti-spam, a file shredder or make security-related decisions (answering popup windows) and several were free of charge.

Browser Security

Browser security is the application of Internet security to web browsers in order to protect networked data and computer systems from breaches of privacy or malware. Security exploits of browsers often use JavaScript — sometimes with cross-site scripting

(XSS) — sometimes with a secondary payload using Adobe Flash. Security exploits can also take advantage of vulnerabilities (security holes) that are commonly exploited in all browsers (including Mozilla Firefox, Google Chrome, Opera, Microsoft Internet Explorer, and Safari).

Security

Web browsers can be breached in one or more of the following ways:

- Operating system is breached and malware is reading/modifying the browser memory space in privilege mode

- Operating system has a malware running as a background process, which is reading/modifying the browser memory space in privileged mode

- Main browser executable can be hacked

- Browser components may be hacked

- Browser plugins can be hacked

- Browser network communications could be intercepted outside the machine

The browser may not be aware of any of the breaches above and may show user a safe connection is made.

Whenever a browser communicates with a website, the website, as part of that communication, collects some information about the browser (in order to process the formatting of the page to be delivered, if nothing else). If malicious code has been inserted into the website's content, or in a worst-case scenario, if that website has been specifically designed to host malicious code, then vulnerabilities specific to a particular browser can allow this malicious code to run processes within the browser application in unintended ways (and remember, one of the bits of information that a website collects from a browser communication is the browser's identity-allowing specific vulnerabilities to be exploited). Once an attacker is able to run processes on the visitor's machine, then exploiting known security vulnerabilities can allow the attacker to gain privileged access (if the browser isn't already running with privileged access) to the "infected" system in order to perform an even greater variety of malicious processes and activities on the machine or even the victim's whole network.

Breaches of web browser security are usually for the purpose of bypassing protections to display pop-up advertising collecting personally identifiable information (PII) for either Internet marketing or identity theft, website tracking or web analytics about a user against their will using tools such as web bugs, Clickjacking, Likejacking (where Facebook's like button is targeted), HTTP cookies, zombie cookies or Flash cookies (Local

Shared Objects or LSOs); installing adware, viruses, spyware such as Trojan horses (to gain access to users' personal computers via cracking) or other malware including on-line banking theft using man-in-the-browser attacks.

Vulnerabilities in the web browser software itself can be minimized by keeping browser software updated, but will not be sufficient if the underlying operating system is compromised, for example, by a rootkit. Some subcomponents of browsers such as scripting, add-ons, and cookies are particularly vulnerable ("the confused deputy problem") and also need to be addressed.

Following the principle of defence in depth, a fully patched and correctly configured browser may not be sufficient to ensure that browser-related security issues cannot occur. For example, a rootkit can capture keystrokes while someone logs into a banking website, or carry out a man-in-the-middle attack by modifying network traffic to and from a web browser. DNS hijacking or DNS spoofing may be used to return false positives for mistyped website names, or to subvert search results for popular search engines. Malware such as RSPlug simply modifies a system's configuration to point at rogue DNS servers.

Browsers can use more secure methods of network communication to help prevent some of these attacks:

- DNS: DNSSec and DNSCrypt, for example with non-default DNS servers such as Google Public DNS or OpenDNS.

- HTTP: HTTP Secure and SPDY with digitally signed public key certificates or Extended Validation Certificates.

Perimeter defenses, typically through firewalls and the use of filtering proxy servers that block malicious websites and perform antivirus scans of any file downloads, are commonly implemented as a best practice in large organizations to block malicious network traffic before it reaches a browser.

The topic of browser security has grown to the point of spawning the creation of entire organizations, such as The Browser Exploitation Framework Project, creating platforms to collect tools to breach browser security, ostensibly in order to test browsers and network systems for vulnerabilities.

Plugins and Extensions

Although not part of the browser per se, browser plugins and extensions extend the attack surface, exposing vulnerabilities in Adobe Flash Player, Adobe (Acrobat) Reader, Java plugin, and ActiveX that are commonly exploited. Malware may also be implemented as a browser extension, such as a browser helper object in the case of Internet Explorer. Browsers like Google Chrome and Mozilla Firefox can block—or warn users of—insecure plugins.

Flash

An August 2009 study by the Social Science Research Network found that 50% of websites using Flash were also employing flash cookies, yet privacy policies rarely disclosed them, and user controls for privacy preferences were lacking. Most browsers' cache and history delete functions do not affect Flash Player's writing Local Shared Objects to its own cache, and the user community is much less aware of the existence and function of Flash cookies than HTTP cookies. Thus, users having deleted HTTP cookies and purged browser history files and caches may believe that they have purged all tracking data from their computers when in fact Flash browsing history remains. As well as manual removal, the BetterPrivacy addon for Firefox can remove Flash cookies. Adblock Plus can be used to filter out specific threats and Flashblock can be used to give an option before allowing content on otherwise trusted sites.

Charlie Miller recommended "not to install Flash" at the computer security conference CanSecWest. Several other security experts also recommend to either not install Adobe Flash Player or to block it.

Password Security Model

The contents of a web page are arbitrary and controlled by the entity owning the domain named displayed in the address bar. If HTTPS is used, then encryption is used to secure against attackers with access to the network from changing the page contents en route. For normal password usage on the WWW, when the user is confronted by a dialog asking for their password, they are supposed to look at the address bar to determine whether the domain name in the address bar is the correct place to send the password.

An un-compromised browser guarantees that the address bar is correct. This guarantee is one reason why browsers will generally display a warning when entering fullscreen mode, on top of where the address bar would normally be, so that a fullscreen website cannot make a fake browser user interface with a fake address bar.

Privacy

Hardware Browser

There have been attempts to market hardware-based browsers running from non-writable, read-only file systems. Data cannot stored on the device and the media cannot be overwritten, presenting a clean executable each time it loads. The first such device was the ZeusGard Secure Hardware Browser, released in late 2013. The ZeusGard website has not been functional since mid-2016. Another device, the iCloak® Stik from the iCloak website provides a complete Live OS which completely replaces the computer's entire operating system and offers two web browsers from the read-only system. With iCloak they provide the Tor browser for Anonymous browsing as well as a regular Firefox browser for non-anonymous browsing. Any non-secured web traffic (not using https, for example), could still be subject to man-in-the-middle alteration or other network traffic-based manipulations.

LiveCD

LiveCDs, which run an operating system from a non-writable source, typically come with internet browsers as part of their default image. If the original LiveCD image is free of malware, all of the software used, including the internet browser, will load free of malware every time the LiveCD image is booted.

Browser Hardening

Browsing the Internet as a least-privilege user account (i.e. without administrator privileges) limits the ability of a security exploit in a web browser from compromising the whole operating system.

Internet Explorer 4 and later allows the blacklisting and whitelisting of ActiveX controls, add-ons and browser extensions in various ways.

Internet Explorer 7 added "protected mode", a technology that hardens the browser through the application of a security sandboxing feature of Windows Vista called Mandatory Integrity Control. Google Chrome provides a sandbox to limit web page access to the operating system.

Suspected malware sites reported to Google, and confirmed by Google, are flagged as hosting malware in certain browsers.

There are third-party extensions and plugins available to harden even the latest browsers, and some for older browsers and operating systems. Whitelist-based software such as NoScript can block JavaScript and Adobe Flash which is used for most attacks on privacy, allowing users to choose only sites they know are safe - AdBlock Plus also uses whitelist ad filtering rules subscriptions, though both the software itself and the filtering list maintainers have come under controversy for by-default allowing some sites to pass the pre-set filters. The US-CERT recommends to block Flash using NoScript.

Remote Browser Isolation

A relatively new approach (started getting a lot of attention in 2017), known as browser isolation or remote browsing, involves executing browsing sessions in a remote location outside the firewall (e.g., in the DMZ or cloud), within an isolated virtual environment such as a container. The securely rendered web content is streamed back to the local browser in real time, providing a seamless and interactive user experience, while ensuring that any malicious code is fully contained—never making its way onto the endpoint. The entire virtual environment can then be reset to a known good state or discarded altogether at the end of the session.

Best Practice

- Load clean software: Boot from a known clean OS that has a known clean internet browser

- Prevent attacks via third-party software: Use a hardened internet browser or add-on-free-browsing mode

- Prevent DNS manipulation: Use trusted and secure DNS

- Avoid website-based exploits: Employ link-checking browser plug-ins commonly found in internet security software

- Avoid malicious content: Employ perimeter defenses and anti-malware software

Trust No One

Trust no one (TNO) is an approach towards Internet and software security issues. In all Internet communication and software packages where some sort of secrecy is needed, usually some sort of encryption is applied. The trust no one approach teaches that no one (but oneself) should be trusted when it comes to the storage of the keys behind the applied encryption technology.

Many encryption technologies rely on the trust of an external party. For instance the security of secure end-to-end SSL connections relies on the trust of a certificate authority (CA).

The trust no one design philosophy requires that the keys for encryption should always be, and stay, in the hands of the user that applies them. This implies that no external party can access the encrypted data (assumed that the encryption is strong enough). It also implies that an external party cannot provide a backup mechanism for password recovery.

Although the philosophy of trust no one at least assures the reliability of the communication of the user that creates it, in real life and in society many communication means rely on a trust relationship between at least two parties.

IP Fragmentation Attack

IP fragmentation is the process of breaking up a single Internet Protocol (IP) datagram into multiple packets of smaller size. Every network link has a characteristic size of messages that may be transmitted, called the maximum transmission unit (MTU).

Part of the TCP/IP suite is the Internet Protocol (IP) which resides at the Internet Layer of this model. IP is responsible for the transmission of packets between network end points. IP includes some features which provide basic measures of fault-tolerance (time to live, checksum), traffic prioritization (type of service) and support for the fragmentation of larger packets into multiple smaller packets (ID field, fragment offset). The support for fragmentation of larger packets provides a protocol allowing routers to fragment a packet into smaller packets when the original packet is too large for the supporting datalink frames. IP fragmentation exploits (attacks) use the fragmentation protocol within IP as an attack vector.

Process

IP datagrams are encapsulated in datalink frames, and, therefore, the link MTU affects larger IP datagrams and forces them to be split into pieces equal to or smaller than the MTU size.

This can be accomplished by several approaches:

- To set the IP datagram size equal or smaller than the directly attached medium and delegate all further fragmentation of datagrams to routers, meaning that routers decide if the current datagram should be re-fragmented or not. This offloads a lot of work on to routers, and can also result in packets being segmented by several IP routers one after another, resulting in very peculiar fragmentation.

- To preview all links between source and destination and select the smallest MTU in this route, assuming there is a unique route. This way we make sure that the fragmentation is done by the sender, using a packet-size smaller than the selected MTU, and there is no further fragmentation en route. This solution, called Path MTU Discovery, allows a sender to fragment/segment a long Internet packet, rather than relying on routers to perform IP-level fragmentation. This is more efficient and more scalable. It is therefore the recommended method in the current Internet. The problem with this approach is that each packet is routed independently; they may well typically follow the same route, but they may not, and so a probe packet to determine fragmentation may follow a path different from paths taken by later packets.

Three fields in the IP header are used to implement fragmentation and reassembly. The "Identification", "Flags" and "Fragment Offset" fields.

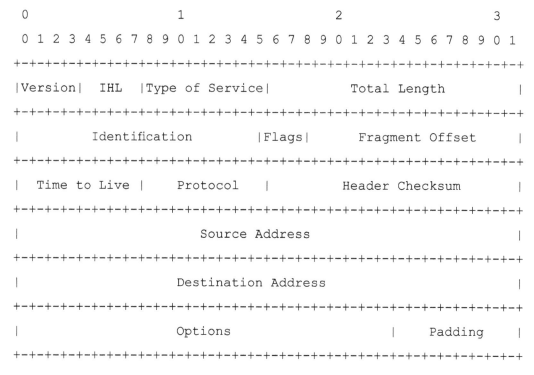

Flags:

> A 3 bit field which says if the datagram is a part of a fragmented data frame or not.
>
> Bit 0: reserved, must be zero (unless datagram is adhering to RFC 3514).
>
> Bit 1: (AF) 0 = May Fragment, 1 = Don't Fragment.
>
> Bit 2: (AF) 0 = Last Fragment, 1 = More Fragments.

```
    0   1   2                      13 bits

  +---+---+---+    +-----------------------------+
  |   | D | M |    |        Fragment Offset      |
  | 0 | F | F |    +-----------------------------+
  +---+---+---+
```

Fragment Offset specifies the fragment's position within the original Datagram, measured in 8-byte units.

Accordingly, every fragment except the last must contain a multiple of 8 bytes of data. It is obvious that Fragment Offset can hold 8192 (2^{13}) units but the datagram can't have 8192 * 8 = 65536 bytes of data because "Total Length" field of IP header records the total size including the header and data. An IP header is at least 20 bytes long, so the maximum value for "Fragment Offset" is restricted to 8189, which leaves room for 3 bytes in the last fragment.

Because an IP internet can be connectionless, fragments from one datagram may be interleaved with those from another at the destination. The "Identification field" uniquely identifies the fragments of a particular datagram.

The source system sets "Identification" field in each datagram to a unique value for all datagrams which use the same source IP address, destination IP address, and "Protocol" values, for the lifetime of the datagram on the internet. This way the destination can distinguish which incoming fragments belong to a unique datagram and buffer all of them until the last fragment is received. The last fragment sets the "More Fragment" bit to 0 and this tells the receiving station to start reassembling the data if all fragments have been received.

The following is a real-life fragmentation example:

The following was obtained using the Ethereal protocol analyzer to capture ICMP echo request packets. To simulate this open up a terminal and type ping ip_dest -n 1 -l 65000.

The results are as follows:

```
    No. Time        Source              Destination         Protocol Info
      1 0.000000     87.247.163.96          66.94.234.13          ICMP
Echo (ping) request
      2 0.000000     87.247.163.96          66.94.234.13            IP
Fragmented IP protocol (proto=ICMP 0x01, off=1480)
      3 0.002929     87.247.163.96          66.94.234.13            IP
Fragmented IP protocol (proto=ICMP 0x01, off=2960)
      4 6.111328     87.247.163.96          66.94.234.13            IP
Fragmented IP protocol (proto=ICMP 0x01, off=4440)
      5 6.123046     87.247.163.96          66.94.234.13            IP
Fragmented IP protocol (proto=ICMP 0x01, off=5920)
      6 6.130859     87.247.163.96          66.94.234.13            IP
Fragmented IP protocol (proto=ICMP 0x01, off=7400)
      7 6.170898     87.247.163.96          66.94.234.13            IP
Fragmented IP protocol (proto=ICMP 0x01, off=8880)
      8 6.214843     87.247.163.96          66.94.234.13            IP
Fragmented IP protocol (proto=ICMP 0x01, off=10360)
      9 6.239257     87.247.163.96          66.94.234.13            IP
Fragmented IP protocol (proto=ICMP 0x01, off=11840)
     10 6.287109     87.247.163.96          66.94.234.13            IP
Fragmented IP protocol (proto=ICMP 0x01, off=13320)
     11 6.302734     87.247.163.96          66.94.234.13            IP
```

```
Fragmented IP protocol (proto=ICMP 0x01, off=14800)

    12 6.327148    87.247.163.96            66.94.234.13        IP
Fragmented IP protocol (proto=ICMP 0x01, off=16280)

    13 6.371093    87.247.163.96            66.94.234.13        IP
Fragmented IP protocol (proto=ICMP 0x01, off=17760)

    14 6.395507    87.247.163.96            66.94.234.13        IP
Fragmented IP protocol (proto=ICMP 0x01, off=19240)

    15 6.434570    87.247.163.96            66.94.234.13        IP
Fragmented IP protocol (proto=ICMP 0x01, off=20720)

    16 6.455078    87.247.163.96            66.94.234.13        IP
Fragmented IP protocol (proto=ICMP 0x01, off=22200)

    17 6.531250    87.247.163.96            66.94.234.13        IP
Fragmented IP protocol (proto=ICMP 0x01, off=23680)

    18 6.550781    87.247.163.96            66.94.234.13        IP
Fragmented IP protocol (proto=ICMP 0x01, off=25160)

    19 6.575195    87.247.163.96            66.94.234.13        IP
Fragmented IP protocol (proto=ICMP 0x01, off=26640)

    20 6.615234    87.247.163.96            66.94.234.13        IP
Fragmented IP protocol (proto=ICMP 0x01, off=28120)

    21 6.634765    87.247.163.96            66.94.234.13        IP
Fragmented IP protocol (proto=ICMP 0x01, off=29600)

    22 6.659179    87.247.163.96            66.94.234.13        IP
Fragmented IP protocol (proto=ICMP 0x01, off=31080)

    23 6.682617    87.247.163.96            66.94.234.13        IP
Fragmented IP protocol (proto=ICMP 0x01, off=32560)

    24 6.699218    87.247.163.96            66.94.234.13        IP
Fragmented IP protocol (proto=ICMP 0x01, off=34040)

    25 6.743164    87.247.163.96            66.94.234.13        IP
Fragmented IP protocol (proto=ICMP 0x01, off=35520)

    26 6.766601    87.247.163.96            66.94.234.13        IP
Fragmented IP protocol (proto=ICMP 0x01, off=37000)

    27 6.783203    87.247.163.96            66.94.234.13        IP
Fragmented IP protocol (proto=ICMP 0x01, off=38480)

    28 6.806640    87.247.163.96            66.94.234.13        IP
Fragmented IP protocol (proto=ICMP 0x01, off=39960)

    29 6.831054    87.247.163.96            66.94.234.13        IP
Fragmented IP protocol (proto=ICMP 0x01, off=41440)

    30 6.850586    87.247.163.96            66.94.234.13        IP
Fragmented IP protocol (proto=ICMP 0x01, off=42920)

    31 6.899414    87.247.163.96            66.94.234.13        IP
Fragmented IP protocol (proto=ICMP 0x01, off=44400)
```

```
    32 6.915039     87.247.163.96          66.94.234.13          IP
Fragmented IP protocol (proto=ICMP 0x01, off=45880)

    33 6.939453     87.247.163.96          66.94.234.13          IP
Fragmented IP protocol (proto=ICMP 0x01, off=47360)

    34 6.958984     87.247.163.96          66.94.234.13          IP
Fragmented IP protocol (proto=ICMP 0x01, off=48840)

    35 6.983398     87.247.163.96          66.94.234.13          IP
Fragmented IP protocol (proto=ICMP 0x01, off=50320)

    36 7.023437     87.247.163.96          66.94.234.13          IP
Fragmented IP protocol (proto=ICMP 0x01, off=51800)

    37 7.046875     87.247.163.96          66.94.234.13          IP
Fragmented IP protocol (proto=ICMP 0x01, off=53280)

    38 7.067382     87.247.163.96          66.94.234.13          IP
Fragmented IP protocol (proto=ICMP 0x01, off=54760)

    39 7.090820     87.247.163.96          66.94.234.13          IP
Fragmented IP protocol (proto=ICMP 0x01, off=56240)

    40 7.130859     87.247.163.96          66.94.234.13          IP
Fragmented IP protocol (proto=ICMP 0x01, off=57720)

    41 7.151367     87.247.163.96          66.94.234.13          IP
Fragmented IP protocol (proto=ICMP 0x01, off=59200)

    42 7.174804     87.247.163.96          66.94.234.13          IP
Fragmented IP protocol (proto=ICMP 0x01, off=60680)

    43 7.199218     87.247.163.96          66.94.234.13          IP
Fragmented IP protocol (proto=ICMP 0x01, off=62160)

    44 7.214843     87.247.163.96          66.94.234.13          IP
Fragmented IP protocol (proto=ICMP 0x01, off=63640)

    45 7.258789     87.247.163.96          66.94.234.13          IP
Fragmented IP protocol (proto=ICMP 0x01, off=65120)
```

The first packet details:

```
    No.Time          Source              Destination         Proto-
col Info

    1 0.000000     87.247.163.96          66.94.234.13          ICMP
Echo (ping) request
```

Frame 1 (1514 bytes on wire, 1514 bytes captured) Ethernet II, Src: OmronTat_00:00:00 (00:00:0a:00:00:00), Dst: 40:0f:20:00:0c:00 (40:0f:20:00:0c:00) Internet Protocol, Src: 87.247.163.96 (87.247.163.96), Dst: 66.94.234.13 (66.94.234.13) Internet Control Message Protocol

Type: 8 (Echo (ping) request)

```
Code: 0

Checksum: 0x6b7d

Identifier: 0x0600

Sequence number: 0x0200

Data (1472 bytes)
```

The second packet details:

```
    No. Time           Source                   Destination           Proto-
col Info

     2 0.000000     87.247.163.96              66.94.234.13              IP
Fragmented IP protocol (proto=ICMP 0x01, off=1480)
```

```
Frame  2  (1514  bytes  on  wire,  1514  bytes  captured)  Ethernet  II,
Src:  OmronTat_00:00:00  (00:00:0a:00:00:00),  Dst:  40:0f:20:00:0c:00
(40:0f:20:00:0c:00)    Internet    Protocol,    Src:    87.247.163.96
(87.247.163.96), Dst: 66.94.234.13 (66.94.234.13) Data (1480 bytes)
```

Note that only the first fragment contains the ICMP header and all remaining fragments are generated without the ICMP header.

Two important points here:

- In some datalink protocols such as Ethernet, only the first fragment contains the full upper layer header, meaning that other fragments look like beheaded datagrams.

- Additional overhead imposed over network because all fragments contains their own IP header. Additional overhead = (number_of_fragments - 1) * (ip_header_len).

Exploits

IP fragment overlapped

The IP fragment overlapped exploit occurs when two fragments contained within the same IP datagram have offsets that indicate that they overlap each other in positioning within the datagram. This could mean that either fragment A is being completely overwritten by fragment B, or that fragment A is partially being overwritten by fragment B. Some operating systems do not properly handle fragments that overlap in this manner and may throw exceptions or behave in other undesirable ways upon receipt of overlapping fragments. This is the basis for the teardrop attack. Overlapping fragments may also be used in an attempt to bypass Intrusion Detection Systems. In this exploit, part of an attack is sent in fragments along with additional random data; future fragments may overwrite the random data with the remainder of the attack. If the completed datagram is not properly reassembled at the IDS, the attack will go undetected.

IP fragmentation buffer full

The IP fragmentation buffer full exploit occurs when there is an excessive amount of incomplete fragmented traffic detected on the protected network. This could be due to an excessive number of incomplete fragmented datagrams, a large number of fragments for individual datagrams or a combination of quantity of incomplete datagrams and size/number of fragments in each datagram. This type of traffic is most likely an attempt to bypass security measures or Intrusion Detection Systems by intentional fragmentation of attack activity.

IP fragment overrun

The IP Fragment Overrun exploit is when a reassembled fragmented datagram exceeds the declared IP data length or the maximum datagram length. By definition, no IP datagram should be larger than 65,535 bytes. Systems that try to process these large datagrams can crash, and can be indicative of a denial of service attempt.

IP fragment too many datagrams

The Too Many Datagrams exploit is identified by an excessive number of incomplete fragmented datagrams detected on the network. This is usually either a denial of service attack or an attempt to bypass security measures. An example of "Too Many Datagrams", "Incomplete Datagram" and "Fragment Too Small" is the Rose Attack.

IP fragment incomplete datagram

This exploit occurs when a datagram can not be fully reassembled due to missing data. This can indicate a denial of service attack or an attempt to defeat packet filter security policies.

IP Fragment Too Small

If an IP fragment is too small it indicates that the fragment is likely intentionally crafted. Any fragment other than the final fragment that is less than 400 bytes could be considered too small. Small fragments may be used in denial of service attacks or in an attempt to bypass security measures or detection.

Fragmentation for Evasion

Network infrastructure equipment such as routers, load-balancers, firewalls and IDS have inconsistent visibility into fragmented packets. For example, a device may subject the initial fragment to rigorous inspection and auditing, but might allow all additional fragments to pass unchecked. Some attacks may use this fact to evade detection by placing incriminating payload data in fragments. Devices operating in "full" proxy mode are generally not susceptible to this subterfuge.

VoIP Vulnerabilities

VoIP is vulnerable to similar types of attacks that Web connection and emails are prone to. VoIP attractiveness, because of its low fixed cost and numerous features, come with some risks that are well known to the developers an are constantly being addressed. But these risks are usually not mentioned to the business which is the most common target.

VoIP also allows the use of fraud and shady practices that most people are not aware of. And while this practices are restricted by most providers, the possibility that someone is using them for his own gain still exists.

Vulnerabilities

Remote Eavesdropping

Unencrypted connections lead to communication and security breaches. Hackers/ trackers can eavesdrops on important or private conversations and extract valuable data. The overheard conversations might be sold to or used by competing businesses. The gathered intelligence can also be used as blackmail for personal gain.

Network Attacks

Attacks to the user network, or internet provider can disrupt or even cut the connection. Since VOIP is highly dependent on our internet connection, direct attacks on the internet connection, or provider, are highly effective way of attack. This kind of attacks are targeting office telephony, since mobile internet is harder to interrupt. Also mobile applications not relying on internet connection to make VOIP calls. are immune to such attacks.

Default Security Settings

Hardphones (a.k.a. VoIP phone) are smart devices, they are more a computer than a phone, and as such they need to be well configured. The Chinese manufacturers, in some cases are using default passwords for each of the manufactured devices leading to vulnerabilities.

VOIP over WiFi

VoIP even while VoIP is relatively secure in 2017, it still needs a source of internet, which in most cases is WIFI network. And while a home/office WIFI can be relatively secure, using public or shared networks will further compromise the connection.

VOIP Exploits

VoIP Spam

Voip has its own spam called SPIT (Spam over Internet Telephony). Using the unlimited extensions provided by VOIP PBX capabilities, the spammer can constantly harass his target from different numbers. The process is not hard to automate and can fill the targets voice mail with notifications. The caller can make calls often enough to block the target from getting important incoming calls. This practices can cost a lot to the caller and are rarely used for other than marketing needs.

VoIP Phishing

VOIP users can change their Caller ID (a.k.a. Caller ID spoofing), allowing caller to represent himself as relative, colleague, or part of the family, in order to extract information, money or benefits form the target.

Transport Layer Security

Transport Layer Security (TLS) – and its predecessor, Secure Sockets Layer (SSL), which is now prohibited from use by the Internet Engineering Task Force (IETF) – are cryptographic protocols that provide communications security over a computer network. Several versions of the protocols find widespread use in applications such as web browsing, email, Internet faxing, instant messaging, and voice over IP (VoIP). Websites are able to use TLS to secure all communications between their servers and web browsers.

The TLS protocol aims primarily to provide privacy and data integrity between two communicating computer applications. When secured by TLS, connections between a client and a server have one or more of the following properties:

- The connection is *private* (or *secure*) because symmetric cryptography is used to encrypt the data transmitted. The keys for this symmetric encryption are generated uniquely for each connection and are based on a shared secret negotiated at the start of the session. The server and client negotiate the details of which encryption algorithm and cryptographic keys to use before the first byte of data is transmitted. The negotiation of a shared secret is both secure (the negotiated secret is unavailable to eavesdroppers and cannot be obtained, even by an attacker who places themselves in the middle of the connection) and reliable (no attacker can modify the communications during the negotiation without being detected).

- The identity of the communicating parties can be *authenticated* using public-key cryptography. This authentication can be made optional, but is generally required for at least one of the parties (typically the server).

- The connection ensures *integrity* because each message transmitted includes a message integrity check using a message authentication code to prevent undetected loss or alteration of the data during transmission.

In addition to the properties above, careful configuration of TLS can provide additional privacy-related properties such as forward secrecy, ensuring that any future disclosure of encryption keys cannot be used to decrypt any TLS communications recorded in the past.

TLS supports many different methods for exchanging keys, encrypting data, and authenticating message integrity. As a result, secure configuration of TLS involves many configurable parameters, and not all choices provide all of the privacy-related properties described in the list above.

Attempts have been made to subvert aspects of the communications security that TLS seeks to provide and the protocol has been revised several times to address these security threats. Developers of web browsers have also revised their products to defend against potential security weaknesses after these were discovered.

The TLS protocol comprises two layers: the TLS record and the TLS handshake protocols.

TLS is a proposed Internet Engineering Task Force (IETF) standard, first defined in 1999 and updated in RFC 5246 (August 2008) and RFC 6176 (March 2011). It builds on the earlier SSL specifications (1994, 1995, 1996) developed by Netscape Communications for adding the HTTPS protocol to their Navigator web browser.

Description

Client-server applications use the TLS protocol to communicate across a network in a way designed to prevent eavesdropping and tampering.

Since applications can communicate either with or without TLS (or SSL), it is necessary for the client to indicate to the server the setup of a TLS connection. One of the main ways of achieving this is to use a different port number for TLS connections, for example port 443 for HTTPS. Another mechanism is for the client to make a protocol-specific request to the server to switch the connection to TLS; for example, by making a

STARTTLS request when using the mail and news protocols.

Once the client and server have agreed to use TLS, they negotiate a stateful connection by using a handshaking procedure. The protocols use a handshake with an asymmetric cipher to establish not only cipher settings but also a session-specific shared key with which further communication is encrypted using a symmetric cipher. During this handshake, the client and server agree on various parameters used to establish the connection's security:

- The handshake begins when a client connects to a TLS-enabled server requesting a secure connection and the client presents a list of supported cipher suites (ciphers and hash functions).

- From this list, the server picks a cipher and hash function that it also supports and notifies the client of the decision.

- The server usually then provides identification in the form of a digital certificate. The certificate contains the server name, the trusted certificate authority (CA) that vouches for the authenticity of the certificate, and the server's public encryption key.

- The client confirms the validity of the certificate before proceeding.

- To generate the session keys used for the secure connection, the client either:

  o encrypts a random number with the server's public key and sends the result to the server (which only the server should be able to decrypt with its private key); both parties then use the random number to generate a unique session key for subsequent encryption and decryption of data during the session.

  o uses Diffie–Hellman key exchange to securely generate a random and unique session key for encryption and decryption that has the additional property of forward secrecy: if the server's private key is disclosed in future, it cannot be used to decrypt the current session, even if the session is intercepted and recorded by a third party.

This concludes the handshake and begins the secured connection, which is encrypted and decrypted with the session key until the connection closes. If any one of the above steps fails, then the TLS handshake fails and the connection is not created.

TLS and SSL do not fit neatly into any single layer of the OSI model or the TCP/IP model. TLS runs "on top of some reliable transport protocol (e.g., TCP)," which would imply that it is above the transport layer. It serves encryption to higher layers, which is normally the function of the presentation layer. However, applications generally use TLS as if it were a transport layer, even though applications using TLS must actively control initiating TLS handshakes and handling of exchanged authentication certificates.

Digital Certificates

A digital certificate certifies the ownership of a public key by the named subject of the certificate, and indicates certain expected usages of that key. This allows others (relying parties) to rely upon signatures or on assertions made by the private key that corresponds to the certified public key.

Certificate Authorities

TLS typically relies on a set of trusted third-party certificate authorities to establish the authenticity of certificates. Trust is usually anchored in a list of certificates distributed with user agent software, and can be modified by the relying party.

According to Netcraft, who monitors active TLS certificates, the market-leading CA has been Symantec since the beginning of their survey (or VeriSign before the authentication services business unit was purchased by Symantec). Symantec currently accounts for just under a third of all certificates and 44% of the valid certificates used by the 1 million busiest websites, as counted by Netcraft.

As a consequence of choosing X.509 certificates, certificate authorities and a public key infrastructure are necessary to verify the relation between a certificate and its owner, as well as to generate, sign, and administer the validity of certificates. While this can be more convenient than verifying the identities via a web of trust, the 2013 mass surveillance disclosures made it more widely known that certificate authorities are a weak point from a security standpoint, allowing man-in-the-middle attacks (MITM).

Algorithm

Key Exchange or Key Agreement

Before a client and server can begin to exchange information protected by TLS, they must securely exchange or agree upon an encryption key and a cipher to use when encrypting data. Among the methods used for key exchange/agreement are: public and private keys generated with RSA (denoted TLS_RSA in the TLS handshake protocol), Diffie–Hellman (TLS_DH), ephemeral Diffie–Hellman (TLS_DHE), Elliptic Curve Diffie–Hellman (TLS_ECDH), ephemeral Elliptic Curve Diffie–Hellman (TLS_ECDHE), anonymous Diffie–Hellman (TLS_DH_anon), pre-shared key (TLS_PSK) and Secure Remote Password (TLS_SRP).

The TLS_DH_anon and TLS_ECDH_anon key agreement methods do not authenticate the server or the user and hence are rarely used because those are vulnerable to man-in-the-middle attack. Only TLS_DHE and TLS_ECDHE provide forward secrecy.

Public key certificates used during exchange/agreement also vary in the size of the public/private encryption keys used during the exchange and hence the robustness of the security provided. In July 2013, Google announced that it would no longer use 1024 bit public keys and would switch instead to 2048 bit keys to increase the security of the TLS encryption it provides to its users because the encryption strength is directly related to the key size.

Key exchange/agreement and authentication							
Algorithm	SSL 2.0	SSL 3.0	TLS 1.0	TLS 1.1	TLS 1.2	TLS 1.3 (Draft)	Status
RSA	Yes	Yes	Yes	Yes	Yes	No	
DH-RSA	No	Yes	Yes	Yes	Yes	No	
DHE-RSA (forward secrecy)	No	Yes	Yes	Yes	Yes	Yes	
ECDH-RSA	No	No	Yes	Yes	Yes	No	
ECDHE-RSA (forward secrecy)	No	No	Yes	Yes	Yes	Yes	
DH-DSS	No	Yes	Yes	Yes	Yes	No	
DHE-DSS (forward secrecy)	No	Yes	Yes	Yes	Yes	No	
ECDH-ECDSA	No	No	Yes	Yes	Yes	No	
ECDHE-ECDSA (forward secrecy)	No	No	Yes	Yes	Yes	Yes	Defined for TLS 1.2 in RFCs
PSK	No	No	Yes	Yes	Yes		
PSK-RSA	No	No	Yes	Yes	Yes		
DHE-PSK (forward secrecy)	No	No	Yes	Yes	Yes		
ECDHE-PSK (forward secrecy)	No	No	Yes	Yes	Yes		
SRP	No	No	Yes	Yes	Yes		
SRP-DSS	No	No	Yes	Yes	Yes		
SRP-RSA	No	No	Yes	Yes	Yes		
Kerberos	No	No	Yes	Yes	Yes		
DH-ANON (insecure)	No	Yes	Yes	Yes	Yes		
ECDH-ANON (insecure)	No	No	Yes	Yes	Yes		
GOST R 34.10-94 / 34.10-2001	No	No	Yes	Yes	Yes		Proposed in RFC drafts

Cipher

Cipher security against publicly known feasible attacks									
Cipher			Protocol version						Status
Type	Algorithm	Nominal strength (bits)	SSL 2.0	SSL 3.0 [n 1][n 2][n 3][n 4]	TLS 1.0 [n 1][n 3]	TLS 1.1 [n 1]	TLS 1.2 [n 1]	TLS 1.3 (Draft)	
Block cipher with mode of operation	AES GCM[n 5]	256, 128	N/A	N/A	N/A	N/A	Secure	Secure	Defined for TLS 1.2 in RFCs
	AES CCM[n 5]		N/A	N/A	N/A	N/A	Secure	Secure	
	AES CBC[n 6]		N/A	N/A	Depends on mitigations	Secure	Secure	N/A	
	Camellia GCM[n 5]	256, 128	N/A	N/A	N/A	N/A	Secure	Secure	
	Camellia CBC[n 6]		N/A	N/A	Depends on mitigations	Secure	Secure	N/A	
	ARIA GCM[n 5]	256, 128	N/A	N/A	N/A	N/A	Secure	Secure	
	ARIA CBC[n 6]		N/A	N/A	Depends on mitigations	Secure	Secure	N/A	
	SEED CBC[n 6]	128	N/A	N/A	Depends on mitigations	Secure	Secure	N/A	
	3DES EDE CBC[n 6][n 7]	112[n 8]	Insecure	Insecure	Insecure	Insecure	Insecure	N/A	
	GOST 28147-89 CNT[n 7]	256	N/A	N/A	Insecure	Insecure	Insecure		Defined in RFC 4357
	IDEA CBC[n 6][n 7][n 9]	128	Insecure	Insecure	Insecure	Insecure	N/A	N/A	Removed from TLS 1.2
	DES CBC[n 6][n 7][n 9]	056	Insecure	Insecure	Insecure	Insecure	N/A	N/A	
		040[n 10]	Insecure	Insecure	Insecure	N/A	N/A	N/A	Forbidden in TLS 1.1 and later
	RC2 CBC[n 6][n 7]	040[n 10]	Insecure	Insecure	Insecure	N/A	N/A	N/A	
Stream cipher	ChaCha20-Poly1305[n 5]	256	N/A	N/A	N/A	N/A	Secure	Secure	Defined for TLS 1.2 in RFCs
	RC4[n 11]	128	Insecure	Insecure	Insecure	Insecure	Insecure	N/A	Prohibited in all versions of TLS by RFC 7465
		040[n 10]	Insecure	Insecure	Insecure	N/A	N/A	N/A	
None	Null[n 12]	–	N/A	Insecure	Insecure	Insecure	Insecure	Insecure	Defined for TLS 1.2 in RFCs

Data Integrity

Message authentication code (MAC) is used for data integrity. HMAC is used for CBC mode of block ciphers and stream ciphers. AEAD is used for authenticated encryption such as GCM mode and CCM mode.

Data integrity							
Algorithm	SSL 2.0	SSL 3.0	TLS 1.0	TLS 1.1	TLS 1.2	TLS 1.3 (Draft)	Status
HMAC-MD5	Yes	Yes	Yes	Yes	Yes	No	Defined for TLS 1.2 in RFCs
HMAC-SHA1	No	Yes	Yes	Yes	Yes	No	
HMAC-SHA256/384	No	No	No	No	Yes	No	
AEAD	No	No	No	No	Yes	Yes	
GOST 28147-89 IMIT	No	No	Yes	Yes	Yes		Proposed in RFC drafts
GOST R 34.11-94	No	No	Yes	Yes	Yes		

Security

SSL 2.0

SSL 2.0 is flawed in a variety of ways:

- Identical cryptographic keys are used for message authentication and encryption. (In SSL 3.0, MAC secrets may be larger than encryption keys, so messages can remain tamper resistant even if encryption keys are broken.)

- SSL 2.0 has a weak MAC construction that uses the MD5 hash function with a secret prefix, making it vulnerable to length extension attacks.

- SSL 2.0 does not have any protection for the handshake, meaning a man-in-the-middle downgrade attack can go undetected.

- SSL 2.0 uses the TCP connection close to indicate the end of data. This means that truncation attacks are possible: the attacker simply forges a TCP FIN, leaving the recipient unaware of an illegitimate end of data message (SSL 3.0 fixes this problem by having an explicit closure alert).

- SSL 2.0 assumes a single service and a fixed domain certificate, which clashes with the standard feature of virtual hosting in Web servers. This means that most websites are practically impaired from using SSL.

SSL 2.0 is disabled by default, beginning with Internet Explorer 7, Mozilla Firefox 2, Opera 9.5, and Safari. After it sends a TLS "ClientHello", if Mozilla Firefox finds that the server is unable to complete the handshake, it will attempt to fall back to using SSL 3.0 with an SSL 3.0 "ClientHello" in SSL 2.0 format to maximize the likelihood of successfully handshaking with older servers. Support for SSL 2.0 (and weak 40-bit and 56-bit ciphers) has been removed completely from Opera as of version 10.

SSL 3.0

SSL 3.0 improved upon SSL 2.0 by adding SHA-1–based ciphers and support for certificate authentication.

From a security standpoint, SSL 3.0 should be considered less desirable than TLS 1.0. The SSL 3.0 cipher suites have a weaker key derivation process; half of the master key that is established is fully dependent on the MD5 hash function, which is not resistant to collisions and is, therefore, not considered secure. Under TLS 1.0, the master key that is established depends on both MD5 and SHA-1 so its derivation process is not currently considered weak. It is for this reason that SSL 3.0 implementations cannot be validated under FIPS 140-2.

In October 2014, the vulnerability in the design of SSL 3.0 was reported, which makes CBC mode of operation with SSL 3.0 vulnerable to the padding attack.

TLS

TLS has a variety of security measures:

- Protection against a downgrade of the protocol to a previous (less secure) version or a weaker cipher suite.

- Numbering subsequent Application records with a sequence number and using this sequence number in the message authentication codes (MACs).

- Using a message digest enhanced with a key (so only a key-holder can check the MAC). The HMAC construction used by most TLS cipher suites is specified in RFC 2104 (SSL 3.0 used a different hash-based MAC).

- The message that ends the handshake ("Finished") sends a hash of all the exchanged handshake messages seen by both parties.

- The pseudorandom function splits the input data in half and processes each one with a different hashing algorithm (MD5 and SHA-1), then XORs them together to create the MAC. This provides protection even if one of these algorithms is found to be vulnerable.

Attacks against TLS/SSL

Significant attacks against TLS/SSL are listed below:

Note: In February 2015, IETF issued an informational RFC summarizing the various known attacks against TLS/SSL.

Renegotiation Attack

A vulnerability of the renegotiation procedure was discovered in August 2009 that can lead to plaintext injection attacks against SSL 3.0 and all current versions of TLS. For example, it allows an attacker who can hijack an https connection to splice their own requests into the beginning of the conversation the client has with the web server. The attacker can't actually decrypt the client–server communication, so it is different from a typical man-in-the-middle attack. A short-term fix is for web servers to stop allowing renegotiation, which typically will not require other changes unless client certificate authentication is used. To fix the vulnerability, a renegotiation indication extension was proposed for TLS. It will require the client and server to include and verify information about previous handshakes in any renegotiation handshakes. This extension has become a proposed standard and has been assigned the number RFC 5746. The RFC has been implemented by several libraries.

Downgrade Attacks: FREAK Attack and Logjam Attack

A protocol downgrade attack (also called a version rollback attack) tricks a web server into negotiating connections with previous versions of TLS (such as SSLv2) that have long since been abandoned as insecure.

Previous modifications to the original protocols, like False Start (adopted and enabled by Google Chrome) or Snap Start, reportedly introduced limited TLS protocol downgrade attacks or allowed modifications to the cipher suite list sent by the client to the server. In doing so, an attacker might succeed in influencing the cipher suite selection in an attempt to downgrade the cipher suite negotiated to use either a weaker symmetric encryption algorithm or a weaker key exchange. A paper presented at an ACM conference on computer and communications security in 2012 demonstrated that the False Start extension was at risk: in certain circumstances it could allow an attacker to recover the encryption keys offline and to access the encrypted data.

Encryption downgrade attacks can force servers and clients to negotiate a connection using cryptographically weak keys. In 2014, a man-in-the-middle attack called FREAK was discovered affecting the OpenSSL stack, the default Android web browser, and some Safari browsers. The attack involved tricking servers into negotiating a TLS connection using cryptographically weak 512 bit encryption keys.

Logjam is a security exploit discovered in May 2015 that exploits the option of using legacy "export-grade" 512-bit Diffie–Hellman groups dating back to the 1990s. It forces susceptible servers to downgrade to cryptographically weak 512-bit Diffie–Hellman groups. An attacker can then deduce the keys the client and server determine using the Diffie–Hellman key exchange.

Cross-protocol Attacks: DROWN

The DROWN attack is an exploit that attacks servers supporting contemporary SSL/TLS protocol suites by exploiting their support for the obsolete, insecure, SSLv2 protocol to leverage an attack on connections using up-to-date protocols that would otherwise be secure. DROWN exploits a vulnerability in the protocols used and the configuration of the server, rather than any specific implementation error. Full details of

DROWN were announced in March 2016, together with a patch for the exploit. At that time, more than 81,000 of the top 1 million most popular websites were among the TLS protected websites that were vulnerable to the DROWN attack.

BEAST Attack

On September 23, 2011 researchers Thai Duong and Juliano Rizzo demonstrated a proof of concept called BEAST (Browser Exploit Against SSL/TLS) using a Java applet to violate same origin policy constraints, for a long-known cipher block chaining (CBC) vulnerability in TLS 1.0: an attacker observing 2 consecutive ciphertext blocks C_0, C_1 can test if the plaintext block P_1 is equal to x by choosing the next plaintext block $P_2 = x \wedge C_0 \wedge C_1$; due to how CBC works C_2 will be equal to C_1 if $x = P_1$. Practical exploits had not been previously demonstrated for this vulnerability, which was originally discovered by Phillip Rogaway in 2002. The vulnerability of the attack had been fixed with TLS 1.1 in 2006, but TLS 1.1 had not seen wide adoption prior to this attack demonstration.

RC4 as a stream cipher is immune to BEAST attack. Therefore, RC4 was widely used as a way to mitigate BEAST attack on the server side. However, in 2013, researchers found more weaknesses in RC4. Thereafter enabling RC4 on server side was no longer recommended.

Chrome and Firefox themselves are not vulnerable to BEAST attack, however, Mozilla updated their NSS libraries to mitigate BEAST-like attacks. NSS is used by Mozilla Firefox and Google Chrome to implement SSL. Some web servers that have a broken implementation of the SSL specification may stop working as a result.

Microsoft released Security Bulletin MS12-006 on January 10, 2012, which fixed the BEAST vulnerability by changing the way that the Windows Secure Channel (SChannel) component transmits encrypted network packets from the server end. Users of Internet Explorer (prior to version 11) that run on older versions of Windows (Windows 7, Windows 8 and Windows Server 2008 R2) can restrict use of TLS to 1.1 or higher.

Apple fixed BEAST vulnerability by implementing 1/n-1 split and turning it on by default in OS X Mavericks, released on October 22, 2013.

CRIME and BREACH attacks

The authors of the BEAST attack are also the creators of the later CRIME attack, which can allow an attacker to recover the content of web cookies when data compression is used along with TLS. When used to recover the content of secret authentication cookies, it allows an attacker to perform session hijacking on an authenticated web session.

While the CRIME attack was presented as a general attack that could work effectively against a large number of protocols, including but not limited to TLS, and application-layer protocols such as SPDY or HTTP, only exploits against TLS and SPDY were demonstrated and largely mitigated in browsers and servers. The CRIME exploit against HTTP compression has not been mitigated at all, even though the authors of CRIME have warned that this vulnerability might be even more widespread than SPDY and TLS compression combined. In 2013 a new instance of the CRIME attack against HTTP compression, dubbed BREACH, was announced. Based on the CRIME attack a BREACH attack can extract login tokens, email addresses or other sensitive information from TLS encrypted web traffic in as little as 30 seconds (depending on the number of bytes to be extracted), provided the attacker tricks the victim into visiting a malicious web link or is able to inject content into valid pages the user is visiting (ex: a wireless network under the control of the attacker). All versions of TLS and SSL are at risk from BREACH regardless of the encryption algorithm or cipher used. Unlike previous instances of CRIME, which can be successfully defended against by turning off TLS compression or SPDY header compression, BREACH exploits HTTP compression which cannot realistically be turned off, as virtually all web servers rely upon it to improve data transmission speeds for users. This is a known limitation of TLS as it is susceptible to chosen-plaintext attack against the application-layer data it was meant to protect.

Timing Attacks on Padding

Earlier TLS versions were vulnerable against the padding oracle attack discovered in 2002. A novel variant, called the Lucky Thirteen attack, was published in 2013.

Some experts also recommended avoiding Triple-DES CBC. Since the last supported ciphers developed to support any program using Windows XP's SSL/TLS library like Internet Explorer on Windows XP are RC4 and Triple-DES, and since RC4 is now deprecated, this makes it difficult to support any version of SSL for any program using this library on XP.

A fix was released as the Encrypt-then-MAC extension to the TLS specification, released as RFC 7366. The Lucky Thirteen attack can be mitigated in TLS 1.2 by using only AES_GCM ciphers; AES_CBC remains vulnerable.

POODLE Attack

On October 14, 2014, Google researchers published a vulnerability in the design of SSL 3.0, which makes CBC mode of operation with SSL 3.0 vulnerable to a padding attack (CVE-2014-3566). They named this attack POODLE (Padding Oracle On Downgraded Legacy Encryption). On average, attackers only need to make 256 SSL 3.0 requests to reveal one byte of encrypted messages.

Although this vulnerability only exists in SSL 3.0 and most clients and servers support TLS 1.0 and above, all major browsers voluntarily downgrade to SSL 3.0 if the handshakes with newer versions of TLS fail unless they provide the option for a user or administrator to disable SSL 3.0 and the user or administrator does so. Therefore, the man-in-the-middle can first conduct a version rollback attack and then exploit this vulnerability.

In general, graceful security degradation for the sake of interoperability is difficult to carry out in a way that cannot be exploited. This is challenging especially in domains where fragmentation is high.

On December 8, 2014, a variant of POODLE was announced that impacts TLS implementations that do not properly enforce padding byte requirements.

RC4 Attacks

Despite the existence of attacks on RC4 that broke its security, cipher suites in SSL and TLS that were based on RC4 were still considered secure prior to 2013 based on the way in which they were used in SSL and TLS. In 2011, the RC4 suite was actually recommended as a work around for the BEAST attack. New forms of attack disclosed in March 2013 conclusively demonstrated the feasibility of breaking RC4 in TLS, suggesting it was not a good workaround for BEAST. An attack scenario was proposed by AlFardan, Bernstein, Paterson, Poettering and Schuldt that used newly discovered statistical biases in the RC4 key table to recover parts of the plaintext with a large number of TLS encryptions. An attack on RC4 in TLS and SSL that requires 13×2^{20} encryptions to break RC4 was unveiled on 8 July 2013 and later described as "feasible" in the accompanying presentation at a USENIX Security Symposium in August 2013. In July 2015, subsequent improvements in the attack make it increasingly practical to defeat the security of RC4-encrypted TLS.

As many modern browsers have been designed to defeat BEAST attacks (except Safari for Mac OS X 10.7 or earlier, for iOS 6 or earlier, and for Windows), RC4 is no longer a good choice for TLS 1.0. The CBC ciphers which were affected by the BEAST attack in the past have become a more popular choice for protection. Mozilla and Microsoft recommend disabling RC4 where possible. RFC 7465 prohibits the use of RC4 cipher suites in all versions of TLS.

On September 1, 2015, Microsoft, Google and Mozilla announced that RC4 cipher suites would be disabled by default in their browsers (Microsoft Edge, Internet Explorer 11 on Windows 7/8.1/10, Firefox, and Chrome) in early 2016.

Truncation Attack

A TLS (logout) truncation attack blocks a victim's account logout requests so that the user unknowingly remains logged into a web service. When the request to sign out is sent, the attacker injects an unencrypted TCP FIN message (no more data from sender) to close the connection. The server therefore doesn't receive the logout request and is unaware of the abnormal termination.

Published in July 2013, the attack causes web services such as Gmail and Hotmail to display a page that informs the user that they have successfully signed-out, while ensuring that the user's browser maintains authorization with the service, allowing an attacker with subsequent access to the browser to access and take over control of the user's logged-in account. The attack does not rely on installing malware on the victim's computer; attackers need only place themselves between the victim and the web server (e.g., by setting up a rogue wireless hotspot). This vulnerability also requires access to the victim's computer. Another possibility is when using FTP the data connection can have a false FIN in the data stream, and if the protocol rules for exchanging close_notify alerts is not adhered to a file can be truncated.

Unholy PAC Attack

This attack, discovered in mid-2016, exploits weaknesses in the Web Proxy Autodiscovery Protocol (WPAD) to expose the URL that a web user is attempting to reach via a TLS-enabled web link. Disclosure of a URL can violate a user's privacy, not only because of the website accessed, but also because URLs are sometimes used to authenticate users. Document sharing services, such as those offered by Google and Dropbox, also work by sending a user a security token that's included in the URL. An attacker who obtains such URLs may be able to gain full access to a victim's account or data.

The exploit works against almost all browsers and operating systems.

Sweet32 Attack

The Sweet32 attack breaks all 64-bit block ciphers used in CBC mode as used in TLS by exploiting a birthday attack and either a man-in-the-middle attack or injection of a malicious JavaScript into a web page. The purpose of the man-in-the-middle attack or the JavaScript injection is to allow the attacker to capture enough traffic to mount a birthday attack.

Implementation Errors: Heartbleed Bug, BERserk Attack, Cloudflare Bug

The Heartbleed bug is a serious vulnerability specific to the implementation of SSL/TLS in the popular OpenSSL cryptographic software library, affecting versions 1.0.1 to 1.0.1f. This weakness, reported in April 2014, allows attackers to steal private keys from servers that should normally be protected. The Heartbleed bug allows anyone on the Internet to read the memory of the systems protected by the vulnerable versions of the OpenSSL software. This compromises the secret private keys associated with the public certificates used to identify the service providers and to encrypt the traffic, the names and passwords of the users and the actual content. This allows attackers to eavesdrop on communications, steal data directly from the services and users and to impersonate services and users. The vulnerability is caused by a buffer over-read bug in the OpenSSL software, rather than a defect in the SSL or TLS protocol specification.

In September 2014, a variant of Daniel Bleichenbacher's PKCS#1 v1.5 RSA Signature Forgery vulnerability was announced by Intel Security Advanced Threat Research. This attack, dubbed BERserk, is a result of incomplete ASN.1 length decoding of public key signatures in some SSL implementations, and allows a man-in-the-middle attack by forging a public key signature.

In February 2015, after media reported the hidden pre-installation of Superfish adware on some Lenovo notebooks, a researcher found a trusted root certificate on affected Lenovo machines to be insecure, as the keys could easily be accessed using the company name, Komodia, as a passphrase. The Komodia library was designed to intercept client-side TLS/SSL traffic for parental control and surveillance, but it was also used in numerous adware programs, including Superfish, that were often surreptitiously installed unbeknownst to the computer user. In turn, these potentially unwanted programs installed the corrupt root certificate, allowing attackers to completely control web traffic and confirm false websites as authentic.

In May 2016, it was reported that dozens of Danish HTTPS-protected websites belonging to Visa Inc. were vulnerable to attacks allowing hackers to inject malicious code and forged content into the browsers of visitors. The attacks worked because the TLS implementation used on the affected servers incorrectly reused random numbers (nonces) that are intended be used only once, ensuring that each TLS handshake is unique.

In February 2017, an implementation error caused by a single mistyped character in code used to parse HTML created a buffer overflow error on Cloudflare servers. Similar in its effects to the Heartbleed bug discovered in 2014, this overflow error, widely known as Cloudbleed, allowed unauthorized third parties to read data in the memory of programs running on the servers—data that should otherwise have been protected by TLS.

Survey of Websites Vulnerable to Attacks

As of October 2016, Trustworthy Internet Movement estimate the ratio of websites that are vulnerable to TLS attacks.

Survey of the TLS vulnerabilities of the most popular websites				
Attacks	Security			
	Insecure	Depends	Secure	Other
Renegotiation attack	1.2% (−0.1%) support insecure renegotiation	0.4% (±0.0%) support both	96.2% (+0.1%) support secure renegotiation	2.2% (±0.0%) no support

RC4 attacks	<0.1% (±0.0%) support only RC4 suites	6.0% (−0.3%) support RC4 suites used with modern browsers	28.5% (−0.7%) support some RC4 suites	65.5% (+1.0%) no support	N/A
CRIME attack	2.4% (−0.1%) vulnerable		N/A	N/A	N/A
Heartbleed	0.1% (±0.0%) vulnerable		N/A	N/A	N/A
ChangeCipherSpec injection attack	0.8% (±0.0%) vulnerable and exploitable		4.7% (−0.2%) vulnerable, not exploit-able	92.6% (+0.4%) not vulnerable	1.9% (+0.1%) un-known
POODLE attack against TLS (Original POODLE against SSL 3.0 is not included)	2.1% (−0.1%) vulnerable and exploitable		N/A	97.1% (+0.2%) not vulnerable	0.8% (−0.1%) un-known
Protocol downgrade	23.2% (−0.4%) TLS_FALLBACK_SCSV not supported		N/A	67.6% (+0.7%) TLS_FALLBACK_ SCSV supported	9.1% (−0.4%) un-known

Forward Secrecy

Forward secrecy is a property of cryptographic systems which ensures that a session key derived from a set of public and private keys will not be compromised if one of the private keys is compromised in the future. Without forward secrecy, if the server's private key is compromised, not only will all future TLS-encrypted sessions using that server certificate be compromised, but also any past sessions that used it as well (provided of course that these past sessions were intercepted and stored at the time of transmission). An implementation of TLS can provide forward secrecy by requiring the use of ephemeral Diffie–Hellman key exchange to establish session keys, and some notable TLS implementations do so exclusively: e.g., Gmail and other Google HTTPS services that use OpenSSL. However, many clients and servers supporting TLS (including browsers and web servers) are not configured to implement such restrictions. In practice, unless a web service uses Diffie–Hellman key exchange to implement forward secrecy, all of the encrypted web traffic to and from that service can be decrypted by a third party if it obtains the server's master (private) key; e.g., by means of a court order.

Even where Diffie–Hellman key exchange is implemented, server-side session management mechanisms can impact forward secrecy. The use of TLS session tickets (a TLS extension) causes the session to be protected by AES128-CBC-SHA256 regardless of any other negotiated TLS parameters, including forward secrecy ciphersuites, and the long-lived TLS session ticket keys defeat the attempt to implement forward secrecy.

Stanford University research in 2014 also found that of 473,802 TLS servers surveyed, 82.9% of the servers deploying ephemeral Diffie–Hellman (DHE) key exchange to support forward secrecy were using weak Diffie–Hellman parameters. These weak parameter choices could potentially compromise the effectiveness of the forward secrecy that the servers sought to provide.

Since late 2011, Google has provided forward secrecy with TLS by default to users of its Gmail service, along with Google Docs and encrypted search among other services. Since November 2013, Twitter has provided forward secrecy with TLS to users of its service. As of June 2016, 51.9% of TLS-enabled websites are configured to use cipher suites that provide forward secrecy to modern web browsers.

Dealing with Man-in-the-middle Attacks

Certificate Pinning

One way to detect and block many kinds of man-in-the-middle attacks is "certificate pinning", sometimes called "SSL pinning", but more accurately called "public key pinning". A client that does key pinning adds an extra step beyond the normal X.509 certificate validation: After obtaining the server's certificate in the standard way, the client checks the public key(s) in the server's certificate chain against a set of (hashes of) public keys for the server name. Typically the public key hashes are bundled with the application. For example, Google Chrome includes public key hashes for the *.google.com certificate that detected fraudulent certificates in 2011. (Chromium does not enforce the hardcoded key pins.) Since then, Mozilla has introduced public key pinning to its Firefox browser.

In other systems the client hopes that the first time it obtains a server's certificate it is trustworthy and stores it; during later sessions with that server, the client checks the server's certificate against the stored certificate to guard against later MITM attacks.

Perspectives Project

The Perspectives Project operates network notaries that clients can use to detect if a site's certificate has changed. By their nature, man-in-the-middle attacks place the attacker between the destination and a single specific target. As such, Perspectives would warn the target that the certificate delivered to the web browser does not match the certificate seen from other perspectives – the perspectives of other users in different times and places. Use of network notaries from a multitude of perspectives makes it possible for a target to detect an attack even if a certificate appears to be completely valid. Other projects, such as the EFF's SSL Observatory, also make use of notaries or similar reporters in discovering man-in-the-middle attacks.

DNSChain

DNSChain relies on the security that blockchains provide to distribute public keys. It uses one pin to secure the connection to the DNSChain server itself, after which all other public keys (that are stored in a block chain) become accessible over a secure channel.

Protocol Details

The TLS protocol exchanges *records*—which encapsulate the data to be exchanged in a specific format. Each record can be compressed, padded, appended with a message authentication code (MAC), or encrypted, all depending on the state of the connection. Each record has a *content type* field that designates the type of data encapsulated, a length field and a TLS version field. The data encapsulated may be control or procedural messages of the TLS itself, or simply the application data needed to be transferred by TLS. The specifications (cipher suite, keys etc.) required to exchange application data by TLS, are agreed upon in the "TLS handshake" between the client requesting the data and the server responding to requests. The protocol therefore defines both the structure of payloads transferred in TLS and the procedure to establish and monitor the transfer.

TLS Handshake

When the connection starts, the record encapsulates a "control" protocol—the handshake messaging protocol (*content type* 22). This protocol is used to exchange all the information required by both sides for the exchange of the actual application data by TLS. It defines the format of messages and the order of their exchange. These may vary according to the demands of the client and server—i.e., there are several possible procedures to set up the connection. This initial exchange results in a successful TLS connection (both parties ready to transfer application data with TLS) or an alert message (as specified below).

Basic TLS Handshake

A typical connection example follows, illustrating a handshake where the server (but not the client) is authenticated by its certificate:

1. Negotiation phase:

   o A client sends a ClientHello message specifying the highest TLS protocol version it supports, a random number, a list of suggested cipher suites and suggested compression methods. If the client is attempting to perform a resumed handshake, it may send a *session ID*. If the client can use Application-Layer Protocol Negotiation, it may include a list of supported application protocols, such as HTTP/2.

   o The server responds with a ServerHello message, containing the chosen protocol version, a random number, CipherSuite and compression method from the choices offered by the client. To confirm or allow resumed handshakes the server may send a *session ID*. The chosen protocol version should be the highest that both the client and server support. For example, if the client supports TLS version 1.1 and the server supports version 1.2, version 1.1 should be selected; version 1.2 should not be selected.

o The server sends its Certificate message (depending on the selected cipher suite, this may be omitted by the server).

o The server sends its ServerKeyExchange message (depending on the selected cipher suite, this may be omitted by the server). This message is sent for all DHE and DH_anon ciphersuites.

o The server sends a ServerHelloDone message, indicating it is done with handshake negotiation.

o The client responds with a ClientKeyExchange message, which may contain a *PreMasterSecret*, public key, or nothing. (Again, this depends on the selected cipher.) This *PreMasterSecret* is encrypted using the public key of the server certificate.

o The client and server then use the random numbers and *PreMasterSecret* to compute a common secret, called the "master secret". All other key data for this connection is derived from this master secret (and the client- and server-generated random values), which is passed through a carefully designed pseudorandom function.

2. The client now sends a ChangeCipherSpec record, essentially telling the server, "Everything I tell you from now on will be authenticated (and encrypted if encryption parameters were present in the server certificate)." The ChangeCipherSpec is itself a record-level protocol with content type of 20.

o Finally, the client sends an authenticated and encrypted Finished message, containing a hash and MAC over the previous handshake messages.

o The server will attempt to decrypt the client's *Finished* message and verify the hash and MAC. If the decryption or verification fails, the handshake is considered to have failed and the connection should be torn down.

3. Finally, the server sends a ChangeCipherSpec, telling the client, "Everything I tell you from now on will be authenticated (and encrypted, if encryption was negotiated)."

o The server sends its authenticated and encrypted Finished message.

o The client performs the same decryption and verification procedure as the server did in the previous step.

4. Application phase: at this point, the "handshake" is complete and the application protocol is enabled, with content type of 23. Application messages exchanged between client and server will also be authenticated and optionally encrypted exactly like in their *Finished* message. Otherwise, the content type will return 25 and the client will not authenticate.

Client-authenticated TLS Handshake

The following *full* example shows a client being authenticated (in addition to the server as in the example above) via TLS using certificates exchanged between both peers.

1. Negotiation Phase:

   o A client sends a ClientHello message specifying the highest TLS protocol version it supports, a random number, a list of suggested cipher suites and compression methods.

   o The server responds with a ServerHello message, containing the chosen protocol version, a random number, cipher suite and compression method from the choices offered by the client. The server may also send a *session id* as part of the message to perform a resumed handshake.

   o The server sends its Certificate message (depending on the selected cipher suite, this may be omitted by the server).

   o The server sends its ServerKeyExchange message (depending on the selected cipher suite, this may be omitted by the server). This message is sent for all DHE and DH_anon ciphersuites.

   o The server requests a certificate from the client, so that the connection can be mutually authenticated, using a CertificateRequest message.

   o The server sends a ServerHelloDone message, indicating it is done with handshake negotiation.

   o The client responds with a Certificate message, which contains the client's certificate.

   o The client sends a ClientKeyExchange message, which may contain a *PreMasterSecret*, public key, or nothing. (Again, this depends on the selected cipher.) This *PreMasterSecret* is encrypted using the public key of the server certificate.

   o The client sends a CertificateVerify message, which is a signature over the previous handshake messages using the client's certificate's private key. This signature can be verified by using the client's certificate's public key.

This lets the server know that the client has access to the private key of the certificate and thus owns the certificate.

- o The client and server then use the random numbers and *PreMasterSecret* to compute a common secret, called the "master secret". All other key data for this connection is derived from this master secret (and the client- and server-generated random values), which is passed through a carefully designed pseudorandom function.

2. The client now sends a ChangeCipherSpec record, essentially telling the server, "Everything I tell you from now on will be authenticated (and encrypted if encryption was negotiated). " The ChangeCipherSpec is itself a record-level protocol and has type 20 and not 22.

- o Finally, the client sends an encrypted Finished message, containing a hash and MAC over the previous handshake messages.

- o The server will attempt to decrypt the client's *Finished* message and verify the hash and MAC. If the decryption or verification fails, the handshake is considered to have failed and the connection should be torn down.

3. Finally, the server sends a ChangeCipherSpec, telling the client, "Everything I tell you from now on will be authenticated (and encrypted if encryption was negotiated)."

- o The server sends its own encrypted Finished message.

- o The client performs the same decryption and verification procedure as the server did in the previous step.

4. Application phase: at this point, the "handshake" is complete and the application protocol is enabled, with content type of 23. Application messages exchanged between client and server will also be encrypted exactly like in their *Finished* message.

Resumed TLS Handshake

Public key operations (e.g., RSA) are relatively expensive in terms of computational power. TLS provides a secure shortcut in the handshake mechanism to avoid these operations: resumed sessions. Resumed sessions are implemented using session IDs or session tickets.

Apart from the performance benefit, resumed sessions can also be used for single sign-on, as it guarantees that both the original session and any resumed session originate from the same client. This is of particular importance for the FTP over TLS/SSL protocol, which would otherwise suffer from a man-in-the-middle attack in which an attacker could intercept the contents of the secondary data connections.

Session IDs

In an ordinary *full* handshake, the server sends a *session id* as part of the ServerHello message. The client associates this *session id* with the server's IP address and TCP port, so that when the client connects again to that server, it can use the *session id* to shortcut the handshake. In the server, the *session id* maps to the cryptographic parameters previously negotiated, specifically the "master secret". Both sides must have the same "master secret" or the resumed handshake will fail (this prevents an eavesdropper from using a *session id*). The random data in the ClientHello and ServerHello messages virtually guarantee that the generated connection keys will be different from in the previous connection. In the RFCs, this type of handshake is called an *abbreviated* handshake. It is also described in the literature as a *restart* handshake.

1. Negotiation phase:

   o A client sends a ClientHello message specifying the highest TLS protocol version it supports, a random number, a list of suggested cipher suites and compression methods. Included in the message is the *session id* from the previous TLS connection.

   o The server responds with a ServerHello message, containing the chosen protocol version, a random number, cipher suite and compression method from the choices offered by the client. If the server recognizes the *session id* sent by the client, it responds with the same *session id*. The client uses this to recognize that a resumed handshake is being performed. If the server does not recognize the *session id* sent by the client, it sends a different value for its *session id*. This tells the client that a resumed handshake will not be performed. At this point, both the client and server have the "master secret" and random data to generate the key data to be used for this connection.

2. The server now sends a ChangeCipherSpec record, essentially telling the client, "Everything I tell you from now on will be encrypted." The ChangeCipherSpec is itself a record-level protocol and has type 20 and not 22.

   o Finally, the server sends an encrypted Finished message, containing a hash and MAC over the previous handshake messages.

   o The client will attempt to decrypt the server's *Finished* message and verify the hash and MAC. If the decryption or verification fails, the handshake is considered to have failed and the connection should be torn down.

3. Finally, the client sends a ChangeCipherSpec, telling the server, "Everything I tell you from now on will be encrypted."

   o The client sends its own encrypted Finished message.

- o The server performs the same decryption and verification procedure as the client did in the previous step.

4. Application phase: at this point, the "handshake" is complete and the application protocol is enabled, with content type of 23. Application messages exchanged between client and server will also be encrypted exactly like in their *Finished* message.

Session Tickets

RFC 5077 extends TLS via use of session tickets, instead of session IDs. It defines a way to resume a TLS session without requiring that session-specific state is stored at the TLS server.

When using session tickets, the TLS server stores its session-specific state in a session ticket and sends the session ticket to the TLS client for storing. The client resumes a TLS session by sending the session ticket to the server, and the server resumes the TLS session according to the session-specific state in the ticket. The session ticket is encrypted and authenticated by the server, and the server verifies its validity before using its contents.

One particular weakness of this method with OpenSSL is that it always limits encryption and authentication security of the transmitted TLS session ticket to AES128-CBC-SHA256, no matter what other TLS parameters were negotiated for the actual TLS session. This means that the state information (the TLS session ticket) is not as well protected as the TLS session itself. Of particular concern is OpenSSL's storage of the keys in an application-wide context (SSL_CTX), i.e. for the life of the application, and not allowing for re-keying of the AES128-CBC-SHA256 TLS session tickets without resetting the application-wide OpenSSL context (which is uncommon, error-prone and often requires manual administrative intervention).

TLS Record

This is the general format of all TLS records.

+	Byte +0	Byte +1	Byte +2	Byte +3
Byte 0	Content type			
Bytes 1..4	Version		Length	
	(Major)	(Minor)	(bits 15..8)	(bits 7..0)
Bytes 5..$(m-1)$	Protocol message(s)			
Bytes $m..(p-1)$	MAC (optional)			
Bytes $p..(q-1)$	Padding (block ciphers only)			

Content type

This field identifies the Record Layer Protocol Type contained in this Record.

Content types		
Hex	Dec	Type
0x14	20	ChangeCipherSpec
0x15	21	Alert
0x16	22	Handshake
0x17	23	Application
0x18	24	Heartbeat

Legacy Version

This field identifies the major and minor version of TLS for the contained message. For a ClientHello message, this need not be the *highest* version supported by the client.

Versions		
Major version	Minor version	Version type
3	0	SSL 3.0
3	1	TLS 1.0
3	2	TLS 1.1
3	3	TLS 1.2

Length

The length of "protocol message(s)", "MAC" and "padding" fields combined (i.e. $q-5$), not to exceed 2^{14} bytes (16 KiB).

Protocol message(s)

One or more messages identified by the Protocol field. Note that this field may be encrypted depending on the state of the connection.

MAC and padding

A message authentication code computed over the "protocol message(s)" field, with additional key material included. Note that this field may be encrypted, or not included entirely, depending on the state of the connection.

No "MAC" or "padding" fields can be present at end of TLS records before all cipher algorithms and parameters have been negotiated and handshaked and then confirmed by sending a CipherStateChange record for signalling that these parameters will take effect in all further records sent by the same peer.

Handshake Protocol

Most messages exchanged during the setup of the TLS session are based on this record, unless an error or warning occurs and needs to be signaled by an Alert protocol record, or the encryption mode of the session is modified by another record.

+	Byte +0	Byte +1	Byte +2	Byte +3
Byte 0	22			
Bytes 1..4	Version		Length	
	(Major)	(Minor)	(bits 15..8)	(bits 7..0)
Bytes 5..8	Message type	Handshake message data length		
		(bits 23..16)	(bits 15..8)	(bits 7..0)
Bytes 9..(n−1)	Handshake message data			
Bytes n..(n+3)	Message type	Handshake message data length		
		(bits 23..16)	(bits 15..8)	(bits 7..0)
Bytes (n+4)..	Handshake message data			

Message type

   This field identifies the handshake message type.

Message types	
Code	Description
0	HelloRequest
1	ClientHello
2	ServerHello
4	NewSessionTicket
11	Certificate
12	ServerKeyExchange
13	CertificateRequest
14	ServerHelloDone
15	CertificateVerify
16	ClientKeyExchange
20	Finished

Handshake message data length

   This is a 3-byte field indicating the length of the handshake data, not including the header.

Note that multiple handshake messages may be combined within one record.

Alert Protocol

This record should normally not be sent during normal handshaking or application exchanges. However, this message can be sent at any time during the handshake and up to the closure of the session. If this is used to signal a fatal error, the session will be closed immediately after sending this record, so this record is used to give a reason for this closure. If the alert level is flagged as a warning, the remote can decide to close the session if it decides that the session is not reliable enough for its needs (before doing so, the remote may also send its own signal).

+	Byte +0	Byte +1	Byte +2	Byte +3
Byte 0	21			
Bytes 1..4	Version		Length	
	(Major)	(Minor)	0	2
Bytes 5..6	Level	Description		
Bytes 7..(p−1)	MAC (optional)			
Bytes p..(q−1)	Padding (block ciphers only)			

Level

>   This field identifies the level of alert. If the level is fatal, the sender should close the session immediately. Otherwise, the recipient may decide to terminate the session itself, by sending its own fatal alert and closing the session itself immediately after sending it. The use of Alert records is optional, however if it is missing before the session closure, the session may be resumed automatically (with its handshakes).

>   Normal closure of a session after termination of the transported application should preferably be alerted with at least the *Close notify* Alert type (with a simple warning level) to prevent such automatic resume of a new session. Signalling explicitly the normal closure of a secure session before effectively closing its transport layer is useful to prevent or detect attacks (like attempts to truncate the securely transported data, if it intrinsically does not have a predetermined length or duration that the recipient of the secured data may expect).

Alert level types		
Code	Level type	Connection state
1	warning	connection or security may be unstable.
2	fatal	connection or security may be compromised, or an unrecoverable error has occurred.

Description

This field identifies which type of alert is being sent.

Alert description types			
Code	Description	Level types	Note
0	Close notify	warning/fatal	
10	Unexpected message	fatal	
20	Bad record MAC	fatal	Possibly a bad SSL implementation, or payload has been tampered with e.g. FTP firewall rule on FTPS server.
21	Decryption failed	fatal	TLS only, reserved
22	Record overflow	fatal	TLS only
30	Decompression failure	fatal	
40	Handshake failure	fatal	
41	No certificate	warning/fatal	SSL 3.0 only, reserved
42	Bad certificate	warning/fatal	
43	Unsupported certificate	warning/fatal	e.g. certificate has only Server authentication usage enabled and is presented as a client certificate
44	Certificate revoked	warning/fatal	
45	Certificate expired	warning/fatal	Check server certificate expire also check no certificate in the chain presented has expired
46	Certificate unknown	warning/fatal	
47	Illegal parameter	fatal	
48	Unknown CA (Certificate authority)	fatal	TLS only
49	Access denied	fatal	TLS only – e.g. no client certificate has been presented (TLS: Blank certificate message or SSLv3: No Certificate alert), but server is configured to require one.
50	Decode error	fatal	TLS only
51	Decrypt error	warning/fatal	TLS only
60	Export restriction	fatal	TLS only, reserved
70	Protocol version	fatal	TLS only
71	Insufficient security	fatal	TLS only
80	Internal error	fatal	TLS only
86	Inappropriate Fallback	fatal	TLS only
90	User canceled	fatal	TLS only
100	No renegotiation	warning	TLS only
110	Unsupported extension	warning	TLS only
111	Certificate unobtainable	warning	TLS only
112	Unrecognized name	warning/fatal	TLS only; client's Server Name Indicator specified a hostname not supported by the server

113	Bad certificate status response	fatal	TLS only
114	Bad certificate hash value	fatal	TLS only
115	Unknown PSK identity (used in TLS-PSK and TLS-SRP)	fatal	TLS only
120	No Application Protocol	fatal	TLS only, client's ALPN did not contain any server-supported protocols

ChangeCipherSpec protocol

+	Byte +0	Byte +1	Byte +2	Byte +3
Byte 0	20			
Bytes 1..4	Version		Length	
	(Major)	*(Minor)*	0	1
Byte 5	CCS protocol type			

CCS protocol type

> Currently only 1.

Application protocol

+	Byte +0	Byte +1	Byte +2	Byte +3
Byte 0	23			
Bytes 1..4	Version		Length	
	(Major)	*(Minor)*	*(bits 15..8)*	*(bits 7..0)*
Bytes 5..(m−1)	Application data			
Bytes m..(p−1)	MAC (optional)			
Bytes p..(q−1)	Padding (block ciphers only)			

Length

> Length of application data (excluding the protocol header and including the MAC and padding trailers).

MAC

> 20 bytes for the SHA-1-based HMAC, 16 bytes for the MD5-based HMAC.

Padding

Variable length; last byte contains the padding length.

Support for Name-based Virtual Servers

From the application protocol point of view, TLS belongs to a lower layer, although the TCP/IP model is too coarse to show it. This means that the TLS handshake is usually (except in the STARTTLS case) performed before the application protocol can start. In the name-based virtual server feature being provided by the application layer, all co-hosted virtual servers share the same certificate because the server has to select and send a certificate immediately after the ClientHello message. This is a big problem in hosting environments because it means either sharing the same certificate among all customers or using a different IP address for each of them.

There are two known workarounds provided by X.509:

- If all virtual servers belong to the same domain, a wildcard certificate can be used. Besides the loose host name selection that might be a problem or not, there is no common agreement about how to match wildcard certificates. Different rules are applied depending on the application protocol or software used.

- Add every virtual host name in the subjectAltName extension. The major problem being that the certificate needs to be reissued whenever a new virtual server is added.

To provide the server name, RFC 4366 Transport Layer Security (TLS) Extensions allow clients to include a Server Name Indication extension (SNI) in the extended ClientHello message. This extension hints the server immediately which name the client wishes to connect to, so the server can select the appropriate certificate to send to the clients.

RFC 2817, also documents a method to implement name-based virtual hosting by upgrading HTTP to TLS via an HTTP/1.1 Upgrade header. Normally this is to securely implement HTTP over TLS within the main "http" URI scheme (which avoids forking the URI space and reduces the number of used ports), however, few implementations currently support this.

Standards

Primary Standards

The current approved version of TLS is version 1.2, which is specified in:

- RFC 5246: "The Transport Layer Security (TLS) Protocol Version 1.2".

The current standard replaces these former versions, which are now considered obsolete:

- RFC 2246: "The TLS Protocol Version 1.0".

- RFC 4346: "The Transport Layer Security (TLS) Protocol Version 1.1".

As well as the never standardized SSL 2.0 and 3.0, which are considered obsolete:

- Internet Draft (1995), SSL Version 2.0.

- RFC 6101: "The Secure Sockets Layer (SSL) Protocol Version 3.0".

Extensions

Other RFCs subsequently extended TLS.

Extensions to TLS 1.0 include:

- RFC 2595: "Using TLS with IMAP, POP3 and ACAP". Specifies an extension to the IMAP, POP3 and ACAP services that allow the server and client to use transport-layer security to provide private, authenticated communication over the Internet.

- RFC 2712: "Addition of Kerberos Cipher Suites to Transport Layer Security (TLS)". The 40-bit cipher suites defined in this memo appear only for the purpose of documenting the fact that those cipher suite codes have already been assigned.

- RFC 2817: "Upgrading to TLS Within HTTP/1.1", explains how to use the Upgrade mechanism in HTTP/1.1 to initiate Transport Layer Security (TLS) over an existing TCP connection. This allows unsecured and secured HTTP traffic to share the same *well known* port (in this case, http: at 80 rather than https: at 443).

- RFC 2818: "HTTP Over TLS", distinguishes secured traffic from insecure traffic by the use of a different 'server port'.

- RFC 3207: "SMTP Service Extension for Secure SMTP over Transport Layer Security". Specifies an extension to the SMTP service that allows an SMTP server and client to use transport-layer security to provide private, authenticated communication over the Internet.

- RFC 3268: "AES Ciphersuites for TLS". Adds Advanced Encryption Standard (AES) cipher suites to the previously existing symmetric ciphers.

- RFC 3546: "Transport Layer Security (TLS) Extensions", adds a mechanism for negotiating protocol extensions during session initialisation and defines some extensions. Made obsolete by RFC 4366.

- RFC 3749: "Transport Layer Security Protocol Compression Methods", specifies the framework for compression methods and the DEFLATE compression method.

- RFC 3943: "Transport Layer Security (TLS) Protocol Compression Using Lempel-Ziv-Stac (LZS)".

- RFC 4132: "Addition of Camellia Cipher Suites to Transport Layer Security (TLS)".

- RFC 4162: "Addition of SEED Cipher Suites to Transport Layer Security (TLS)".

- RFC 4217: "Securing FTP with TLS".

- RFC 4279: "Pre-Shared Key Ciphersuites for Transport Layer Security (TLS)", adds three sets of new cipher suites for the TLS protocol to support authentication based on pre-shared keys.

Extensions to TLS 1.1 include:

- RFC 4347: "Datagram Transport Layer Security" specifies a TLS variant that works over datagram protocols (such as UDP).

- RFC 4366: "Transport Layer Security (TLS) Extensions" describes both a set of specific extensions and a generic extension mechanism.

- RFC 4492: "Elliptic Curve Cryptography (ECC) Cipher Suites for Transport Layer Security (TLS)".

- RFC 4680: "TLS Handshake Message for Supplemental Data".

- RFC 4681: "TLS User Mapping Extension".

- RFC 4785: "Pre-Shared Key (PSK) Ciphersuites with NULL Encryption for Transport Layer Security (TLS)".

- RFC 5054: "Using the Secure Remote Password (SRP) Protocol for TLS Authentication". Defines the TLS-SRP ciphersuites.

- RFC 5077: "Transport Layer Security (TLS) Session Resumption without Server-Side State".

- RFC 5081: "Using OpenPGP Keys for Transport Layer Security (TLS) Authentication", obsoleted by RFC 6091.

Extensions to TLS 1.2 include:

- RFC 5288: "AES Galois Counter Mode (GCM) Cipher Suites for TLS".

- RFC 5289: "TLS Elliptic Curve Cipher Suites with SHA-256/384 and AES Galois Counter Mode (GCM)".

- RFC 5746: "Transport Layer Security (TLS) Renegotiation Indication Extension".

- RFC 5878: "Transport Layer Security (TLS) Authorization Extensions".

- RFC 5932: "Camellia Cipher Suites for TLS".

- RFC 6066: "Transport Layer Security (TLS) Extensions: Extension Definitions", includes Server Name Indication and OCSP stapling.

- RFC 6091: "Using OpenPGP Keys for Transport Layer Security (TLS) Authentication".

- RFC 6176: "Prohibiting Secure Sockets Layer (SSL) Version 2.0".

- RFC 6209: "Addition of the ARIA Cipher Suites to Transport Layer Security (TLS)".

- RFC 6347: "Datagram Transport Layer Security Version 1.2".

- RFC 6367: "Addition of the Camellia Cipher Suites to Transport Layer Security (TLS)".

- RFC 6460: "Suite B Profile for Transport Layer Security (TLS)".

- RFC 6655: "AES-CCM Cipher Suites for Transport Layer Security (TLS)".

- RFC 7027: "Elliptic Curve Cryptography (ECC) Brainpool Curves for Transport Layer Security (TLS)".

- RFC 7251: "AES-CCM Elliptic Curve Cryptography (ECC) Cipher Suites for TLS".

- RFC 7301: "Transport Layer Security (TLS) Application-Layer Protocol Negotiation Extension".

- RFC 7366: "Encrypt-then-MAC for Transport Layer Security (TLS) and Datagram Transport Layer Security (DTLS)".

- RFC 7465: "Prohibiting RC4 Cipher Suites".

- RFC 7507: "TLS Fallback Signaling Cipher Suite Value (SCSV) for Preventing Protocol Downgrade Attacks".

- RFC 7568: "Deprecating Secure Sockets Layer Version 3.0".

- RFC 7627: "Transport Layer Security (TLS) Session Hash and Extended Master Secret Extension".

- RFC 7685: "A Transport Layer Security (TLS) ClientHello Padding Extension".

Encapsulations of TLS include:

- RFC 5216: "The EAP-TLS Authentication Protocol".

Informational RFCs

- RFC 7457: "Summarizing Known Attacks on Transport Layer Security (TLS) and Datagram TLS (DTLS)".

- RFC 7525: "Recommendations for Secure Use of Transport Layer Security (TLS) and Datagram Transport Layer Security (DTLS)".

References

- Conway, Richard (204). Code Hacking: A Developer's Guide to Network Security. Hingham, Massachusetts: Charles River Media. p. 281. ISBN 1-58450-314-9

- Chang, Rocky (October 2002). "Defending Against Flooding-Based Distributed Denial-of-Service Attacks: A Tutorial". IEEE Communications Magazine. 40 (10): 42–43. doi:10.1109/mcom.2002.1039856

- Ingham, Kenneth; Forrest, Stephanie (2002). "A History and Survey of Network Firewalls" (PDF). Retrieved 2011-11-25

- Abdullah A. Mohamed, «Design Intrusion Detection System Based On Image Block Matching», International Journal of Computer and Communication Engineering, IACSIT Press, Vol. 2, No. 5, September 2013.

- Boudriga, Noureddine (2010). Security of mobile communications. Boca Raton: CRC Press. pp. 32–33. ISBN 0849379423

- Proceedings of National Conference on Recent Developments in Computing and Its Applications, August 12–13, 2009. I.K. International Pvt. Ltd. 2009-01-01. Retrieved 2014-04-22

- McGraw, Gary (May 2007). "Silver Bullet Talks with Becky Bace" (PDF). IEEE Security & Privacy Magazine. 5 (3): 6–9. doi:10.1109/MSP.2007.70. Retrieved 18 April 2017

Malicious Software: Computer Threats

Malware is the software that is designed to damage a computer, server or a computer network. This chapter discusses about some common malicious software such as virus, worm, Trojan horses, adware and spyware besides many others. This chapter has been carefully written to provide an easy understanding of the varied kinds of malicious software.

Malware

Malware, short for malicious software, is an umbrella term used to refer to a variety of forms of harmful or intrusive software, including computer viruses, worms, Trojan horses, ransomware, spyware, adware, scareware, and other malicious programs. It can take the form of executable code, scripts, active content, and other software. Malware is defined by its malicious intent, acting against the requirements of the computer user — and so does not include software that causes unintentional harm due to some deficiency.

Programs supplied officially by companies can be considered malware if they secretly act against the interests of the computer user. An example is the Sony rootkit, a Trojan horse embedded into CDs sold by Sony, which silently installed and concealed itself on purchasers' computers with the intention of preventing illicit copying; it also reported on users' listening habits, and unintentionally created vulnerabilities that were exploited by unrelated malware.

Antivirus software and firewalls are used to protect against malicious activity, and to recover from attacks.

Purposes

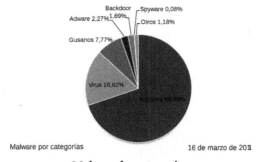

Malware by categories.

Many early infectious programs, including the first Internet Worm, were written as experiments or pranks. Today, malware is used by both black hat hackers and governments, to steal personal, financial, or business information.

Malware is sometimes used broadly against government or corporate websites to gather guarded information, or to disrupt their operation in general. However, malware can be used against individuals to gain information such as personal identification numbers or details, bank or credit card numbers, and passwords.

Since the rise of widespread broadband Internet access, malicious software has more frequently been designed for profit. Since 2003, the majority of widespread viruses and worms have been designed to take control of users' computers for illicit purposes. Infected "zombie computers" can be used to send email spam, to host contraband data such as child pornography, or to engage in distributed denial-of-service attacks as a form of extortion.

Programs designed to monitor users' web browsing, display unsolicited advertisements, or redirect affiliate marketing revenues are called spyware. Spyware programs do not spread like viruses; instead they are generally installed by exploiting security holes. They can also be hidden and packaged together with unrelated user-installed software.

Ransomware affects an infected computer system in some way, and demands payment to bring it back to its normal state. For example, programs such as CryptoLocker encrypt files securely, and only decrypt them on payment of a substantial sum of money.

Some malware is used to generate money by click fraud, making it appear that the computer user has clicked an advertising link on a site, generating a payment from the advertiser. It was estimated in 2012 that about 60 to 70% of all active malware used some kind of click fraud, and 22% of all ad-clicks were fraudulent.

In addition to criminal money-making, malware can be used for sabotage, often for political motives. Stuxnet, for example, was designed to disrupt very specific industrial equipment. There have been politically motivated attacks that have spread over and shut down large computer networks, including massive deletion of files and corruption of master boot records, described as "computer killing". Such attacks were made on Sony Pictures Entertainment (25 November 2014, using malware known as Shamoon or W32.Disttrack) and Saudi Aramco (August 2012).

Infectious Malware

The best-known types of malware, viruses and worms, are known for the manner in which they spread, rather than any specific types of behavior. A computer virus is software that embeds itself in some other executable software (including the operating system itself) on the target system without the user's consent and when it is run, the virus is spread to other executables. On the other hand, a *worm* is a stand-alone malware software that *actively* transmits itself over a network to infect other computers. These definitions lead to the observation that a virus requires the user to run an infected software or operating system for the virus to spread, whereas a worm spreads itself.

Concealment

These categories are not mutually exclusive, so malware may use multiple techniques. This section only applies to malware designed to operate undetected, not sabotage and ransomware.

Viruses

A computer virus is software usually hidden within another seemingly innocuous program that can produce copies of itself and insert them into other programs or files, and that usually performs a harmful action (such as destroying data). An example of this is a PE infection, a technique, usually used to spread malware, that inserts extra data or executable code into PE files.

Lock-screens

Lock-screens, or screen lockers is a type of "cyber police" ransomware that blocks screens on Windows or Android devices with a false accusation in harvesting illegal content, trying to scare the victims into paying up a fee. Jisut and SLocker impact Android devices more than other lock-screens, with Jisut making up nearly 60 percent of all Android ransomware detections.

Trojan Horses

A Trojan horse is a malicious program which misrepresents itself to appear useful, routine, or interesting in order to persuade a victim to install it. The term is derived from the Ancient Greek story of the Trojan horse used to invade the city of Troy by stealth.

Trojan horses are generally spread by some form of social engineering, for example, where a user is duped into executing an e-mail attachment disguised to be unsuspicious, (e.g., a routine form to be filled in), or by drive-by download. Although their payload can be anything, many modern forms act as a backdoor, contacting a controller which can then have unauthorized access to the affected computer. While Trojan horses and backdoors are not easily detectable by themselves, computers may appear to run slower due to heavy processor or network usage.

Unlike computer viruses and worms, Trojan horses generally do not attempt to inject themselves into other files or otherwise propagate themselves.

In spring 2017 Mac users were hit by the new version of Proton Remote Access Trojan

(RAT) trained to extract password data from various sources, such as browser auto-fill data, the Mac-OS keychain, and password vaults.

Rootkits

Once malicious software is installed on a system, it is essential that it stays concealed, to avoid detection. Software packages known as *rootkits* allow this concealment, by modifying the host's operating system so that the malware is hidden from the user. Rootkits can prevent a malicious process from being visible in the system's list of processes, or keep its files from being read.

Some malicious software contains routines to defend against removal, not merely to hide themselves. An early example of this behavior is recorded in the Jargon File tale of a pair of programs infesting a Xerox CP-V time sharing system:

> Each ghost-job would detect the fact that the other had been killed, and would start a new copy of the recently stopped program within a few milliseconds. The only way to kill both ghosts was to kill them simultaneously (very difficult) or to deliberately crash the system.

Backdoors

A backdoor is a method of bypassing normal authentication procedures, usually over a connection to a network such as the Internet. Once a system has been compromised, one or more backdoors may be installed in order to allow access in the future, invisibly to the user.

The idea has often been suggested that computer manufacturers preinstall backdoors on their systems to provide technical support for customers, but this has never been reliably verified. It was reported in 2014 that US government agencies had been diverting computers purchased by those considered "targets" to secret workshops where software or hardware permitting remote access by the agency was installed, considered to be among the most productive operations to obtain access to networks around the world. Backdoors may be installed by Trojan horses, worms, implants, or other methods.

Evasion

Since the beginning of 2015, a sizable portion of malware utilizes a combination of many techniques designed to avoid detection and analysis.

- The most common evasion technique is when the malware evades analysis and detection by fingerprinting the environment when executed.

- The second most common evasion technique is confusing automated tools' detection methods. This allows malware to avoid detection by technologies such as signature-based antivirus software by changing the server used by the malware.

- The third most common evasion technique is timing-based evasion. This is when malware runs at certain times or following certain actions taken by the user, so it executes during certain vulnerable periods, such as during the boot process, while remaining dormant the rest of the time.

- The fourth most common evasion technique is done by obfuscating internal data so that automated tools do not detect the malware.

- An increasingly common technique is adware that uses stolen certificates to disable anti-malware and virus protection; technical remedies are available to deal with the adware.

Nowadays, one of the most sophisticated and stealthy ways of evasion is to use information hiding techniques, namely stegomalware.

Vulnerability

- In this context, and throughout, what is called the "system" under attack may be anything from a single application, through a complete computer and operating system, to a large network.

- Various factors make a system more vulnerable to malware.

Security Defects in Software

Malware exploits security defects (security bugs or vulnerabilities) in the design of the operating system, in applications (such as browsers, e.g. older versions of Microsoft Internet Explorer supported by Windows XP), or in vulnerable versions of browser plugins such as Adobe Flash Player, Adobe Acrobat or Reader, or Java SE. Sometimes even installing new versions of such plugins does not automatically uninstall old versions. Security advisories from plug-in providers announce security-related updates. Common vulnerabilities are assigned CVE IDs and listed in the US National Vulnerability Database. Secunia PSI is an example of software, free for personal use, that will check a PC for vulnerable out-of-date software, and attempt to update it.

Malware authors target bugs, or loopholes, to exploit. A common method is exploitation of a buffer overrun vulnerability, where software designed to store data in a specified region of memory does not prevent more data than the buffer can accommodate being supplied. Malware may provide data that overflows the buffer, with malicious executable code or data after the end; when this payload is accessed it does what the attacker, not the legitimate software, determines.

Insecure Design or user Error

Early PCs had to be booted from floppy disks. When built-in hard drives became common, the operating system was normally started from them, but it was possible to boot from another boot device if available, such as a floppy disk, CD-ROM, DVD-ROM, USB flash drive or network. It was common to configure the computer to boot from one of these devices when available. Normally none would be available; the user would intentionally insert, say, a CD into the optical drive to boot the computer in some special way, for example, to install an operating system. Even without booting, computers can be configured to execute software on some media as soon as they become available, e.g. to autorun a CD or USB device when inserted.

Malicious software distributors would trick the user into booting or running from an infected device or medium. For example, a virus could make an infected computer add autorunnable code to any USB stick plugged into it. Anyone who then attached the stick to another computer set to autorun from USB would in turn become infected, and also pass on the infection in the same way. More generally, any device that plugs into a USB port - even lights, fans, speakers, toys, or peripherals such as a digital microscope - can be used to spread malware. Devices can be infected during manufacturing or supply if quality control is inadequate.

This form of infection can largely be avoided by setting up computers by default to boot from the internal hard drive, if available, and not to autorun from devices. Intentional booting from another device is always possible by pressing certain keys during boot.

Older email software would automatically open HTML email containing potentially malicious JavaScript code. Users may also execute disguised malicious email attachments and infected executable files supplied in other ways.

Over-privileged users and Over-privileged Code

In computing, privilege refers to how much a user or program is allowed to modify a system. In poorly designed computer systems, both users and programs can be assigned more privileges than they should be, and malware can take advantage of this. The two ways that malware does this is through overprivileged users and overprivileged code.

Some systems allow all users to modify their internal structures, and such users today would be considered over-privileged users. This was the standard operating procedure for early microcomputer and home computer systems, where there was no distinction between an *administrator* or *root*, and a regular user of the system. In some systems, non-administrator users are over-privileged by design, in the sense that they are allowed to modify internal structures of the system. In some environments, users are over-privileged because they have been inappropriately granted administrator or equivalent status.

Some systems allow code executed by a user to access all rights of that user, which is known as over-privileged code. This was also standard operating procedure for early microcomputer and home computer systems. Malware, running as over-privileged code, can use this privilege to subvert the system. Almost all currently popular operating systems, and also many scripting applications allow code too many privileges, usually in the sense that when a user executes code, the system allows that code all rights of that user. This makes users vulnerable to malware in the form of e-mail attachments, which may or may not be disguised.

Use of the Same Operating System

- Homogeneity can be a vulnerability. For example, when all computers in a network run the same operating system, upon exploiting one, one worm can exploit them all: In particular, Microsoft Windows or Mac OS X have such a large share of the market that an exploited vulnerability concentrating on either operating system could subvert a large number of systems. Introducing diversity purely for the sake of robustness, such as adding Linux computers, could increase short-term costs for training and maintenance. However, as long as all the nodes are not part of the same directory service for authentication, having a few diverse nodes could deter total shutdown of the network and allow those nodes to help with recovery of the infected nodes. Such separate, functional redundancy could avoid the cost of a total shutdown, at the cost of increased complexity and reduced usability in terms of single sign-on authentication.

Anti-malware Strategies

As malware attacks become more frequent, attention has begun to shift from viruses and spyware protection, to malware protection, and programs that have been specifically developed to combat malware. (Other preventive and recovery measures, such as backup and recovery methods, are mentioned in the computer virus).

Anti-virus and Anti-malware Software

A specific component of anti-virus and anti-malware software, commonly referred to as an on-access or real-time scanner, hooks deep into the operating system's core or kernel and functions in a manner similar to how certain malware itself would attempt to operate, though with the user's informed permission for protecting the system. Any time the operating system accesses a file, the on-access scanner checks if the file is a 'legitimate' file or not. If the file is identified as malware by the scanner, the access operation will be stopped, the file will be dealt with by the scanner in a pre-defined way (how the anti-virus program was configured during/post installation), and the user will be notified. This may have a considerable performance impact on the operating system, though the degree of impact is dependent on how well the scanner was programmed. The goal is to stop any operations the malware may attempt on the system before they occur, including activities which might exploit bugs or trigger unexpected operating system behavior.

Anti-malware programs can combat malware in two ways:

1. They can provide real time protection against the installation of malware

software on a computer. This type of malware protection works the same way as that of antivirus protection in that the anti-malware software scans all incoming network data for malware and blocks any threats it comes across.

2. Anti-malware software programs can be used solely for detection and removal of malware software that has already been installed onto a computer. This type of anti-malware software scans the contents of the Windows registry, operating system files, and installed programs on a computer and will provide a list of any threats found, allowing the user to choose which files to delete or keep, or to compare this list to a list of known malware components, removing files that match.

Real-time protection from malware works identically to real-time antivirus protection: the software scans disk files at download time, and blocks the activity of components known to represent malware. In some cases, it may also intercept attempts to install start-up items or to modify browser settings. Because many malware components are installed as a result of browser exploits or user error, using security software (some of which are anti-malware, though many are not) to "sandbox" browsers (essentially isolate the browser from the computer and hence any malware induced change) can also be effective in helping to restrict any damage done.

Examples of Microsoft Windows antivirus and anti-malware software include the optional Microsoft Security Essentials (for Windows XP, Vista, and Windows 7) for real-time protection, the Windows Malicious Software Removal Tool (now included with Windows (Security) Updates on "Patch Tuesday", the second Tuesday of each month), and Windows Defender (an optional download in the case of Windows XP, incorporating MSE functionality in the case of Windows 8 and later). Additionally, several capable antivirus software programs are available for free download from the Internet (usually restricted to non-commercial use). Tests found some free programs to be competitive with commercial ones. Microsoft's System File Checker can be used to check for and repair corrupted system files.

Some viruses disable System Restore and other important Windows tools such as Task Manager and Command Prompt. Many such viruses can be removed by rebooting the computer, entering Windows safe mode with networking, and then using system tools or Microsoft Safety Scanner.

Hardware implants can be of any type, so there can be no general way to detect them.

Website Security Scans

As malware also harms the compromised websites (by breaking reputation, blacklisting in search engines, etc.), some websites offer vulnerability scanning. Such scans check the website, detect malware, may note outdated software, and may report known security issues.

"Air Gap" Isolation or "Parallel Network"

As a last resort, computers can be protected from malware, and infected computers can be prevented from disseminating trusted information, by imposing an "air gap" (i.e. completely disconnecting them from all other networks). However, malware can still cross the air gap in some situations. For example, removable media can carry malware across the gap. In December 2013 researchers in Germany showed one way that an apparent air gap can be defeated.

"AirHopper", "BitWhisper", "GSMem" and "Fansmitter" are four techniques introduced by researchers that can leak data from air-gapped computers using electromagnetic, thermal and acoustic emissions.

Grayware

Grayware is a term applied to unwanted applications or files that are not classified as malware, but can worsen the performance of computers and may cause security risks.

It describes applications that behave in an annoying or undesirable manner, and yet are less serious or troublesome than malware. Grayware encompasses spyware, adware, fraudulent dialers, joke programs, remote access tools and other unwanted programs that may harm the performance of computers or cause inconvenience. The term came into use around 2004.

Another term, potentially unwanted program (PUP) or potentially unwanted application (PUA), refers to applications that would be considered unwanted despite often having been downloaded by the user, possibly after failing to read a download agreement. PUPs include spyware, adware, and fraudulent dialers. Many security products classify unauthorised key generators as grayware, although they frequently carry true malware in addition to their ostensible purpose.

Software maker Malwarebytes lists several criteria for classifying a program as a PUP. Some types of adware (using stolen certificates) turn off anti-malware and virus protection; technical remedies are available.

History of Viruses and Worms

Before Internet access became widespread, viruses spread on personal computers by infecting the executable boot sectors of floppy disks. By inserting a copy of itself into the machine code instructions in these executables, a virus causes itself to be run whenever a program is run or the disk is booted. Early computer viruses were written for the Apple II and Macintosh, but they became more widespread with the dominance of the IBM PC and MS-DOS system. Executable-infecting viruses are dependent on users exchanging software or boot-able floppies and thumb drives so they spread rapidly in computer hobbyist circles.

The first worms, network-borne infectious programs, originated not on personal computers, but on multitasking Unix systems. The first well-known worm was the Internet Worm of 1988, which infected SunOS and VAX BSD systems. Unlike a virus, this worm did not insert itself into other programs. Instead, it exploited security holes (vulnerabilities) in network server programs and started itself running as a separate process. This same behavior is used by today's worms as well.

With the rise of the Microsoft Windows platform in the 1990s, and the flexible macros of its applications, it became possible to write infectious code in the macro language of Microsoft Word and similar programs. These *macro viruses* infect documents and templates rather than applications (executables), but rely on the fact that macros in a Word document are a form of executable code.

Academic Research

The notion of a self-reproducing computer program can be traced back to initial theories about the operation of complex automata. John von Neumann showed that in theory a program could reproduce itself. This constituted a plausibility result in computability theory. Fred Cohen experimented with computer viruses and confirmed Neumann's postulate and investigated other properties of malware such as detectability and self-obfuscation using rudimentary encryption. His doctoral dissertation was on the subject of computer viruses. The combination of cryptographic technology as part of the payload of the virus, exploiting it for attack purposes was initialized and investigated from the mid 1990s, and includes initial ransomware and evasion ideas.

Computer Virus

Hex dump of the Blaster worm, showing a message left for Microsoft co-founder Bill Gates by the worm's programmer

A computer virus is a type of malicious software program ("malware") that, when executed, replicates itself by modifying other computer programs and inserting its own code. When this replication succeeds, the affected areas are then said to be "infected" with a computer virus.

Virus writers use social engineering deceptions and exploit detailed knowledge of security vulnerabilities to initially infect systems and to spread the virus. The vast majority of viruses target systems running Microsoft Windows, employing a variety of mechanisms to infect new hosts, and often using complex anti-detection/stealth strategies to evade antivirus software. Motives for creating viruses can include seeking profit (e.g., with ransomware), desire to send a political message, personal amusement, to demonstrate that a vulnerability exists in software, for sabotage and denial of service, or simply because they wish to explore cybersecurity issues, artificial life and evolutionary algorithms.

Computer viruses currently cause billions of dollars' worth of economic damage each year, due to causing system failure, wasting computer resources, corrupting data, increasing maintenance costs, etc. In response, free, open-source antivirus tools have been developed, and an industry of antivirus software has cropped up, selling or freely distributing virus protection to users of various operating systems. As of 2005, even though no currently existing antivirus software was able to uncover all computer viruses (especially new ones), computer security researchers are actively searching for new ways to enable antivirus solutions to more effectively detect emerging viruses, before they have already become widely distributed.

The term "virus" is also commonly, but erroneously, used to refer to other types of malware. "Malware" encompasses computer viruses along with many other forms of malicious software, such as computer "worms", ransomware, spyware, adware, trojan horses, keyloggers, rootkits, bootkits, malicious Browser Helper Object (BHOs) and other malicious software. The majority of active malware threats are actually trojan horse programs or computer worms rather than computer viruses. The term computer virus, coined by Fred Cohen in 1985, is a misnomer. Viruses often perform some type of harmful activity on infected host computers, such as acquisition of hard disk space or central processing unit (CPU) time, accessing private information (e.g., credit card numbers), corrupting data, displaying political or humorous messages on the user's screen, spamming their e-mail contacts, logging their keystrokes, or even rendering the computer useless. However, not all viruses carry a destructive "payload" and attempt to hide themselves—the defining characteristic of viruses is that they are self-replicating computer programs which modify other software without user consent.

Operations and Functions

Parts

A viable computer virus must contain a search routine, which locates new files or new disks which are worthwhile targets for infection. Secondly, every computer virus must contain a routine to copy itself into the program which the search routine locates. The three main virus parts are:

Infection Mechanism

Infection mechanism (also called 'infection vector'), is how the virus spreads or propagates. A virus typically has a search routine, which locates new files or new disks for infection.

Trigger

The trigger, which is also known as logic bomb, is the compiled version that could be activated any time an executable file with the virus is run that determines the event or condition for the malicious "payload" to be activated or delivered such as a particular date, a particular time, particular presence of another program, capacity of the disk exceeding some limit, or a double-click that opens a particular file.

Payload

The "payload" is the actual body or data that perform the actual malicious purpose of the virus. Payload activity might be noticeable (e.g., because it causes the system to slow down or "freeze"), as most of the time the "payload" itself is the harmful activity, or some times non-destructive but distributive, which is called Virus hoax.

Phases

Virus phases is the life cycle of the computer virus, described by using an analogy to biology. This life cycle can be divided into four phases:

Dormant Phase

The virus program is idle during this stage. The virus program has managed to access the target user's computer or software, but during this stage, the virus does not take any action. The virus will eventually be activated by the "trigger" which states which event will execute the virus, such as a date, the presence of another program or file, the capacity of the disk exceeding some limit or the user taking a certain action (e.g., double-clicking on a certain icon, opening an e-mail, etc.). Not all viruses have this stage.

Propagation Phase

The virus starts propagating, that is multiplying and replicating itself. The virus places a copy of itself into other programs or into certain system areas on the disk. The copy may not be identical to the propagating version; viruses often "morph" or change to evade detection by IT professionals and anti-virus software. Each infected program will now contain a clone of the virus, which will itself enter a propagation phase.

Triggering Phase

A dormant virus moves into this phase when it is activated, and will now perform the function for which it was intended. The triggering phase can be caused by a variety of system events, including a count of the number of times that this copy of the virus has made copies of itself.

Execution Phase

This is the actual work of the virus, where the "payload" will be released. It can be destructive such as deleting files on disk, crashing the system, or corrupting files or relatively harmless such as popping up humorous or political messages on screen.

Infection Targets and Replication Techniques

Computer viruses infect a variety of different subsystems on their host computers and software. One manner of classifying viruses is to analyze whether they reside in binary executables (such as .EXE or .COM files), data files (such as Microsoft Word documents or PDF files), or in the boot sector of the host's hard drive (or some combination of all of these).

Resident vs. Non-resident Viruses

A *memory-resident virus* (or simply "resident virus") installs itself as part of the operating system when executed, after which it remains in RAM from the time the computer is booted up to when it is shut down. Resident viruses overwrite interrupt handling code or other functions, and when the operating system attempts to access the target file or disk sector, the virus code intercepts the request and redirects the control flow to the replication module, infecting the target. In contrast, a *non-memory-resident virus* (or "non-resident virus"), when executed, scans the disk for targets, infects them, and then exits (i.e. it does not remain in memory after it is done executing).

Macro Viruses

Many common applications, such as Microsoft Outlook and Microsoft Word, allow macro programs to be embedded in documents or emails, so that the programs may be run automatically when the document is opened. A *macro virus* (or "document virus") is a virus that is written in a macro language, and embedded into these documents so that when users open the file, the virus code is executed, and can infect the user's computer. This is one of the reasons that it is dangerous to open unexpected or suspicious attachments in e-mails. While not opening attachments in e-mails from unknown persons or organizations can help to reduce the likelihood of contracting a virus, in some cases, the virus is designed so that the e-mail appears to be from a reputable organization (e.g., a major bank or credit card company).

Boot Sector Viruses

Boot sector viruses specifically target the boot sector and/or the Master Boot Record

(MBR) of the host's hard drive or removable storage media (flash drives, floppy disks, etc.).

Email Virus

Email virus – A virus that intentionally, rather than accidentally, uses the email system to spread. While virus infected files may be accidentally sent as email attachments, email viruses are aware of email system functions. They generally target a specific type of email system (Microsoft's Outlook is the most commonly used), harvest email addresses from various sources, and may append copies of themselves to all email sent, or may generate email messages containing copies of themselves as attachments.

Stealth Techniques

In order to avoid detection by users, some viruses employ different kinds of deception. Some old viruses, especially on the MS-DOS platform, make sure that the "last modified" date of a host file stays the same when the file is infected by the virus. This approach does not fool antivirus software, however, especially those which maintain and date cyclic redundancy checks on file changes. Some viruses can infect files without increasing their sizes or damaging the files. They accomplish this by overwriting unused areas of executable files. These are called *cavity viruses*. For example, the CIH virus, or Chernobyl Virus, infects Portable Executable files. Because those files have many empty gaps, the virus, which was 1 KB in length, did not add to the size of the file. Some viruses try to avoid detection by killing the tasks associated with antivirus software before it can detect them (for example, Conficker). In the 2010s, as computers and operating systems grow larger and more complex, old hiding techniques need to be updated or replaced. Defending a computer against viruses may demand that a file system migrate towards detailed and explicit permission for every kind of file access.

Read Request Intercepts

While some kinds of antivirus software employ various techniques to counter stealth mechanisms, once the infection occurs any recourse to "clean" the system is unreliable. In Microsoft Windows operating systems, the NTFS file system is proprietary. This leaves antivirus software little alternative but to send a "read" request to Windows OS files that handle such requests. Some viruses trick antivirus software by intercepting its requests to the Operating system (OS). A virus can hide by intercepting the request to read the infected file, handling the request itself, and returning an uninfected version of the file to the antivirus software. The interception can occur by code injection of the actual operating system files that would handle the read request. Thus, an antivirus software attempting to detect the virus will either not be given permission to read the infected file, or, the "read" request will be served with the uninfected version of the same file.

The only reliable method to avoid "stealth" viruses is to "reboot" from a medium that is known to be "clear". Security software can then be used to check the dormant operating system files. Most security software relies on virus signatures, or they employ heuristics. Security software may also use a database of file "hashes" for Windows OS files, so the security software can identify altered files, and request Windows installation media to replace them with authentic versions. In older versions of Windows, file cryptographic hash functions of Windows OS files stored in Windows—to allow file integrity/authenticity to be checked—could be overwritten so that the System File Checker would report that altered system files are authentic, so using file hashes to scan for altered files would not always guarantee finding an infection.

Self-modification

Most modern antivirus programs try to find virus-patterns inside ordinary programs by scanning them for so-called *virus signatures*. Unfortunately, the term is misleading, in that viruses do not possess unique signatures in the way that human beings do. Such a virus "signature" is merely a sequence of bytes that an antivirus program looks for because it is known to be part of the virus. A better term would be "search strings". Different antivirus programs will employ different search strings, and indeed different search methods, when identifying viruses. If a virus scanner finds such a pattern in a file, it will perform other checks to make sure that it has found the virus, and not merely a coincidental sequence in an innocent file, before it notifies the user that the file is infected. The user can then delete, or (in some cases) "clean" or "heal" the infected file. Some viruses employ techniques that make detection by means of signatures difficult but probably not impossible. These viruses modify their code on each infection. That is, each infected file contains a different variant of the virus.

Encrypted Viruses

One method of evading signature detection is to use simple encryption to encipher (encode) the body of the virus, leaving only the encryption module and a static cryptographic key in cleartext which does not change from one infection to the next. In this case, the virus consists of a small decrypting module and an encrypted copy of the virus code. If the virus is encrypted with a different key for each infected file, the only part of the virus that remains constant is the decrypting module, which would (for example) be appended to the end. In this case, a virus scanner cannot directly detect the virus using signatures, but it can still detect the decrypting module, which still makes indirect detection of the virus possible. Since these would be symmetric keys, stored on the infected host, it is entirely possible to decrypt the final virus, but this is probably not required, since self-modifying code is such a rarity that it may be reason for virus scanners to at least "flag" the file as suspicious. An old but compact way will be the use of arithmetic operation like addition or subtraction and the use of logical conditions such as XORing, where each byte in a virus is with a constant, so that the exclusive-or operation had only to be repeated for decryption. It is suspicious for a code to modify itself, so the code to do the encryption/decryption may be part of the signature in many virus definitions. A simpler older approach did not use a key, where the encryption consisted only of operations with no parameters, like incrementing and decrementing, bitwise rotation, arithmetic negation, and logical NOT. Some viruses will employ a means of encryption inside an executable in which the virus is encrypted under certain events, such as the virus scanner being disabled for updates or the computer being rebooted. This is called cryptovirology. At said times, the executable will decrypt the virus and execute its hidden runtimes, infecting the computer and sometimes disabling the antivirus software.

Polymorphic Code

Polymorphic code was the first technique that posed a serious threat to virus scanners. Just like regular encrypted viruses, a polymorphic virus infects files with an encrypted copy of itself, which is decoded by a decryption module. In the case of polymorphic viruses, however, this decryption module is also modified on each infection. A well-written polymorphic virus therefore has no parts which remain identical between infections, making it very difficult to detect directly using "signatures". Antivirus software can detect it by decrypting the viruses using an emulator, or by statistical pattern analysis of the encrypted virus body. To enable polymorphic code, the virus has to have a polymorphic engine (also called "mutating engine" or "mutation engine") somewhere in its encrypted body.

Some viruses employ polymorphic code in a way that constrains the mutation rate of the virus significantly. For example, a virus can be programmed to mutate only slightly over time, or it can be programmed to refrain from mutating when it infects a file on a computer that already contains copies of the virus. The advantage of using such slow polymorphic code is that it makes it more difficult for antivirus professionals and investigators to obtain representative samples of the virus, because "bait" files that are infected in one run will typically contain identical or similar samples of the virus. This will make it more likely that the detection by the virus scanner will be unreliable, and that some instances of the virus may be able to avoid detection.

Metamorphic Code

To avoid being detected by emulation, some viruses rewrite themselves completely each time they are to infect new executables. Viruses that utilize this technique are said to be in metamorphic code. To enable metamorphism, a "metamorphic engine" is needed. A metamorphic virus is usually very large and complex. For example, W32/Simile consisted of over 14,000 lines of assembly language code, 90% of which is part of the metamorphic engine.

Vulnerabilities and Infection Vectors

Software Bugs

As software is often designed with security features to prevent unauthorized use of system resources, many viruses must exploit and manipulate security bugs, which are security defects in a system or application software, to spread themselves and infect other computers. Software development strategies that produce large numbers of "bugs" will generally also produce potential exploitable "holes" or "entrances" for the virus.

Social Engineering and Poor Security Practices

In order to replicate itself, a virus must be permitted to execute code and write to memory. For this reason, many viruses attach themselves to executable files that may be part of legitimate programs. If a user attempts to launch an infected program, the virus' code may be executed simultaneously. In operating systems that use file extensions to determine program associations (such as Microsoft Windows), the extensions may be hidden from the user by default. This makes it possible to create a file that is of a different type than it appears to the user. For example, an executable may be created and named "picture.png.exe", in which the user sees only "picture.png" and therefore assumes that this file is a digital image and most likely is safe, yet when opened, it runs the executable on the client machine.

Vulnerability of Different Operating Systems

The vast majority of viruses target systems running Microsoft Windows. This is due to Microsoft's large market share of desktop computer users. The diversity of software systems on a network limits the destructive potential of viruses and malware. Open-source operating systems such as Linux allow users to choose from a variety of desktop environments, packaging tools, etc., which means that malicious code targeting any of these systems will only affect a subset of all users. Many Windows users are running the same set of applications, enabling viruses to rapidly spread among Microsoft Windows systems by targeting the same exploits on large numbers of hosts.

While Linux and Unix in general have always natively prevented normal users from making changes to the operating system environment without permission, Windows users are generally not prevented from making these changes, meaning that viruses can easily gain control of the entire system on Windows hosts. This difference has continued partly due to the widespread use of administrator accounts in contemporary versions like Windows XP. In 1997, researchers created and released a virus for Linux—known as "Bliss". Bliss, however, requires that the user run it explicitly, and it can only infect programs that the user has the access to modify. Unlike Windows users, most Unix users do not log in as an administrator, or "root user", except to install or configure software; as a result, even if a user ran the virus, it could not harm their operating system. The Bliss virus never became widespread, and remains chiefly a research curiosity. Its creator later posted the source code to Usenet, allowing researchers to see how it worked.

Countermeasures

Antivirus Software

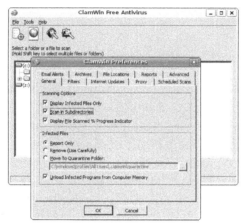

Screenshot of the open source ClamWin antivirus software running in Wine on Ubuntu Linux

Many users install antivirus software that can detect and eliminate known viruses when the computer attempts to download or run the executable file (which may be distributed as an email attachment, or on USB flash drives, for example). Some antivirus software blocks known malicious websites that attempt to install malware. Antivirus software does not change the underlying capability of hosts to transmit viruses. Users must update their software regularly to patch security vulnerabilities ("holes"). Antivirus software also needs to be regularly updated in order to recognize the latest threats. This is because malicious hackers and other individuals are always creating new viruses. The German AV-TEST Institute publishes evaluations of antivirus software for Windows and Android.

Examples of Microsoft Windows anti virus and anti-malware software include the optional Microsoft Security Essentials (for Windows XP, Vista and Windows 7) for real-time protection, the Windows Malicious Software Removal Tool (now included with Windows (Security) Updates on "Patch Tuesday", the second Tuesday of each month), and Windows Defender (an optional download in the case of Windows XP). Additionally, several capable antivirus software programs are available for free download from the Internet (usually restricted to non-commercial use). Some such free programs are almost as good as commercial competitors. Common security vulnerabilities are assigned CVE IDs and listed in the US National Vulnerability Database. Secunia PSI is an example of software, free for personal use, that will check a PC for vulnerable out-of-date software, and attempt to update it. Ransomware and phishing scam alerts appear as press releases on the Internet Crime Complaint Center noticeboard. Ransomware is a virus that posts a message on the user's screen saying that the screen or system will remain locked or unusable until a ransom payment is made. Phishing is a deception in which the malicious individual pretends to be a friend, computer security expert, or other benevolent individual, with the goal of convincing the targeted individual to reveal passwords or other personal information.

Other commonly used preventative measures include timely operating system updates, software updates, careful Internet browsing (avoiding shady websites), and installation of only trusted software. Certain browsers flag sites that have been reported to Google and that have been confirmed as hosting malware by Google.

There are two common methods that an antivirus software application uses to detect viruses, as described in the antivirus software topic. The first, and by far the most common method of virus detection is using a list of virus signature definitions. This works by examining the content of the computer's memory (its Random Access Memory (RAM), and boot sectors) and the files stored on fixed or removable drives (hard drives, floppy drives, or USB flash drives), and comparing those files against a database of known virus "signatures". Virus signatures are just strings of code that are used to identify individual viruses; for each virus, the antivirus designer tries to choose a unique signature string that will not be found in a legitimate program. Different antivirus programs use different "signatures" to identify viruses. The disadvantage of this detection method is that users are only protected from viruses that are detected by signatures in their most recent virus definition update, and not protected from new viruses.

A second method to find viruses is to use a heuristic algorithm based on common virus behaviors. This method has the ability to detect new viruses for which antivirus security firms have yet to define a "signature", but it also gives rise to more false positives than using signatures. False positives can be disruptive, especially in a commercial environment, because it may lead to a company instructing staff not to use the company computer system until IT services has checked the system for viruses. This can slow down productivity for regular workers.

Recovery Strategies and Methods

One may reduce the damage done by viruses by making regular backups of data (and the operating systems) on different media, that are either kept unconnected to the system (most of the time, as in a hard drive), read-only or not accessible for other reasons, such as using different file systems. This way, if data is lost through a virus, one can start again using the backup (which will hopefully be recent). If a backup session on optical media like CD and DVD is closed, it becomes read-only and can no longer be affected by a virus (so long as a virus or infected file was not copied onto the CD/DVD). Likewise, an operating system on a bootable CD can be used to start the computer if the installed operating systems become unusable. Backups on removable media must be carefully inspected before restoration. The Gammima virus, for example, propagates via removable flash drives.

Virus Removal

Many websites run by antivirus software companies provide free online virus scanning, with limited "cleaning" facilities (after all, the purpose of the websites is to sell antivirus products and services). Some websites—like Google subsidiary VirusTotal. com—allow users to upload one or more suspicious files to be scanned and checked by one or more antivirus programs in one operation. Additionally, several capable antivirus software programs are available for free download from the Internet (usually restricted to non-commercial use). Microsoft offers an optional free antivirus utility called Microsoft Security Essentials, a Windows Malicious Software Removal Tool that is updated as part of the regular Windows update regime, and an older optional anti-malware (malware removal) tool Windows Defender that has been upgraded to an antivirus product in Windows 8.

Some viruses disable System Restore and other important Windows tools such as Task Manager and CMD. An example of a virus that does this is CiaDoor. Many such viruses can be removed by rebooting the computer, entering Windows "safe mode" with networking, and then using system tools or Microsoft Safety Scanner. System Restore on Windows Me, Windows XP, Windows Vista and Windows 7 can restore the registry and critical system files to a previous checkpoint. Often a virus will cause a system to "hang" or "freeze", and a subsequent hard reboot will render a system restore point from the same day corrupted. Restore points from previous days should work, provided the virus is not designed to corrupt the restore files and does not exist in previous restore points.

Operating System Reinstallation

Microsoft's System File Checker (improved in Windows 7 and later) can be used to check for, and repair, corrupted system files. Restoring an earlier "clean" (virus-free) copy of the entire partition from a cloned disk, a disk image, or a backup copy is one solution—restoring an earlier backup disk "image" is relatively simple to do, usually removes any malware, and may be faster than "disinfecting" the computer—or reinstalling and reconfiguring the operating system and programs from scratch, as described below, then restoring user preferences. Reinstalling the operating system is another approach to virus removal. It may be possible to recover copies of essential user data by booting from a live CD, or connecting the hard drive to another computer and booting from the second computer's operating system, taking great care not to infect that computer by executing any infected programs on the original drive. The original hard drive can then be reformatted and the OS and all programs installed from original media. Once the system has been restored, precautions must be taken to avoid reinfection from any restored executable files.

Viruses and the Internet

Before computer networks became widespread, most viruses spread on removable media, particularly floppy disks. In the early days of the personal computer, many users regularly exchanged information and programs on floppies. Some viruses spread by infecting programs stored on these disks, while others installed themselves into the disk boot sector, ensuring that they would be run when the user booted the computer from the disk, usually inadvertently. Personal computers of the era would attempt to boot first from a floppy if one had been left in the drive. Until floppy disks fell out of use, this was the most successful infection strategy and boot sector viruses were the most common in the "wild" for many years. Traditional computer viruses emerged in the 1980s, driven by the spread of personal computers and the resultant increase in bulletin board system (BBS), modem use, and software sharing. Bulletin board–driven software sharing contributed directly to the spread of Trojan horse programs, and viruses were written to infect popularly traded software. Shareware and bootleg software were equally common vectors for viruses on BBSs. Viruses can increase their chances of spreading to other computers by infecting files on a network file system or a file system that is accessed by other computers.

Macro viruses have become common since the mid-1990s. Most of these viruses are written in the scripting languages for Microsoft programs such as Microsoft Word and Microsoft Excel and spread throughout Microsoft Office by infecting documents and spreadsheets. Since Word and Excel were also available for Mac OS, most could also spread to Macintosh computers. Although most of these viruses did not have the ability to send infected email messages, those viruses which did take advantage of the Microsoft Outlook Component Object Model (COM) interface. Some old versions of Microsoft Word allow macros to replicate themselves with additional blank lines. If two macro viruses simultaneously infect a document, the combination of the two, if also self-replicating, can appear as a "mating" of the two and would likely be detected as a virus unique from the "parents".

A virus may also send a web address link as an instant message to all the contacts (e.g., friends and colleagues' e-mail addresses) stored on an infected machine. If the recipient, thinking the link is from a friend (a trusted source) follows the link to the website, the virus hosted at the site may be able to infect this new computer and continue propagating. Viruses that spread using cross-site scripting were first reported in 2002, and were academically demonstrated in 2005. There have been multiple instances of the cross-site scripting viruses in the "wild", exploiting websites such as MySpace (with the Samy worm) and Yahoo!.

Computer Worm

A computer worm is a standalone malware computer program that replicates itself in order to spread to other computers. Often, it uses a computer network to spread itself, relying on security failures on the target computer to access it. Worms almost always cause at least some harm to the network, even if only by consuming bandwidth, whereas viruses almost always corrupt or modify files on a targeted computer.

```
0 00 00-6D 73 62 6C                              msbl
0 6A 75-73 74 20 77    ast.exe I just w
9 20 4C-4F 56 45 20    ant to say LOVE
0 62 69-6C 6C 79 20    YOU SAN!! billy
0 64 6F-20 79 6F 75    gates why do you
3 20 70-6F 73 73 69     make this possi
0 20 6D-61 6B 69 6E    ble ? Stop makin
E 64 20-66 69 78 20    g money and fix
7 61 72-65 21 21 00    your software!!
0 00 00-7F 00 00 00
0 00 00-01 00 01 00
0 00 00-00 00 00 46
C C9 11-9F E8 08 00
0 00 03-10 00 00 00
3 00 00-01 00 04 00
```

Hex dump of the Blaster worm, showing a message left for Microsoft CEO Bill Gates by the worm programmer

Worm:Win32 Conficker

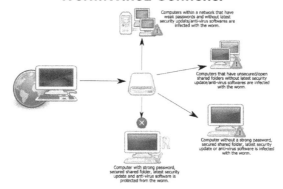

Spread of Conficker worm

Many worms that have been created are designed only to spread, and do not attempt to change the systems they pass through. However, as the Morris worm and Mydoom showed, even these "payload-free" worms can cause major disruption by increasing network traffic and other unintended effects.

Harm

Any code designed to do more than spread the worm is typically referred to as the "payload". Typical malicious payloads might delete files on a host system (e.g., the ExploreZip worm), encrypt files in a ransomware attack, or exfiltrate data such as confidential documents or passwords.

Probably the most common payload for worms is to install a backdoor. This allows the computer to be remotely controlled by the worm author as a "zombie". Networks of such machines are often referred to as botnets and are very commonly used for a range of malicious purposes, including sending spam or performing DoS attacks.

Countermeasures

Worms spread by exploiting vulnerabilities in operating systems. Vendors with security problems supply regular security updates and if these are installed to a machine then the majority of worms are unable to spread to it. If a vulnerability is disclosed before the security patch released by the vendor, a zero-day attack is possible.

Users need to be wary of opening unexpected email, and should not run attached files or programs, or visit web sites that are linked to such emails. However, as with the ILOVEYOU worm, and with the increased growth and efficiency of phishing attacks, it remains possible to trick the end-user into running malicious code.

Anti-virus and anti-spyware software are helpful, but must be kept up-to-date with new pattern files at least every few days. The use of a firewall is also recommended.

In the April–June 2008 issue of *IEEE Transactions on Dependable and Secure Computing*, computer scientists described a new and potentially effective way to combat internet worms. The researchers discovered how to contain worms that scanned the Internet randomly, looking for vulnerable hosts to infect. They found that the key was to use software to monitor the number of scans that machines on a network send out. When a machine started to send out too many scans, it was a sign that it has been infected, which allowed administrators to take it off line and check it for malware. In addition, machine learning techniques can be used to detect new worms, by analyzing the behavior of the suspected computer.

Users can minimize the threat posed by worms by keeping their computers' operating system and other software up to date, avoiding opening unrecognized or unexpected emails and running firewall and antivirus software.

Mitigation techniques include:

- ACLs in routers and switches
- Packet-filters
- TCP Wrapper/ACL enabled network service daemons
- Nullroute

Worms with Good Intent

Beginning with the very first research into worms at Xerox PARC, there have been attempts to create useful worms. Those worms allowed testing by John Shoch and Jon Hupp of the Ethernet principles on their network of Xerox Alto computers. The Nachi family of worms tried to download and install patches from Microsoft's website to fix vulnerabilities in the host system—by exploiting those same vulnerabilities. In practice, although this may have made these systems more secure, it generated considerable network traffic, rebooted the machine in the course of patching it, and did its work without the consent of the computer's owner or user. Regardless of their payload or their writers' intentions, most security experts regard all worms as malware.

Several worms, like XSS worms, have been written to research how worms spread. For example, the effects of changes in social activity or user behavior. One study proposed what seems to be the first computer worm that operates on the second layer of the OSI model (Data link Layer), it utilizes topology information such as Content-addressable memory (CAM) tables and Spanning Tree information stored in switches to propagate and probe for vulnerable nodes until the enterprise network is covered.

Trojan Horse

In computing, a Trojan horse, or Trojan, is any malicious computer program which misleads users of its true intent. The term is derived from the Ancient Greek story of the deceptive wooden horse that led to the fall of the city of Troy.

Trojans are generally spread by some form of social engineering, for example where a user is duped into executing an e-mail attachment disguised to be unsuspicious, (e.g., a routine form to be filled in), or by drive-by download. Although their payload can be anything, many modern forms act as a backdoor, contacting a controller which can then have unauthorized access to the affected computer. Trojans may allow an attacker to access users' personal information such as banking information, passwords, or personal identity (IP address). It can infect other devices connected to the network. Ransomware attacks are often carried out using a Trojan.

Unlike computer viruses and worms, Trojans generally do not attempt to inject themselves into other files or otherwise propagate themselves.

Origin of the Concept

Ken Thompson

This terminology occurs for the first time in a US Air Force report in 1974 on the analysis of vulnerability in computer systems. It was made popular by Ken Thompson in his Turing lecture which he gave at the reception of the Turing Award in 1983, attributed to him for having created UNIX. His conference is subtitled:

> *To what extent should one trust a statement that a program is free of Trojan horses? Perhaps it is more important to trust: the people who wrote the software.*

He mentioned that he knew about the possible existence of Trojan horses in a report on the security of Multics of which he was unfortunately unable to find a reference. However Paul Karger and Roger Schell affirm that this is their above cited report.

Malicious uses

Trojan in this way may require interaction with a malicious controller (not necessarily distributing the Trojan) to fulfill their purpose. It is possible for those involved with Trojans to scan computers on a network to locate any with a Trojan installed, which the hacker can then control.

Some Trojans take advantage of a security flaw in older versions of Internet Explorer and Google Chrome to use the host computer as an anonymizer proxy to effectively hide Internet usage, enabling the controller to use the Internet for illegal purposes while all potentially incriminating evidence indicates the infected computer or its IP address. The host's computer may or may not show the internet history of the sites viewed using the computer as a proxy. The first generation of anonymizer Trojan horses tended to leave their tracks in the page view histories of the host computer. Later generations of the Trojan tend to "cover" their tracks more efficiently. Several versions of Sub7 have been widely circulated in the US and Europe and became the most widely distributed examples of this type of Trojan.

In German-speaking countries, spyware used or made by the government is sometimes called *govware*. Govware is typically a Trojan software used to intercept communications from the target computer. Some countries like Switzerland and Germany have a legal framework governing the use of such software. Examples of govware Trojans include the Swiss MiniPanzer and MegaPanzer and the German "state trojan" nicknamed R2D2. German govware works by exploiting security gaps unknown to the general public and accessing smartphone data before it becomes encrypted via other applications.

Due to the popularity of botnets among hackers and the availability of advertising services that permit authors to violate their users' privacy, Trojans are becoming more common. According to a survey conducted by BitDefender from January to June 2009, "Trojan-type malware is on the rise, accounting for 83-percent of the global malware detected in the world." Trojans have a relationship with worms, as they spread with the help given by worms and travel across the internet with them. BitDefender has stated that approximately 15% of computers are members of a botnet, usually recruited by a Trojan infection.

Ransomware

Ransomware is a type of malicious software from cryptovirology that threatens to publish the victim's data or perpetually block access to it unless a ransom is paid. While some simple ransomware may lock the system in a way which is not difficult for a knowledgeable person to reverse, more advanced malware uses a technique called cryptoviral extortion, in which it encrypts the victim's files, making them inaccessible, and demands a ransom payment to decrypt them. In a properly implemented cryptoviral extortion attack, recovering the files without the decryption key is an intractable problem – and difficult to trace digital currencies such as Ukash and Bitcoin are used for the ransoms, making tracing and prosecuting the perpetrators difficult.

Ransomware attacks are typically carried out using a Trojan that is disguised as a legitimate file that the user is tricked into downloading or opening when it arrives as an email attachment. However, one high-profile example, the "WannaCry worm", traveled automatically between computers without user interaction.

Starting from around 2012 the use of ransomware scams has grown internationally. in June 2013, vendor McAfee released data showing that it had collected more than double the number of samples of ransomware that quarter than it had in the same quarter of the previous year. CryptoLocker was particularly successful, procuring an estimated US $3 million before it was taken down by authorities, and CryptoWall was estimated by the US Federal Bureau of Investigation (FBI) to have accrued over US $18m by June 2015.

Operation

The concept of file encrypting ransomware was invented and implemented by Young and Yung at Columbia University and was presented at the 1996 IEEE Security & Privacy conference. It is called *cryptoviral extortion* and it was inspired by the fictional facehugger in the movie *Alien*. Cryptoviral extortion is the following three-round protocol carried out between the attacker and the victim.

1. [attacker→victim] The attacker generates a key pair and places the corresponding public key in the malware. The malware is released.

2. [victim→attacker] To carry out the cryptoviral extortion attack, the malware generates a random symmetric key and encrypts the victim's data with it. It uses the public key in the malware to encrypt the symmetric key. This is known as hybrid encryption and it results in a small asymmetric ciphertext as well as the symmetric ciphertext of the victim's data. It zeroizes the symmetric key and the original plaintext data to prevent recovery. It puts up a message to the user that includes the asymmetric ciphertext and how to pay the ransom. The victim sends the asymmetric ciphertext and e-money to the attacker.

3. [attacker→victim] The attacker receives the payment, deciphers the asymmetric ciphertext with the attacker's private key, and sends the symmetric key to the victim. The victim deciphers the encrypted data with the needed symmetric key thereby completing the cryptovirology attack.

The symmetric key is randomly generated and will not assist other victims. At no point is the attacker's private key exposed to victims and the victim need only send a very small ciphertext (the encrypted symmetric-cipher key) to the attacker.

Ransomware attacks are typically carried out using a Trojan, entering a system through, for example, a downloaded file or a vulnerability in a network service. The program then runs a payload, which locks the system in some fashion, or claims to lock the system but does not (e.g., a scareware program). Payloads may display a fake warning purportedly by an entity such as a law enforcement agency, falsely claiming that the system has been used for illegal activities, contains content such as pornography and "pirated" media.

Some payloads consist simply of an application designed to lock or restrict the system until payment is made, typically by setting the Windows Shell to itself, or even modifying the master boot record and/or partition table to prevent the operating system from booting until it is repaired. The most sophisticated payloads encrypt files, with many using strong encryption to encrypt the victim's files in such a way that only the malware author has the needed decryption key.

Payment is virtually always the goal, and the victim is coerced into paying for the ransomware to be removed—which may or may not actually occur—either by supplying a program that can decrypt the files, or by sending an unlock code that undoes the payload's changes. A key element in making ransomware work for the attacker is a convenient payment system that is hard to trace. A range of such payment methods have been used, including wire transfers, premium-rate text messages, pre-paid voucher services such as Paysafecard, and the digital currency Bitcoin. A 2016 survey commissioned by Citrix claimed that larger businesses are holding bitcoin as contingency plans.

Notable Examples

Reveton

In 2012, a major ransomware Trojan known as Reveton began to spread. Based on the Citadel Trojan (which itself, is based on the Zeus Trojan), its payload displays a warning purportedly from a law enforcement agency claiming that the computer has been used for illegal activities, such as downloading unlicensed software or child pornography. Due to this behaviour, it is commonly referred to as the "Police Trojan". The warning informs the user that to unlock their system, they would have to pay a fine using a voucher from an anonymous prepaid cash service such as Ukash or Paysafecard. To increase the illusion that the computer is being tracked by law enforcement, the screen also displays the computer's IP address, while some versions display footage from a victim's webcam to give the illusion that the user is being recorded.

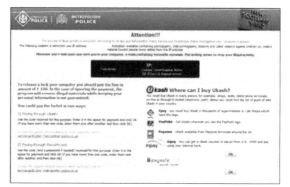

A Reveton payload, fraudulently claiming that the user must pay a fine to the Metropolitan Police Service

Reveton initially began spreading in various European countries in early 2012. Variants were localized with templates branded with the logos of different law enforcement organizations based on the user's country; for example, variants used in the United Kingdom contained the branding of organizations such as the Metropolitan Police Service and the Police National E-Crime Unit. Another version contained the logo of the royalty collection society PRS for Music, which specifically accused the user of illegally downloading music. In a statement warning the public about the malware, the Metropolitan Police clarified that they would never lock a computer in such a way as part of an investigation.

In May 2012, Trend Micro threat researchers discovered templates for variations for the United States and Canada, suggesting that its authors may have been planning to target users in North America. By August 2012, a new variant of Reveton began to spread in the United States, claiming to require the payment of a $200 fine to the FBI using a MoneyPak card. In February 2013, a Russian citizen was arrested in Dubai by Spanish authorities for his connection to a crime ring that had been using Reveton; ten other individuals were arrested on money laundering charges. In August 2014, Avast Software reported that it had found new variants of Reveton that also distribute password stealing malware as part of its payload.

CryptoLocker

Encrypting ransomware reappeared in September 2013 with a Trojan known as *CryptoLocker*, which generated a 2048-bit RSA key pair and uploaded in turn to a command-and-control server, and used to encrypt files using a whitelist of specific file extensions. The malware threatened to delete the private key if a payment of Bitcoin or a pre-paid cash voucher was not made within 3 days of the infection. Due to the extremely large key size it uses, analysts and those affected by the Trojan considered CryptoLocker extremely difficult to repair. Even after the deadline passed, the private key could still be obtained using an online tool, but the price would increase to 10 BTC—which cost approximately US\$2300 as of November 2013.

CryptoLocker was isolated by the seizure of the Gameover ZeuS botnet as part of Operation Tovar, as officially announced by the U.S. Department of Justice on 2 June 2014. The Department of Justice also publicly issued an indictment against the Russian hacker Evgeniy Bogachev for his alleged involvement in the botnet. It was estimated that at least US\$3 million was extorted with the malware before the shutdown.

CryptoLocker.F and TorrentLocker

In September 2014, a wave of ransomware Trojans surfaced that first targeted users in Australia, under the names *CryptoWall* and *CryptoLocker* (which is, as with CryptoLocker 2.0, unrelated to the original CryptoLocker). The Trojans spread via fraudulent e-mails claiming to be failed parcel delivery notices from Australia Post; to evade detection by automatic e-mail scanners that follow all links on a page to scan for malware, this variant was designed to require users to visit a web page and enter a CAPTCHA code before the payload is actually downloaded, preventing such automated processes from being able to scan the payload. Symantec determined that these new variants, which it identified as *CryptoLocker.F*, were again, unrelated to the original CryptoLocker due to differences in their operation. A notable victim of the Trojans was the Australian Broadcasting Corporation; live programming on its television news channel ABC News 24 was disrupted for half an hour and shifted to Melbourne studios due to a CryptoWall infection on computers at its Sydney studio.

Another Trojan in this wave, TorrentLocker, initially contained a design flaw comparable to CryptoDefense; it used the same keystream for every infected computer, making the encryption trivial to overcome. However, this flaw was later fixed. By late-November 2014, it was estimated that over 9,000 users had been infected by TorrentLocker in Australia alone, trailing only Turkey with 11,700 infections.

CryptoWall

Another major ransomware Trojan targeting Windows, CryptoWall, first appeared in 2014. One strain of CryptoWall was distributed as part of a malvertising campaign on the Zedo ad network in late-September 2014 that targeted several major websites; the ads redirected to rogue websites that used browser plugin exploits to download the payload. A Barracuda Networks researcher also noted that the payload was signed with a digital signature in an effort to appear trustworthy to security software. CryptoWall 3.0 used a payload written in JavaScript as part of an email attachment, which downloads executables disguised as JPG images. To further evade detection, the malware creates new instances of explorer.exe and svchost.exe to communicate with its servers.

When encrypting files, the malware also deletes volume shadow copies, and installs spyware that steals passwords and Bitcoin wallets.

The FBI reported in June 2015 that nearly 1,000 victims had contacted the bureau's Internet Crime Complaint Center to report CryptoWall infections, and estimated losses of at least $18 million.

The most recent version, CryptoWall 4.0, enhanced its code to avoid antivirus detection, and encrypts not only the data in files but also the file names.

Fusob

Fusob is one of the major mobile ransomware families. Between April 2015 and March 2016, about 56 percent of accounted mobile ransomware was Fusob.

Like a typical mobile ransomware, it employs scare tactics to extort people to pay a ransom. The program pretends to be an accusatory authority, demanding the victim to pay a fine from $100 to $200 USD or otherwise face a fictitious charge. Rather surprisingly, Fusob suggests using iTunes gift cards for payment. Also, a timer clicking down on the screen adds to the users' anxiety as well.

In order to infect devices, Fusob masquerades as a pornographic video player. Thus, victims, thinking it is harmless, unwittingly download Fusob.

When Fusob is installed, it first checks the language used in the device. If it uses Russian or certain Eastern European languages, Fusob does nothing. Otherwise, it proceeds on to lock the device and demand ransom. Among victims, about 40% of them are in Germany with the United Kingdom and the United States following with 14.5% and 11.4% respectively.

Fusob has lots in common with Small, which is another major family of mobile ransomware. They represented over 93% of mobile ransomwares between 2015 and 2016.

WannaCry

In May 2017, the WannaCry ransomware attack spread through the Internet, using an exploit vector named EternalBlue, which was leaked from the U.S. National Security Agency. The ransomware attack, unprecedented in scale, infected more than 230,000 computers in over 150 countries, using 20 different languages to demand money from users using Bitcoin cryptocurrency. WannaCrypt demanded US$300 per computer. The attack affected Telefónica and several other large companies in Spain, as well as parts of the British National Health Service (NHS), where at least 16 hospitals had to turn away patients or cancel scheduled operations, FedEx, Deutsche Bahn, Honda, Renault, as well as the Russian Interior Ministry and Russian telecom MegaFon. The attackers gave their victims a 7-day deadline from the day their computers got infected, after which the encrypted files would be deleted.

Petya

Petya was first discovered in March 2016; unlike other forms of encrypting ransomware, the malware aimed to infect the master boot record, installing a payload which encrypts the file tables of the NTFS file system the next time that the infected system boots, blocking the system from booting into Windows at all until the ransom is paid. Check Point reported that despite what it believed to be an innovative evolution in ransomware design, it had resulted in relatively-fewer infections than other ransomware active around the same time frame.

On June 27, 2017, a heavily modified version of Petya was used for a global cyberattack primarily targeting Ukraine. This version had been modified to propagate using the same EternalBlue exploit that was used by WannaCry. Due to another design change, it is also unable to actually unlock a system after the ransom is paid; this led to security analysts speculating that the attack was not meant to generate illicit profit, but to simply cause disruption.

Bad Rabbit

On October 24, 2017, some users in Russia and Ukraine reported a new ransomware attack, named "Bad Rabbit", which follows a similar pattern to WannaCry and Petya by encrypting the user's file tables and then demands a BitCoin payment to decrypt them. ESET believed the ransomware to have been distributed by a bogus update to Adobe Flash software. Among agencies that were affected by the ransomware included Interfax, Odessa International Airport, Kiev Metro, and the Ministry of Infrastructure of Ukraine. As it used corporate network structures to spread, the ransomware was also discovered in other countries, including Turkey, Germany, Poland, Japan, South Korea, and the United States. Experts believed the ransomware attack was tied to the Petya attack in the Ukraine, though the only identity to the culprits are the names of characters from the *Game of Thrones* series embedded within the code.

Security experts found that the ransomware did not use the EternalBlue exploit to spread, and a simple method to vaccinate an unaffected machine running older Windows versions was found by October 24, 2017. Further, the sites that had been used to spread the bogus Flash updating have gone offline or removed the problematic files within a few days of its discovery, effectively killing off the spread of Bad Rabbit.

Mitigation

As with other forms of malware, security software (antivirus software) might not detect a ransomware payload, or, especially in the case of encrypting payloads, only after encryption is under way or complete, particularly if a new version unknown to the protective software is distributed. If an attack is suspected or detected in its early stages, it takes some time for encryption to take place; immediate removal of the malware (a relatively simple process) before it has completed would stop further damage to data, without salvaging any already lost.

Security experts have suggested precautionary measures for dealing with ransomware. Using software or other security policies to block known payloads from launching will help to prevent infection, but will not protect against all attacks Keeping "offline" backups of data stored in locations inaccessible from any potentially infected computer, such as external storage drives or devices that do not have any access to any network (including the Internet), prevents them from being accessed by the ransomware. Installing security updates issued by software vendors can mitigate the vulnerabilities leveraged by certain strains to propagate. Other measures include cyber hygiene – exercising caution when opening e-mail attachments and links, network segmentation, and keeping critical computers isolated from networks. Furthermore, to mitigate the spread of ransomware measures of infection control can be applied. Such may include disconnecting infected machines from all networks, educational programs, effective communication channels, malware surveillance and ways of collective participation.

There are a number of tools intended specifically to decrypt files locked by ransomware, although successful recovery may not be possible. If the same encryption key is used for all files, decryption tools use files for which there are both uncorrupted backups and encrypted copies (a known-plaintext attack in the jargon of cryptanalysis); recovery of the key, if it is possible, may take several days. Free ransomware decryption tools can help decrypt files encrypted by the following forms of ransomware: AES_NI, Alcatraz Locker, Apocalypse, BadBlock, Bart, BTCWare, Crypt888, CryptoMix, CrySiS, EncrypTile, FindZip, Globe, Hidden Tear, Jigsaw, LambdaLocker, Legion, NoobCrypt, Stampado, SZFLocker, TeslaCrypt, XData.

Freedom of Speech Challenges and Criminal Punishment

The publication of proof-of-concept attack code is common among academic researchers and vulnerability researchers. It teaches the nature of the threat, conveys the gravity of the issues, and enables countermeasures to be devised and put into place. However, lawmakers with the support of law-enforcement bodies are contemplating making the creation of ransomware illegal. In the state of Maryland the original draft of HB 340 made it a felony to create ransomware, punishable by up to 10 years in prison. However, this provision was removed from the final version of the bill. A minor in Japan was arrested for creating and distributing ransomware code. Young and Yung have had the ANSI C source code to a ransomware cryptotrojan on-line, at cryptovirology.com, since 2005 as part of a cryptovirology book being written.

Spyware

Spyware is software that aims to gather information about a person or organization without their knowledge, that may send such information to another entity without the consumer's consent, or that asserts control over a device without the consumer's knowledge.

"Spyware" is mostly classified into four types: adware, system monitors, tracking cookies, and trojans; examples of other notorious types include digital rights management capabilities that "phone home", keyloggers, rootkits, and web beacons.

Spyware is mostly used for the purposes of tracking and storing Internet users' movements on the Web and serving up pop-up ads to Internet users. Whenever spyware is used for malicious purposes, its presence is typically hidden from the user and can be difficult to detect. Some spyware, such as keyloggers, may be installed by the owner of a shared, corporate, or public computer intentionally in order to monitor users.

While the term *spyware* suggests software that monitors a user's computing, the functions of spyware can extend beyond simple monitoring. Spyware can collect almost any type of data, including personal information like internet surfing habits, user logins, and bank or credit account information. Spyware can also interfere with a user's control of a computer by installing additional software or redirecting web browsers. Some spyware can change computer settings, which can result in slow Internet connection speeds, un-authorized changes in browser settings, or changes to software settings.

Sometimes, spyware is included along with genuine software, and may come from a malicious website or may have been added to the intentional functionality of genuine software. In response to the emergence of spyware, a small industry has sprung up dealing in anti-spyware software. Running anti-spyware software has become a widely recognized element of computer security practices, especially for computers running Microsoft Windows. A number of jurisdictions have passed anti-spyware laws, which usually target any software that is surreptitiously installed to control a user's computer.

In German-speaking countries, spyware used or made by the government is called *govware* by computer experts (in common parlance: *Regierungstrojaner*, literally "Government Trojan"). Govware is typically a trojan horse software used to intercept communications from the target computer. Some countries, like Switzerland and Germany, have a legal framework governing the use of such software. In the US, the term "policeware" has been used for similar purposes.

Use of the term "spyware" has eventually declined as the practice of tracking users has been pushed ever further into the mainstream by major websites and data mining companies; these generally break no known laws and compel users to be tracked, not by fraudulent practices *per se*, but by the default settings created for users and the language of terms-of-service agreements. In one documented example, on CBS/ CNet News reported, on March 7, 2011, on a *Wall Street Journal* analysis revealing the practice of Facebook and other websites of tracking users' browsing activity, linked to their identity, far beyond users' visits and activity within the Facebook site itself. The report stated: "Here's how it works. You go to Facebook, you log in, you spend some time there, and then ... you move on without logging out. Let's say the next site you go to is *New York Times*. Those buttons, without you clicking on them, have just reported back to Facebook and Twitter that you went there and also your identity within those accounts. Let's say you moved on to something like a site about depression. This one also has a tweet button, a Google widget, and those, too, can report back who you are and that you went there." The *WSJ* analysis was researched by Brian Kennish, founder of Disconnect, Inc.

Routes of Infection

Spyware does not necessarily spread in the same way as a virus or worm because infected systems generally do not attempt to transmit or copy the software to other computers. Instead, spyware installs itself on a system by deceiving the user or by exploiting software vulnerabilities.

Most spyware is installed without knowledge, or by using deceptive tactics. Spyware may try to deceive users by bundling itself with desirable software. Other common tactics are using a Trojan horse, spy gadgets that look like normal devices but turn out to be something else, such as a USB Keylogger. These devices actually are connected to the device as memory units but are capable of recording each stroke made on the keyboard. Some spyware authors infect a system through security holes in the Web browser or in other software. When the user navigates to a Web page controlled by the spyware author, the page contains code which attacks the browser and forces the download and installation of spyware.

The installation of spyware frequently involves Internet Explorer. Its popularity and history of security issues have made it a frequent target. Its deep integration with the Windows environment make it susceptible to attack into the Windows operating system. Internet Explorer also serves as a point of attachment for spyware in the form of Browser Helper Objects, which modify the browser's behavior.

Effects and Behaviors

A spyware program rarely operates alone on a computer; an affected machine usually has multiple infections. Users frequently notice unwanted behavior and degradation of system performance. A spyware infestation can create significant unwanted CPU activity, disk usage, and network traffic. Stability issues, such as applications freezing, failure to boot, and system-wide crashes are also common. Spyware, which interferes with networking software commonly causes difficulty connecting to the Internet.

In some infections, the spyware is not even evident. Users assume in those situations that the performance issues relate to faulty hardware, Windows installation problems, or another malware infection. Some owners of badly infected systems resort to contacting technical support experts, or even buying a new computer because the existing system "has become too slow". Badly infected systems may require a clean reinstallation of all their software in order to return to full functionality.

Moreover, some types of spyware disable software firewalls and antivirus software, and/or reduce browser security settings, which opens the system to further opportunistic infections. Some spyware disables or even removes competing spyware programs, on the grounds that more spyware-related annoyances increase the likelihood that users will take action to remove the programs.

Keyloggers are sometimes part of malware packages downloaded onto computers without the owners' knowledge. Some keylogger software is freely available on the internet, while others are commercial or private applications. Most keyloggers allow not only keyboard keystrokes to be captured, they also are often capable of collecting screen captures from the computer.

A typical Windows user has administrative privileges, mostly for convenience. Because of this, any program the user runs has unrestricted access to the system. As with other operating systems, Windows users are able to follow the principle of least privilege and use non-administrator accounts. Alternatively, they can reduce the privileges of specific vulnerable Internet-facing processes, such as Internet Explorer.

Since Windows Vista is, by default, a computer administrator that runs everything under limited user privileges, when a program requires administrative privileges, a User Account Control pop-up will prompt the user to allow or deny the action. This improves on the design used by previous versions of Windows.

Remedies and Prevention

As the spyware threat has worsened, a number of techniques have emerged to counteract it. These include programs designed to remove or block spyware, as well as various user practices which reduce the chance of getting spyware on a system.

Nonetheless, spyware remains a costly problem. When a large number of pieces of spyware have infected a Windows computer, the only remedy may involve backing up user data, and fully reinstalling the operating system. For instance, some spyware cannot be completely removed by Symantec, Microsoft, PC Tools.

Anti-spyware Programs

Many programmers and some commercial firms have released products dedicated to remove or block spyware. Programs such as PC Tools' Spyware Doctor, Lavasoft's

Ad-Aware SE and Patrick Kolla's *Spybot - Search & Destroy* rapidly gained popularity as tools to remove, and in some cases intercept, spyware programs. On December 16, 2004, Microsoft acquired the *GIANT AntiSpyware* software, rebranding it as *Windows AntiSpyware beta* and releasing it as a free download for Genuine Windows XP and Windows 2003 users. (In 2006 it was renamed Windows Defender).

Major anti-virus firms such as Symantec, PC Tools, McAfee and Sophos have also added anti-spyware features to their existing anti-virus products. Early on, anti-virus firms expressed reluctance to add anti-spyware functions, citing lawsuits brought by spyware authors against the authors of web sites and programs which described their products as "spyware". However, recent versions of these major firms home and business anti-virus products do include anti-spyware functions, albeit treated differently from viruses. Symantec Anti-Virus, for instance, categorizes spyware programs as "extended threats" and now offers real-time protection against these threats.

How Anti-spyware Software Works

Anti-spyware programs can combat spyware in two ways:

1. They can provide real-time protection in a manner similar to that of anti-virus protection: they scan all incoming network data for spyware and blocks any threats it detects.

2. Anti-spyware software programs can be used solely for detection and removal of spyware software that has already been installed into the computer. This kind of anti-spyware can often be set to scan on a regular schedule.

Such programs inspect the contents of the Windows registry, operating system files, and installed programs, and remove files and entries which match a list of known spyware. Real-time protection from spyware works identically to real-time anti-virus protection: the software scans disk files at download time, and blocks the activity of components known to represent spyware. In some cases, it may also intercept attempts to install start-up items or to modify browser settings. Earlier versions of anti-spyware programs focused chiefly on detection and removal. Javacool Software's SpywareBlaster, one of the first to offer real-time protection, blocked the installation of ActiveX-based spyware.

Like most anti-virus software, many anti-spyware/adware tools require a frequently updated database of threats. As new spyware programs are released, anti-spyware developers discover and evaluate them, adding to the list of known spyware, which allows the software to detect and remove new spyware. As a result, anti-spyware software is of limited usefulness without regular updates. Updates may be installed automatically or manually.

A popular generic spyware removal tool used by those that requires a certain degree of expertise is HijackThis, which scans certain areas of the Windows OS where spyware often resides and presents a list with items to delete manually. As most of the items are legitimate windows files/registry entries it is advised for those who are less knowledgeable on this subject to post a HijackThis log on the numerous antispyware sites and let the experts decide what to delete.

If a spyware program is not blocked and manages to get itself installed, it may resist attempts to terminate or uninstall it. Some programs work in pairs: when an anti-spyware scanner (or the user) terminates one running process, the other one respawns the killed program. Likewise, some spyware will detect attempts to remove registry keys and immediately add them again. Usually, booting the infected computer in safe mode allows an anti-spyware program a better chance of removing persistent spyware. Killing the process tree may also work.

Security Practices

To detect spyware, computer users have found several practices useful in addition to installing anti-spyware programs. Many users have installed a web browser other than Internet Explorer, such as Mozilla Firefox or Google Chrome. Though no browser is completely safe, Internet Explorer was once at a greater risk for spyware infection due to its large user base as well as vulnerabilities such as ActiveX but these three major browsers are now close to equivalent when it comes to security.

Some ISPs—particularly colleges and universities—have taken a different approach to blocking spyware: they use their network firewalls and web proxies to block access to Web sites known to install spyware. On March 31, 2005, Cornell University's Information Technology department released a report detailing the behavior of one particular piece of proxy-based spyware, *Marketscore*, and the steps the university took to intercept it. Many other educational institutions have taken similar steps.

Individual users can also install firewalls from a variety of companies. These monitor the flow of information going to and from a networked computer and provide protection against spyware and malware. Some users install a large hosts file which prevents the user's computer from connecting to known spyware-related web addresses. Spyware may get installed via certain shareware programs offered for download. Downloading programs only from reputable sources can provide some protection from this source of attack.

Applications

"Stealware" and Affiliate Fraud

A few spyware vendors, notably 180 Solutions, have written what the *New York Times* has dubbed "stealware", and what spyware researcher Ben Edelman terms *affiliate fraud*, a form of click fraud. Stealware diverts the payment of affiliate marketing revenues from the legitimate affiliate to the spyware vendor.

Spyware which attacks affiliate networks places the spyware operator's affiliate tag on the user's activity – replacing any other tag, if there is one. The spyware operator is the only party that gains from this. The user has their choices thwarted, a legitimate affiliate loses revenue, networks' reputations are injured, and vendors are harmed by having to pay out affiliate revenues to an "affiliate" who is not party to a contract. Affiliate fraud is a violation of the terms of service of most affiliate marketing networks. As a result, spyware operators such as 180 Solutions have been terminated from affiliate networks including LinkShare and ShareSale. Mobile devices can also be vulnerable to chargeware, which manipulates users into illegitimate mobile charges.

Identity Theft and Fraud

In one case, spyware has been closely associated with identity theft. In August 2005, researchers from security software firm Sunbelt Software suspected the creators of the common CoolWebSearch spyware had used it to transmit "chat sessions, user names, passwords, bank information, etc."; however it turned out that "it actually (was) its own sophisticated criminal little trojan that's independent of CWS." This case is currently under investigation by the FBI.

The Federal Trade Commission estimates that 27.3 million Americans have been victims of identity theft, and that financial losses from identity theft totaled nearly $48 billion for businesses and financial institutions and at least $5 billion in out-of-pocket expenses for individuals.

Digital Rights Management

Some copy-protection technologies have borrowed from spyware. In 2005, Sony BMG Music Entertainment was found to be using rootkits in its XCP digital rights management technology Like spyware, not only was it difficult to detect and uninstall, it was so poorly written that most efforts to remove it could have rendered computers unable to function. Texas Attorney General Greg Abbott filed suit, and three separate class-action suits were filed. Sony BMG later provided a workaround on its website to help users remove it.

Beginning on April 25, 2006, Microsoft's Windows Genuine Advantage Notifications application was installed on most Windows PCs as a "critical security update". While the main purpose of this deliberately uninstallable application is to ensure the copy of Windows on the machine was lawfully purchased and installed, it also installs software that has been accused of "phoning home" on a daily basis, like spyware. It can be removed with the RemoveWGA tool.

Personal Relationships

Spyware has been used to monitor electronic activities of partners in intimate relationships. At least one software package, Loverspy, was specifically marketed for this purpose. Depending on local laws regarding communal/marital property, observing a partner's online activity without their consent may be illegal; the author of Loverspy and several users of the product were indicted in California in 2005 on charges of wiretapping and various computer crimes.

Browser Cookies

Anti-spyware programs often report Web advertisers' HTTP cookies, the small text files that track browsing activity, as spyware. While they are not always inherently malicious, many users object to third parties using space on their personal computers for their business purposes, and many anti-spyware programs offer to remove them.

Examples

These common spyware programs illustrate the diversity of behaviors found in these attacks. Note that as with computer viruses, researchers give names to spyware programs which may not be used by their creators. Programs may be grouped into "families" based not on shared program code, but on common behaviors, or by "following the money" of apparent financial or business connections. For instance, a number of the spyware programs distributed by Claria are collectively known as "Gator". Likewise, programs that are frequently installed together may be described as parts of the same spyware package, even if they function separately.

- CoolWebSearch, a group of programs, takes advantage of Internet Explorer vulnerabilities. The package directs traffic to advertisements on Web sites including *coolwebsearch.com*. It displays pop-up ads, rewrites search engine results, and alters the infected computer's hosts file to direct DNS lookups to these sites.

- FinFisher, sometimes called FinSpy is a high-end surveillance suite sold to law enforcement and intelligence agencies. Support services such as training and technology updates are part of the package.

- GO Keyboard virtual Android keyboard apps (GO Keyboard - Emoji keyboard and GO Keyboard - Emoticon keyboard) transmit personal information to its remote servers without explicit users' consent. This information includes user's Google account email, language, IMSI, location, network type, Android version and build, and device's model and screen size. The apps also download and execute a code from a remote server, breaching the Malicious Behavior section of the Google Play privacy policies. Some of these plugins are detected as Adware or PUP by many Anti-Virus engines, while the developer, a Chinese company GOMO Dev Team, claims in the apps' description that they will never collect personal data including credit card information. The apps with about 2 million users in total were caught on spying on September 2017 by security researches from AdGuard who then reported their findings to Google.

- HuntBar, aka WinTools or Adware.Websearch, was installed by an ActiveX drive-by download at affiliate Web sites, or by advertisements displayed by other spyware programs—an example of how spyware can install more spyware. These programs add toolbars to IE, track aggregate browsing behavior, redirect affiliate references, and display advertisements.

- Internet Optimizer, also known as DyFuCa, redirects Internet Explorer error pages to advertising. When users follow a broken link or enter an erroneous URL, they see a page of advertisements. However, because password-protected Web sites (HTTP Basic authentication) use the same mechanism as HTTP errors, Internet Optimizer makes it impossible for the user to access password-protected sites.

- Spyware such as Look2Me hides inside system-critical processes and start up even in safe mode. With no process to terminate they are harder to detect and remove, which is a combination of both spyware and a rootkit. Rootkit technology is also seeing increasing use, as newer spyware programs also have specific countermeasures against well known anti-malware products and may prevent them from running or being installed, or even uninstall them.

- Movieland, also known as Moviepass.tv and Popcorn.net, is a movie download service that has been the subject of thousands of complaints to the Federal Trade Commission (FTC), the Washington State Attorney General's Office, the Better Business Bureau, and other agencies. Consumers complained they were held hostage by a cycle of oversized pop-up windows demanding payment of at least $29.95, claiming that they had signed up for a three-day free trial but had not cancelled before the trial period was over, and were thus obligated to pay. The FTC filed a complaint, since settled, against Movieland and eleven other defendants charging them with having "engaged in a nationwide scheme to use deception and coercion to extract payments from consumers."

- WeatherStudio has a plugin that displays a window-panel near the *bottom* of a browser window. The official website notes that it is easy to remove (uninstall) WeatherStudio from a computer, using its own uninstall-program, such as under C:\Program Files\WeatherStudio. Once WeatherStudio is removed, a browser returns to the prior display appearance, without the need to modify the browser settings.

- Zango (formerly 180 Solutions) transmits detailed information to advertisers about the Web sites which users visit. It also alters HTTP requests for affiliate advertisements linked from a Web site, so that the advertisements make unearned profit for the 180 Solutions company. It opens pop-up ads that cover

over the Web sites of competing companies (as seen in their [Zango End User License Agreement]).

- Zlob trojan, or just Zlob, downloads itself to a computer via an ActiveX codec and reports information back to Control Server. Some information can be the search-history, the Websites visited, and even keystrokes. More recently, Zlob has been known to hijack routers set to defaults.

Programs Distributed with Spyware

- Kazaa
- Morpheus
- WeatherBug
- WildTangent

Programs Formerly Distributed with Spyware

- AOL Instant Messenger (AOL Instant Messenger still packages Viewpoint Media Player, and WildTangent)
- DivX
- FlashGet
- magicJack

Rogue Anti-spyware Programs

Malicious programmers have released a large number of rogue (fake) anti-spyware programs, and widely distributed Web banner ads can warn users that their computers have been infected with spyware, directing them to purchase programs which do not actually remove spyware—or else, may add more spyware of their own.

The recent proliferation of fake or spoofed antivirus products that bill themselves as antispyware can be troublesome. Users may receive popups prompting them to install them to protect their computer, when it will in fact add spyware. This software is called rogue software. It is recommended that users do not install any freeware claiming to be anti-spyware unless it is verified to be legitimate. Some known offenders include:

- AntiVirus 360
- Antivirus 2009
- AntiVirus Gold
- ContraVirus
- MacSweeper
- Pest Trap
- PSGuard
- Spy Wiper

- Spydawn
- Spylocked
- Spysheriff
- SpyShredder
- Spyware Quake
- SpywareStrike

- UltimateCleaner
- WinAntiVirus Pro 2006
- Windows Police Pro
- WinFixer
- WorldAntiSpy

Fake antivirus products constitute 15 percent of all malware.

On January 26, 2006, Microsoft and the Washington state attorney general filed suit against Secure Computer for its Spyware Cleaner product.

Legal Issues

Criminal Law

Unauthorized access to a computer is illegal under computer crime laws, such as the U.S. Computer Fraud and Abuse Act, the U.K.'s Computer Misuse Act, and similar laws in other countries. Since owners of computers infected with spyware generally claim that they never authorized the installation, a *prima facie* reading would suggest that the promulgation of spyware would count as a criminal act. Law enforcement has often pursued the authors of other malware, particularly viruses. However, few spyware developers have been prosecuted, and many operate openly as strictly legitimate businesses, though some have faced lawsuits.

Spyware producers argue that, contrary to the users' claims, users do in fact give consent to installations. Spyware that comes bundled with shareware applications may be described in the legalese text of an end-user license agreement (EULA). Many users habitually ignore these purported contracts, but spyware companies such as Claria say these demonstrate that users have consented.

Despite the ubiquity of EULAs agreements, under which a single click can be taken as consent to the entire text, relatively little caselaw has resulted from their use. It has been established in most common law jurisdictions that this type of agreement can be a binding contract *in certain circumstances*. This does not, however, mean that every such agreement is a contract, or that every term in one is enforceable.

Some jurisdictions, including the U.S. states of Iowa and Washington, have passed laws criminalizing some forms of spyware. Such laws make it illegal for anyone other than the owner or operator of a computer to install software that alters Web-browser settings, monitors keystrokes, or disables computer-security software.

In the United States, lawmakers introduced a bill in 2005 entitled the Internet Spyware Prevention Act, which would imprison creators of spyware.

Administrative Sanctions

US FTC Actions

The US Federal Trade Commission has sued Internet marketing organizations under the "unfairness doctrine" to make them stop infecting consumers' PCs with spyware. In one case, that against Seismic Entertainment Productions, the FTC accused the defendants of developing a program that seized control of PCs nationwide, infected them with spyware and other malicious software, bombarded them with a barrage of pop-up advertising for Seismic's clients, exposed the PCs to security risks, and caused them to malfunction. Seismic then offered to sell the victims an "antispyware" program to fix the computers, and stop the popups and other problems that Seismic had caused. On November 21, 2006, a settlement was entered in federal court under which a $1.75 million judgment was imposed in one case and $1.86 million in another, but the defendants were insolvent.

In a second case, brought against CyberSpy Software LLC, the FTC charged that CyberSpy marketed and sold "RemoteSpy" keylogger spyware to clients who would then secretly monitor unsuspecting consumers' computers. According to the FTC, Cyberspy touted RemoteSpy as a "100% undetectable" way to "Spy on Anyone. From Anywhere." The FTC has obtained a temporary order prohibiting the defendants from selling the software and disconnecting from the Internet any of their servers that collect, store, or provide access to information that this software has gathered. The case is still in its preliminary stages. A complaint filed by the Electronic Privacy Information Center (EPIC) brought the RemoteSpy software to the FTC's attention.

Netherlands OPTA

An administrative fine, the first of its kind in Europe, has been issued by the Independent Authority of Posts and Telecommunications (OPTA) from the Netherlands. It applied fines in total value of Euro 1,000,000 for infecting 22 million computers. The spyware concerned is called DollarRevenue. The law articles that have been violated are art. 4.1 of the Decision on universal service providers and on the interests of end users; the fines have been issued based on art. 15.4 taken together with art. 15.10 of the Dutch telecommunications law.

Civil Law

Former New York State Attorney General and former Governor of New York Eliot Spitzer has pursued spyware companies for fraudulent installation of software. In a suit brought in 2005 by Spitzer, the California firm Intermix Media, Inc. ended up settling, by agreeing to pay US$7.5 million and to stop distributing spyware.

The hijacking of Web advertisements has also led to litigation. In June 2002, a number of large Web publishers sued Claria for replacing advertisements, but settled out of court.

Courts have not yet had to decide whether advertisers can be held liable for spyware that displays their ads. In many cases, the companies whose advertisements appear in spyware pop-ups do not directly do business with the spyware firm. Rather, they have contracted with an advertising agency, which in turn contracts with an online subcontractor who gets paid by the number of "impressions" or appearances of the advertisement. Some major firms such as Dell Computer and Mercedes-Benz have sacked advertising agencies that have run their ads in spyware.

Libel Suits by Spyware Developers

Litigation has gone both ways. Since "spyware" has become a common pejorative, some makers have filed libel and defamation actions when their products have been so described. In 2003, Gator (now known as Claria) filed suit against the website PC Pitstop for describing its program as "spyware". PC Pitstop settled, agreeing not to use the word "spyware", but continues to describe harm caused by the Gator/Claria software. As a result, other anti-spyware and anti-virus companies have also used other terms such as "potentially unwanted programs" or greyware to denote these products.

WebcamGate

In the 2010 WebcamGate case, plaintiffs charged two suburban Philadelphia high schools secretly spied on students by surreptitiously and remotely activating webcams embedded in school-issued laptops the students were using at home, and therefore infringed on their privacy rights. The school loaded each student's computer with LANrev's remote activation tracking software. This included the now-discontinued "Theft-Track". While TheftTrack was not enabled by default on the software, the program allowed the school district to elect to activate it, and to choose which of the TheftTrack surveillance options the school wanted to enable.

TheftTrack allowed school district employees to secretly remotely activate the webcam embedded in the student's laptop, above the laptop's screen. That allowed school officials to secretly take photos through the webcam, of whatever was in front of it and in its line of sight, and send the photos to the school's server. The LANrev software disabled the webcams for all other uses (*e.g.*, students were unable to use Photo Booth or video chat), so most students mistakenly believed their webcams did not work at all. In addition to webcam surveillance, TheftTrack allowed school officials to take screenshots, and send them to the school's server. In addition, LANrev allowed school officials to take snapshots of instant messages, web browsing, music playlists, and written compositions. The schools admitted to secretly snapping over 66,000 webshots and screenshots, including webcam shots of students in their bedrooms.

Adware

Adware, or advertising-supported software, is software that generates revenue for its developer by automatically generating online advertisements in the user interface of the software or on a screen presented to the user during the installation process. The software may generate two types of revenue: one is for the display of the advertisement and another on a "pay-per-click" basis, if the user clicks on the advertisement. The software may implement advertisements in a variety of ways, including a static box display, a banner display, full screen, a video, pop-up ad or in some other form.

Some software developers offer their software free of charge, and rely on revenue from advertising to recoup their expenses and generate income. Some also offer a version of the software at a fee without advertising.

The software's functions may be designed to analyze the user's location and which Internet sites the user visits and to present advertising pertinent to the types of goods or services featured there. The term is sometimes used to refer to software that displays unwanted advertisements known as malware.

Advertising-supported Software

In legitimate software, the advertising functions are integrated into or bundled with the program. Adware is usually seen by the developer as a way to recover development costs, and to generate revenue. In some cases, the developer may provided the software to the user free of charge or at a reduced price. The income derived from presenting advertisements to the user may allow or motivate the developer to continue to develop, maintain and upgrade the software product. The use of advertising-supported software in business is becoming increasingly popular, with a third of IT and business executives in a 2007 survey by McKinsey & Company planning to be using ad-funded software within the following two years. Advertisement-funded software is also one of the business models for open-source software.

Application Software

Some software is offered in both an advertising-supported mode and a paid, advertisement-free mode. The latter is usually available by an online purchase of a license or registration code for the software that unlocks the mode, or the purchase and download of a separate version of the software.

Some software authors offer advertising-supported versions of their software as an alternative option to business organizations seeking to avoid paying large sums for software licenses, funding the development of the software with higher fees for advertisers.

Examples of advertising-supported software include Adblock Plus ("Acceptable Ads"), the Windows version of the Internet telephony application Skype, and the Amazon Kindle 3 family of e-book readers, which has versions called "Kindle with Special Offers" that display advertisements on the home page and in sleep mode in exchange for substantially lower pricing.

In 2012, Microsoft and its advertising division, Microsoft Advertising,[b] announced that Windows 8, the major release of the Microsoft Windows operating system, would provide built-in methods for software authors to use advertising support as a business model. The idea had been considered since as early as 2005.

Software as a Service

Support by advertising is a popular business model of software as a service (SaaS) on the Web. Notable examples include the email service Gmail and other Google Apps (now G Suite) products, and the social network Facebook. Microsoft has also adopted the advertising-supported model for many of its social software SaaS offerings. The Microsoft Office Live service was also available in an advertising-supported mode.

In the view of Federal Trade Commission staff, there appears to be general agreement that software should be considered "spyware" only if it is downloaded or installed on a computer without the user's knowledge and consent. However, unresolved issues remain concerning how, what, and when consumers need to be told about software installed on their computers for consent to be adequate. For instance, distributors often disclose in an end-user license agreement that there is additional software bundled with primary software, but some panelists and commenters did not view such disclosure as sufficient to infer consent to the installation of the bundled software.

Malware

The term *adware* is frequently used to describe a form of malware (malicious software) which presents unwanted advertisements to the user of a computer. The advertisements produced by adware are sometimes in the form of a pop-up or sometimes in an "unclosable window".

When the term is used in this way, the severity of its implication varies. While some sources rate adware only as an "irritant", others classify it as an "online threat" or even rate it as seriously as computer viruses and trojans. The precise definition of the term in this context also varies.[c] Adware that observes the computer user's activities without their consent and reports it to the software's author is called spyware. However most adware operates legally and some adware manufacturers have even sued antivirus companies for blocking adware.

Programs that have been developed to detect, quarantine, and remove advertisement-displaying malware, including Ad-Aware, Malwarebytes' Anti-Malware, Spyware

Doctor and Spybot – Search & Destroy. In addition, almost all commercial antivirus software currently detect adware and spyware, or offer a separate detection module.

A new wrinkle is adware (using stolen certificates) that disables anti-malware and virus protection; technical remedies are available.

Adware has also been discovered in certain low-cost Android devices, particularly those made by small Chinese firms running on Allwinner systems-on-chip. There are even cases where adware code is embedded deep into files stored on the system and boot partitions, to which removal involves extensive (and complex) modifications to the firmware.

Scareware

Scareware is a form of malware which uses social engineering to cause shock, anxiety, or the perception of a threat in order to manipulate users into buying unwanted software. Scareware is part of a class of malicious software that includes rogue security software, ransomware and other scam software that tricks users into believing their computer is infected with a virus, then suggests that they download and pay for fake antivirus software to remove it. Usually the virus is fictional and the software is non-functional or malware itself. According to the Anti-Phishing Working Group, the number of scareware packages in circulation rose from 2,850 to 9,287 in the second half of 2008. In the first half of 2009, the APWG identified a 585% increase in scareware programs.

The "scareware" label can also apply to any application or virus which pranks users with intent to cause anxiety or panic.

Scam Scareware

Internet security writers use the term "scareware" to describe software products that produce frivolous and alarming warnings or threat notices, most typically for fictitious or useless commercial firewall and registry cleaner software. This class of program tries to increase its perceived value by bombarding the user with constant warning messages that do not increase its effectiveness in any way. Software is packaged with a look and feel that mimics legitimate security software in order to deceive consumers.

Some websites display pop-up advertisement windows or banners with text such as: "Your computer may be infected with harmful spyware programs. Immediate removal may be required. To scan, click 'Yes' below." These websites can go as far as saying that a user's job, career, or marriage would be at risk. Products using advertisements such as these are often considered scareware. Serious scareware applications qualify as rogue software.

Some scareware is not affiliated with any other installed programs. A user can encounter a pop-up on a website indicating that their PC is infected. In some scenarios, it is possible to become infected with scareware even if the user attempts to cancel the notification. These popups are especially designed to look like they come from the user's operating system when they are actually a webpage.

A 2010 study by Google found 11,000 domains hosting fake anti-virus software, accounting for 50% of all malware delivered via internet advertising.

Starting on March 29, 2011, more than 1.5 million web sites around the world have been infected by the LizaMoon SQL injection attack spread by scareware.

Research by Google discovered that scareware was using some of its servers to check for internet connectivity. The data suggested that up to a million machines were infected with scareware. The company has placed a warning in the search results of users whose computers appear to be infected.

Another example of scareware is Smart Fortress. This site scares people into thinking they have lots of viruses on their computer and asks them to buy the professional service.

Spyware

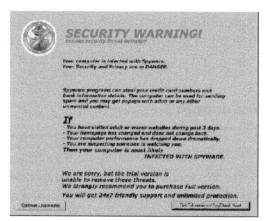

Dialog from SpySheriff, designed to scare users into installing the rogue software

Some forms of spyware also qualify as scareware because they change the user's desktop background, install icons in the computer's notification area (under Microsoft Windows), and claiming that some kind of spyware has infected the user's computer and that the scareware application will help to remove the infection. In some cases, scareware trojans have replaced the desktop of the victim with large, yellow text reading "Warning! You have spyware!" or a box containing similar text, and have even forced the screensaver to change to "bugs" crawling across the screen. Winwebsec is the term usually used to address the malware that attacks the users of Windows operating system and produces fake claims similar to that of genuine anti-malware software.

SpySheriff exemplifies spyware and scareware: it purports to remove spyware, but is actually a piece of spyware itself, often accompanying SmitFraud infections. Other antispyware scareware may be promoted using a phishing scam.

Uninstallation of Security Software

Another approach is to trick users into uninstalling legitimate antivirus software, such as Microsoft Security Essentials, or disabling their firewall. Since antivirus programs typically include protection against being tampered with or disabled by other software, scareware may use social engineering to convince the user to disable programs which would otherwise prevent the malware from working.

Prank Software

Another type of scareware involves software designed to literally scare the user through the use of unanticipated shocking images, sounds or video.

- An early program of this type is NightMare, a program distributed on the Fish Disks for the Amiga computer (Fish #448) in 1991. When NightMare executes, it lies dormant for an extended and random period of time, finally changing the entire screen of the computer to an image of a skull while playing a horrifying shriek on the audio channels.

- Anxiety-based scareware puts users in situations where there are no positive outcomes. For example, a small program can present a dialog box saying "Erase everything on hard drive?" with two buttons, both labeled "OK". Regardless of which button is chosen, nothing is destroyed.

- This tactic was used in an advertisement campaign by Sir-Tech in 1997 to advertise *Virus: The Game*. When the file is run, a full screen representation of the desktop appears. The software then begins simulating deletion of the Windows folder. When this process is complete, a message is slowly typed on screen saying "Thank God this is only a game." A screen with the purchase information appears on screen and then returns to the desktop. No damage is done to the computer during the advertisement.

References

- Young, Adam; Yung, Moti (1997). "Deniable Password Snatching: On the Possibility of Evasive Electronic Espionage". Symp. on Security and Privacy. IEEE. pp. 224–235. ISBN 0-8186-7828-3

- Kovacs, Eduard. "MiniDuke Malware Used Against European Government Organizations". Softpedia. Retrieved 27 February 2013

- Hanspach, Michael; Goetz, Michael (November 2013). "On Covert Acoustical Mesh Networks in Air". Journal of Communications. arXiv:1406.1213 doi:10.12720/jcm.8.11.758-767

- Young, Adam (2006). "Cryptoviral Extortion Using Microsoft's Crypto API: Can Crypto APIs

Help the Enemy?". International Journal of Information Security. Springer-Verlag. 5 (2): 67–76. doi:10.1007/s10207-006-0082-7

- "How Anti-Virus Software Works". Stanford University. Archived from the original on July 7, 2015. Retrieved September 4, 2015

- Peter Szor (3 February 2005). The Art of Computer Virus Research and Defense. Pearson Education. p. 204. ISBN 978-0-672-33390-3

- Young, A.; M. Yung (1996). Cryptovirology: extortion-based security threats and countermeasures. IEEE Symposium on Security and Privacy. pp. 129 140. doi:10.1109/SECPRI.1996.502676. ISBN 0-8186-7417-2

- "Virus Notice: Network Associates' AVERT Discovers First Virus That Can Infect JPEG Files, Assigns Low-Profiled Risk". Archived from the original on 2005-05-04. Retrieved 2002-06-13

- Ludwig, Mark A. (1996). The Little Black Book of Computer Viruses: Volume 1, The Basic Technologies. pp. 16–17. ISBN 0-929408-02-0

Computer Security Software

Computer security software is designed to enhance information security and defence against any intrusion and unauthorized access. This chapter elaborates the different kinds of security software and their applications to provide a holistic understanding of computer security.

Antivirus Software

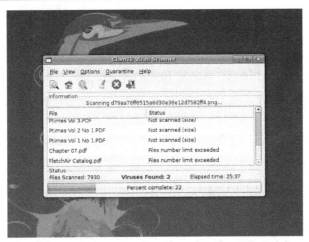

ClamTk, an open source antivirus based on the ClamAV antivirus engine, originally developed by Tomasz Kojm.

Antivirus or anti-virus software (often abbreviated as AV), sometimes known as anti-malware software, is computer software used to prevent, detect and remove malicious software.

Antivirus software was originally developed to detect and remove computer viruses, hence the name. However, with the proliferation of other kinds of malware, antivirus software started to provide protection from other computer threats. In particular, modern antivirus software can protect from: malicious browser helper objects (BHOs), browser hijackers, ransomware, keyloggers, backdoors, rootkits, trojan horses, worms, malicious LSPs, dialers, fraudtools, adware and spyware. Some products also include protection from other computer threats, such as infected and malicious URLs, spam, scam and phishing attacks, online identity (privacy), online banking attacks, social engineering techniques, advanced persistent threat (APT) and botnet DDoS attacks.

Identification Methods

One of the few solid theoretical results in the study of computer viruses is Frederick B. Cohen's 1987 demonstration that there is no algorithm that can perfectly detect all possible viruses. However, using different layers of defense, a good detection rate may be achieved.

There are several methods which antivirus engine can use to identify malware:

- Sandbox detection: is a particular behavioural-based detection technique that, instead of detecting the behavioural fingerprint at run time, it executes the programs in a virtual environment, logging what actions the program performs. Depending on the actions logged, the antivirus engine can determine if the program is malicious or not. If not, then, the program is executed in the real environment. Albeit this technique has shown to be quite effective, given its heaviness and slowness, it is rarely used in end-user antivirus solutions.

- Data mining techniques: are one of the latest approach applied in malware detection. Data mining and machine learning algorithms are used to try to classify the behaviour of a file (as either malicious or benign) given a series of file features, that are extracted from the file itself.

Signature-based Detection

Traditional antivirus software relies heavily upon signatures to identify malware.

Substantially, when a malware arrives in the hands of an antivirus firm, it is analysed by malware researchers or by dynamic analysis systems. Then, once it is determined to be a malware, a proper signature of the file is extracted and added to the signatures database of the antivirus software.

Although the signature-based approach can effectively contain malware outbreaks, malware authors have tried to stay a step ahead of such software by writing "oligomorphic", "polymorphic" and, more recently, "metamorphic" viruses, which encrypt parts of themselves or otherwise modify themselves as a method of disguise, so as to not match virus signatures in the dictionary.

Heuristics

Many viruses start as a single infection and through either mutation or refinements by other attackers, can grow into dozens of slightly different strains, called variants. Generic detection refers to the detection and removal of multiple threats using a single virus definition.

For example, the Vundo trojan has several family members, depending on the antivirus vendor's classification. Symantec classifies members of the Vundo family into two distinct categories, *Trojan.Vundo* and *Trojan.Vundo.B.*

While it may be advantageous to identify a specific virus, it can be quicker to detect a virus family through a generic signature or through an inexact match to an existing signature. Virus researchers find common areas that all viruses in a family share uniquely and can thus create a single generic signature. These signatures often contain non-contiguous code, using wildcard characters where differences lie. These wildcards allow the scanner to detect viruses even if they are padded with extra, meaningless code. A detection that uses this method is said to be "heuristic detection".

Rootkit Detection

Anti-virus software can attempt to scan for rootkits. A rootkit is a type of malware designed to gain administrative-level control over a computer system without being detected. Rootkits can change how the operating system functions and in some cases can tamper with the anti-virus program and render it ineffective. Rootkits are also difficult to remove, in some cases requiring a complete re-installation of the operating system.

Real-time Protection

Real-time protection, on-access scanning, background guard, resident shield, autoprotect, and other synonyms refer to the automatic protection provided by most antivirus, anti-spyware, and other anti-malware programs. This monitors computer systems for suspicious activity such as computer viruses, spyware, adware, and other malicious objects in 'real-time', in other words while data loaded into the computer's active memory: when inserting a CD, opening an email, or browsing the web, or when a file already on the computer is opened or executed.

Issues of Concern

Unexpected Renewal Costs

Some commercial antivirus software end-user license agreements include a clause that the subscription will be automatically renewed, and the purchaser's credit card automatically billed, at the renewal time without explicit approval. For example, McAfee requires users to unsubscribe at least 60 days before the expiration of the present subscription while BitDefender sends notifications to unsubscribe 30 days before the renewal. Norton AntiVirus also renews subscriptions automatically by default.

Rogue Security Applications

Some apparent antivirus programs are actually malware masquerading as legitimate software, such as WinFixer, MS Antivirus, and Mac Defender.

Problems Caused by False Positives

A "false positive" or "false alarm" is when antivirus software identifies a non-malicious file as malware. When this happens, it can cause serious problems. For example, if an antivirus program is configured to immediately delete or quarantine infected files, as is common on Microsoft Windows antivirus applications, a false positive in an essential file can render the Windows operating system or some applications unusable. Recovering from such damage to critical software infrastructure incurs technical support costs and businesses can be forced to close whilst remedial action is undertaken. For example, in May 2007 a faulty virus signature issued by Symantec mistakenly removed essential operating system files, leaving thousands of PCs unable to boot.

Also in May 2007, the executable file required by Pegasus Mail on Windows was falsely detected by Norton AntiVirus as being a Trojan and it was automatically removed, preventing Pegasus Mail from running. Norton AntiVirus had falsely identified three releases of Pegasus Mail as malware, and would delete the Pegasus Mail installer file when that happened. In response to this Pegasus Mail stated:

> On the basis that Norton/Symantec has done this for every one of the last three releases of Pegasus Mail, we can only condemn this product as too flawed to use, and recommend in the strongest terms that our users cease using it in favour of alternative, less buggy anti-virus packages.

In April 2010, McAfee VirusScan detected svchost.exe, a normal Windows binary, as a virus on machines running Windows XP with Service Pack 3, causing a reboot loop and loss of all network access.

In December 2010, a faulty update on the AVG anti-virus suite damaged 64-bit versions of Windows 7, rendering it unable to boot, due to an endless boot loop created.

In October 2011, Microsoft Security Essentials (MSE) removed the Google Chrome web browser, rival to Microsoft's own Internet Explorer. MSE flagged Chrome as a Zbot banking trojan.

In September 2012, Sophos' anti-virus suite identified various update-mechanisms, including its own, as malware. If it was configured to automatically delete detected files, Sophos Antivirus could render itself unable to update, required manual intervention to fix the problem.

In September 2017, the Google Play Protect anti-virus started identifying Motorola's G4 bluetooth application as malware, causing bluetooth functionality to become disabled.

System and Interoperability Related Issues

Running (the real-time protection of) multiple antivirus programs concurrently can degrade performance and create conflicts. However, using a concept called multiscanning, several companies (including G Data Software and Microsoft) have created applications which can run multiple engines concurrently.

It is sometimes necessary to temporarily disable virus protection when installing major updates such as Windows Service Packs or updating graphics card drivers. Active anti-virus protection may partially or completely prevent the installation of a major update. Anti-virus software can cause problems during the installation of an operating system upgrade, e.g. when upgrading to a newer version of Windows "in place" — without erasing the previous version of Windows. Microsoft recommends that anti-virus software be disabled to avoid conflicts with the upgrade installation process.

The functionality of a few computer programs can be hampered by active anti-virus software. For example, TrueCrypt, a disk encryption program, states on its troubleshooting page that anti-virus programs can conflict with TrueCrypt and cause it to malfunction or operate very slowly. Anti-virus software can impair the performance and stability of games running in the Steam platform.

Support issues also exist around antivirus application interoperability with common solutions like SSL VPN remote access and network access control products. These technology solutions often have policy assessment applications which require that an up-to-date antivirus is installed and running. If the antivirus application is not recognized by the policy assessment, whether because the antivirus application has been updated or because it is not part of the policy assessment library, the user will be unable to connect.

Effectiveness

Studies in December 2007 showed that the effectiveness of antivirus software had decreased in the previous year, particularly against unknown or zero day attacks. The computer magazine *c't* found that detection rates for these threats had dropped from 40–50% in 2006 to 20–30% in 2007. At that time, the only exception was the NOD32 antivirus, which managed a detection rate of 68%. According to the *ZeuS tracker* website the average detection rate for all variants of the well-known ZeuS trojan is as low as 40%.

The problem is magnified by the changing intent of virus authors. Some years ago it was obvious when a virus infection was present. The viruses of the day, written by amateurs, exhibited destructive behavior or pop-ups. Modern viruses are often written by professionals, financed by criminal organizations.

In 2008, Eva Chen, CEO of Trend Micro, stated that the anti-virus industry has over-hyped how effective its products are — and so has been misleading customers — for years.

Independent testing on all the major virus scanners consistently shows that none provide 100% virus detection. The best ones provided as high as 99.9% detection for simulated real-world situations, while the lowest provided 91.1% in tests conducted in August 2013. Many virus scanners produce false positive results as well, identifying benign files as malware.

Although methodologies may differ, some notable independent quality testing agencies include AV-Comparatives, ICSA Labs, West Coast Labs, Virus Bulletin, AV-TEST and other members of the Anti-Malware Testing Standards Organization.

New Viruses

Anti-virus programs are not always effective against new viruses, even those that use non-signature-based methods that should detect new viruses. The reason for this is that the virus designers test their new viruses on the major anti-virus applications to make sure that they are not detected before releasing them into the wild.

Some new viruses, particularly ransomware, use polymorphic code to avoid detection by virus scanners. Jerome Segura, a security analyst with ParetoLogic, explained:

> It's something that they miss a lot of the time because this type of [ransomware virus] comes from sites that use a polymorphism, which means they basically randomize the file they send you and it gets by well-known antivirus products very easily. I've seen people firsthand getting infected, having all the pop-ups and yet they have antivirus software running and it's not detecting anything. It actually can be pretty hard to get rid of, as well, and you're never really sure if it's really gone. When we see something like that usually we advise to reinstall the operating system or reinstall backups.

A proof of concept virus has used the Graphics Processing Unit (GPU) to avoid detection from anti-virus software. The potential success of this involves bypassing the CPU in order to make it much harder for security researchers to analyse the inner workings of such malware.

Rootkits

Detecting rootkits is a major challenge for anti-virus programs. Rootkits have full administrative access to the computer and are invisible to users and hidden from the list of running processes in the task manager. Rootkits can modify the inner workings of the operating system and tamper with antivirus programs.

Damaged Files

If a file has been infected by a computer virus, anti-virus software will attempt to remove the virus code from the file during disinfection, but it is not always able to restore the file to its undamaged state. In such circumstances, damaged files can only be restored from existing backups or shadow copies (this is also true for ransomware); installed software that is damaged requires re-installation.

Firmware Issues

Active anti-virus software can interfere with a firmware update process. Any writeable firmware in the computer can be infected by malicious code. This is a major concern, as an infected BIOS could require the actual BIOS chip to be replaced to ensure the malicious code is completely removed. Anti-virus software is not effective at protecting firmware and the motherboard BIOS from infection. In 2014, security researchers discovered that USB devices contain writeable firmware which can be modified with malicious code (dubbed "BadUSB"), which anti-virus software cannot detect or prevent. The malicious code can run undetected on the computer and could even infect the operating system prior to it booting up.

Performance and other Drawbacks

Antivirus software has some drawbacks, first of which that it can impact a computer's performance.

Furthermore, inexperienced users can be lulled into a false sense of security when using the computer, considering themselves to be invulnerable, and may have problems understanding the prompts and decisions that antivirus software presents them with. An incorrect decision may lead to a security breach. If the antivirus software employs heuristic detection, it must be fine-tuned to minimize misidentifying harmless software as malicious (false positive).

Antivirus software itself usually runs at the highly trusted kernel level of the operating system to allow it access to all the potential malicious process and files, creating a potential avenue of attack. The UK and US intelligence agencies, GCHQ and the National Security Agency (NSA), respectively, have been exploiting anti-virus software to spy on users. Anti-virus software has highly privileged and trusted access to the underlying operating system, which makes it a much more appealing target for remote attacks. Additionally anti-virus software is "years behind security-conscious client-side applications like browsers or document readers", according to Joxean Koret, a researcher with Coseinc, a Singapore-based information security consultancy.

Alternative Solutions

Installed antivirus solutions, running on individual computers, although the most used, is only one method of guarding against malware. Other alternative solutions are also used, including: Unified Threat Management (UTM), hardware and network firewalls, Cloud-based antivirus and on-line scanners.

The command-line virus scanner of Clam AV 0.95.2, an open source antivirus originally developed by Tomasz Kojm. Here running a virus signature definition update, scanning a file and identifying a Trojan.

Hardware and Network Firewall

Network firewalls prevent unknown programs and processes from accessing the system. However, they are not antivirus systems and make no attempt to identify or remove anything. They may protect against infection from outside the protected computer or network, and limit the activity of any malicious software which is present by blocking incoming or outgoing requests on certain TCP/IP ports. A firewall is designed to deal with broader system threats that come from network connections into the system and is not an alternative to a virus protection system.

Cloud Antivirus

Cloud antivirus is a technology that uses lightweight agent software on the protected computer, while offloading the majority of data analysis to the provider's infrastructure.

One approach to implementing cloud antivirus involves scanning suspicious files using multiple antivirus engines. This approach was proposed by an early implementation of the cloud antivirus concept called CloudAV. CloudAV was designed to send programs or documents to a network cloud where multiple antivirus and behavioral detection programs are used simultaneously in order to improve detection rates. Parallel scanning of files using potentially incompatible antivirus scanners is achieved by spawning a virtual machine per detection engine and therefore eliminating any possible issues. CloudAV can also perform "retrospective detection," whereby the cloud detection engine rescans all files in its file access history when a new threat is identified thus improving new threat detection speed. Finally, CloudAV is a solution for effective virus scanning on devices that lack the computing power to perform the scans themselves.

Some examples of cloud anti-virus products are Panda Cloud Antivirus, Crowdstrike, Cb Defense and Immunet. Comodo group has also produced cloud-based anti-virus.

Online Scanning

Some antivirus vendors maintain websites with free online scanning capability of the entire computer, critical areas only, local disks, folders or files. Periodic online scanning is a good idea for those that run antivirus applications on their computers because those applications are frequently slow to catch threats. One of the first things that malicious software does in an attack is disable any existing antivirus software and sometimes the only way to know of an attack is by turning to an online resource that is not installed on the infected computer.

Specialist Tools

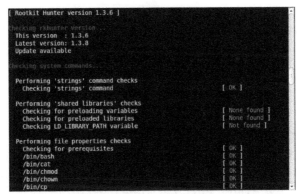

The command-line rkhunter scanner, an engine to scan for Linux rootkits.
Here running the tool on Ubuntu.

Virus removal tools are available to help remove stubborn infections or certain types of infection. Examples include Trend Micro's *Rootkit Buster*, and rkhunter for the detection of rootkits, Avira's *AntiVir Removal Tool*, *PCTools Threat Removal Tool*, and AVG's Anti-Virus Free 2011.

A rescue disk that is bootable, such as a CD or USB storage device, can be used to run antivirus software outside of the installed operating system, in order to remove infections while they are dormant. A bootable antivirus disk can be useful when, for example, the installed operating system is no longer bootable or has malware that is resisting all attempts to be removed by the installed antivirus software. Examples of some of these bootable disks include the *Avira AntiVir Rescue System*, *PCTools Alternate Operating System Scanner*, and *AVG Rescue CD*. The AVG Rescue CD software can also be installed onto a USB storage device, that is bootable on newer computers.

Usage and Risks

According to an FBI survey, major businesses lose $12 million annually dealing with virus incidents. A survey by Symantec in 2009 found that a third of small to medium-sized business did not use antivirus protection at that time, whereas more than 80% of home users had some kind of antivirus installed. According to a sociological survey conducted by G Data Software in 2010 49% of women did not use any antivirus program at all.

Anti-keylogger

An anti-keylogger (or anti–keystroke logger) is a type of software specifically designed for the detection of keystroke logger software; often, such software will also incorporate the ability to delete or at least immobilize hidden keystroke logger software on a computer. In comparison to most anti-virus or anti-spyware software, the primary difference is that an anti-keylogger does not make a distinction between a *legitimate* keystroke-logging program and an *illegitimate* keystroke-logging program (such as malware); all keystroke-logging programs are flagged and optionally removed, whether they appear to be legitimate keystroke-logging software or not.

Use of Anti-keyloggers

Keyloggers are sometimes part of malware packages downloaded onto computers without the owners' knowledge. Detecting the presence of a keylogger on a computer can be difficult. So-called anti- keylogging programs have been developed to thwart keylogging systems, and these are often effective when used properly.

Anti-keyloggers are used both by large organizations as well as individuals in order to scan for and remove (or in some cases simply immobilize) keystroke logging software on a computer. It is generally advised the software developers that anti-keylogging scans be run on a regular basis in order to reduce the amount of time during which a keylogger may record keystrokes. For example, if a system is scanned once every three days, there is a maximum of only three days during which a keylogger could be hidden on the system and recording keystrokes.

Public Computers

Public computers are extremely susceptible to the installation of keystroke logging software and hardware, and there are documented instances of this occurring. Public computers are particularly susceptible to keyloggers because any number of people can gain access to the machine and install both a hardware keylogger and a software keylogger, either or both of which can be secretly installed in a matter of minutes. Anti-keyloggers are often used on a daily basis to ensure that public computers are not infected with keyloggers, and are safe for public use.

Gaming usage

Keyloggers have been prevalent in the online gaming industry, being used to secretly record a gamer's access credentials, user name and password, when logging into an account, this information is sent back to the hacker. The hacker can sign on later to the account and change the password to the account, thus stealing it.

World of Warcraft has been of particular importance to game hackers and has been the target of numerous keylogging viruses. Anti-keyloggers are used by many World of Warcraft and other gaming community members in order to try to keep their gaming accounts secure.

Financial Institutions

Financial institutions have become the target of keyloggers, particularly those institutions which do not use advanced security features such as PIN pads or screen keyboards. Anti-keyloggers are used to run regular scans of any computer on which banking or client information is accessed, protecting passwords, banking information, and credit card numbers from identity thieves.

Personal use

The most common use of an anti-keylogger is by individuals wishing to protect their privacy while using their computer; uses range from protecting financial information used in online banking, any passwords, personal communication, and virtually any other information which may be typed into a computer. Keyloggers are often installed by people known by the computer's owner, and many times have been installed by an ex-partner hoping to spy on their ex-partner's activities, particularly chat.

Types

Signature-based

This type of software has a signature base, that is strategic information that helps to uniquely identify a keylogger, and the list contains as many known keyloggers as possible. Some vendors make some effort or availability of an up-to-date listing for download by customers. Each time a 'System Scan' is run, this software compares the contents of the hard disk drive, item by item, against the list, looking for any matches.

This type of software is a rather widespread one, but it has its own drawbacks The biggest drawback of signature-based anti-keyloggers is that one can only be protected from keyloggers found on the signature-base list, thus staying vulnerable to unknown or unrecognized keyloggers. A criminal can download one of many famous keyloggers, change it just enough, and the anti-keylogger won't recognize it.

Heuristic Analysis

This software doesn't use signature bases, it uses a checklist of known features, attributes, and methods that keyloggers are known use.

It analyzes the methods of work of all the modules in a PC, thus blocking the activity of any module that is similar to the work of keyloggers. Though this method gives better keylogging protection than signature-based anti-keyloggers, it has its own drawbacks. One of them is that this type of software blocks non-keyloggers also. Several 'non-harmful' software modules, either part of the operating system or part of legitimate apps, use processes which keyloggers also use, which can trigger a false positive. Usually all the non signature-based keyloggers have the option to allow the user to unblock selected modules, but this can cause difficulties for inexperienced users who are unable to discern good modules from bad modules when maually choosing to block or unblock.

Anti-Subversion Software

Software subversion is the process of making software perform unintended actions either by tampering with program code or by altering behavior in another fashion. For example, code tampering could be used to change program code to load malicious rules or heuristics, SQL injection is a form of subversion for the purpose of data corruption or theft and buffer overflows are a form of subversion for the purpose of unauthorised access. These attacks are examples of computer hacking.

Anti-Subversion Software detects subversion and attempts to stop the effects of the hack. Software applications are vulnerable to the effects of subversion throughout their lifecycle from development to deployment, but particularly in operation and maintenance.

Anti-subversion protection can be accomplished in both a static and dynamic manner:

- Static anti-subversion is performed during the construction of the code. The code is statically tested and verified against various attack types by examining the program source code. Examples of static anti-subversion include security auditing, code verification, and fuzzing. Static anti-subversion is generally seen as a good coding practice, and is deemed necessary in some compliance regimes. However, static solutions cannot prevent all types of subversion attacks.

- Dynamic anti-subversion is performed during code execution. The code is dynamically protected against subversion by continuously checking for unintended program behaviours. Examples of dynamic anti-subversion include application firewalls, security wrappers, and protection embedded in the software.

Software applications running on desktops, corporate servers, mobile devices and embedded devices are all at risk from subversion.

Anti-tamper Software

Anti-tamper software (or tamper-resistant software) is software which makes it harder for an attacker to modify it. The measures involved can be passive such as obfuscation to make reverse engineering difficult or active tamper-detection techniques which aim to make a program malfunction or not operate at all if modified. It is essentially tamper resistance implemented in the software domain. It shares certain aspects but also differs from related technologies like copy protection and trusted hardware, though it is often used in combination with them. Anti-tampering technology typically makes the software somewhat larger and also has a performance impact. There are no provably secure software anti-tampering methods, thus the field is an arms race between attackers and software anti-tampering technologies.

Tampering is generally malicious, to gain control over some aspect of the software with an unauthorized modification that alters the computer program code and behaviour. Examples include installing rootkits and backdoors, disabling security monitoring, subverting authentication, malicious code injection for the purposes of data theft or to achieve higher user privileges, altering control flow and communication, license code bypassing for the purpose of software piracy, code interference to extract data or algorithms and counterfeiting. Software applications are vulnerable to the effects of tampering and code changes throughout their lifecycle from development and deployment to operation and maintenance.

Anti-tamper protection can be applied as either internally or externally to the application being protected. External anti-tampering is normally accomplished by monitoring the software to detect tampering. This type of defense is commonly expressed as malware scanners and anti-virus applications. Internal anti-tampering is used to turn an application into its own security system and is generally done with specific code within the software that will detect tampering as it happens. This type of tamper proofing defense may take the form of runtime integrity checks such as cyclic redundancy checksums, anti-debugging measures, encryption or obfuscation. Execution inside a virtual machine has become a common anti-tamper method used in recent years for commercial software; it is used for example in StarForce and SecuROM. Some anti-tamper software uses white-box cryptography, so cryptographic keys are not revealed even when cryptographic computations are being observed in complete detail in a debugger. A more recent research trend is tamper-tolerant software, which aims to correct the effects of tampering and allow the program to continue as if unmodified. A simple (and easily defeated) scheme of this kind was used in the Diablo II video game, which stored its critical player data in two copies at different memory locations and if one was modified externally, the game used the lower value.

Anti-tamper software is used in many types of software products including: embedded systems, financial applications, software for mobile devices, network-appliance systems, anti-cheating in games, military, license management software, and digital rights management (DRM) systems. Some general-purpose packages have been developed which can wrap existing code with minimal programing effort; for example the SecuROM and similar kits used in the gaming industry, though they have the downside that semi-generic attacking tools also exist to counter them. Malicious software itself can and has been observed using anti-tampering techniques, for example the Mariposa botnet.

Encryption Software

Encryption software is software that uses cryptography to prevent unauthorized access to digital information. Practically speaking, people use cryptography today to protect the digital information on their computers as well as the digital information that is sent to other computers over the Internet. As software that implements secure cryptography is complex to develop and difficult to get right, most computer users make use of the encryption software that already exists rather than writing their own.

Classification

As encryption software is an important component in providing protection from cyber-crime, there are many, many software products that provide encryption. Because there are so many software products that provide encryption, a good way to begin understanding this topic is classification by categorization.

Software encryption uses a cipher to obscure the content into ciphertext, so one way to classify this type of software is by the type of cipher used. Ciphers can be categorized into two categories: public key ciphers, also known as asymmetric ciphers, and symmetric key ciphers. Thus, encryption software may be said to based on public key or symmetric key encryption.

Another way to classify software encryption is to categorize its purpose. Using this approach, software encryption may be classified into software that encrypts "data in transit" and software that encrypts "data at rest".

As it turns out, these two types of classifications has something in common: that is, data in transit generally uses public key ciphers, and data at rest generally uses symmetric key ciphers.

However, software encryption is not as simple at that.

To begin with, symmetric key ciphers can be further subdivided into stream ciphers and block ciphers. Stream ciphers typically encrypt plaintext a bit or byte at a time, and are most commonly used to encrypt real-time communications, such as audio and video information. The key is used to establish the initial state of a keystream generator, and the output of that generator is used to encrypt the plaintext. Block cipher algorithms split the plaintext into fixed-size blocks and encrypt one block at a time. For example, AES processes 16-byte blocks, while its predecessor DES encrypted blocks of eight bytes.

Also, there is also a well-known case where PKI is used for data in transit of data at rest.

Data in Transit

Data in transit is data that is being sent over a network. When the data is between two endpoints, any confidential information may be vulnerable to snooping. To maintain the confidentiality of the transmission, the payload (confidential information) can be encrypted to protect its confidentiality, as well as its integrity and non-repudiation.

Often, the data in transit is between two entities that do not know each other - such as visiting a website. As establishing a relationship and securely sharing an encryption key to secure the information that will be exchanged, a set of roles, policies, and procedures to accomplish this has been developed; it is known as the public key infrastructure, or PKI. Once PKI has established a secure connection, a symmetric key can be shared between endpoints. A symmetric key is preferred to over the private and public keys as a symmetric cipher is much more efficient (uses less CPU cycles) than an asymmetric cipher.

For Data in Transit

Below are some examples of software that provide this type of encryption.

- IP Security - IPsec
- Secure Copy - SCP
- Secure Email
- Secure Shell - SSH
- SSH File Transfer Protocol - SFTP
- Web Communication - HTTPS

Data at Rest

Data at rest refers data that has been saved to persistent storage. Generally speaking, data at rest is encrypted by a symmetric key.

As mentioned previously, there are many, many software products that provide encryption. While these products are all listed under "disk" encryption, this may be a bit misleading.

In looking at this table that compares whether the encryption software works at the disk, partition, file, etc. layer, there just doesn't seem to be enough room to capture all the options. That's because encryption may be applied at different layers in the storage stack. For example, encryption can be configured at the disk layer, on a subset of a disk called a partition, on a volume, which is a combination of disks or partitions, at the layer of a file system, or within userland applications such as database or other applications that run on the host operating system.

With full disk encryption, the entire disk is encrypted (except for the bits necessary to boot or access the disk when not using an unencrypted boot/preboot partition). As disks can be partitioned into multiple partitions, partition encryption can be used to encrypt individual disk partitions. Volumes, created by combinining two or more partitions, can be encrypted using volume encryption. File systems, also composed of one or more partitions, can be encrypted using file system encryption. Directories are referred to as encrypted when the files within the directory are encrypted. File encryption encrypts a single file. Database encryption acts on the data to be stored, accepting unencrypted information and writing that information to persistent storage only after it has encrypted the data. Device-level encryption, a somewhat vague term that includes encryption-capable tape drives, can be used to offload the encryption tasks from the CPU.

For Data at Rest

There are a large number of encryption software products in this space. For that reason it does not seem prudent to attempt to capture all of that information in this Section. Instead, it is recommended to look into one or more of these section.

- Disk Encryption
- Partition Encryption
- Volume Encryption
- Filesystem Encryption
- File and Directory Encryption
- Database Encryption

Transit of Data at Rest

When there is a need to securely transmit data at rest, without the ability to create a secure connection, userland tools have been developed that support this need. These tools rely upon the receiver publishing their public key, and the sender being able to obtain that public key. The sender is then able to create a symmetric key to encrypt the information, and then use the receivers public key to securely protect the transmission of the information and the symmetric key. This allows secure transmission of information from one party to another.

For the Transit of Data at Rest

Below are some examples of software that provide this type of encryption:

- GNU Privacy Guard (GnuPG or GPG).

- OpenPGP.

- Pretty Good Privacy (PGP).

References

- Szor, Peter (February 13, 2005). The Art of Computer Virus Research and Defense. Addison-Wesley Professional. ISBN 0321304543

- Shabtai, Asaf; Kanonov, Uri; Elovici, Yuval; Glezer, Chanan; Weiss, Yael (2011). ""Andromaly": A behavioral malware detection framework for android devices". Journal of Intelligent Information Systems. 38: 161. doi:10.1007/s10844-010-0148-x

- Ye, Yanfang; Wang, Dingding; Li, Tao; Ye, Dongyi; Jiang, Qingshan (2008). "An intelligent PE-malware detection system based on association mining". Journal in Computer Virology. 4 (4): 323. doi:10.1007/s11416-008-0082-4

- Fox-Brewster, Thomas. "Netflix Is Dumping Anti-Virus, Presages Death Of An Industry". Forbes. Archivedfrom the original on September 6, 2015. Retrieved September 4, 2015

- Cappaert, J.; Preneel, B. (2010). "A general model for hiding control flow". Proceedings of the tenth annual ACM workshop on Digital rights management - DRM '10 (PDF). p. 35. doi:10.1145/1866870.1866877. ISBN 9781450300919

- Oorschot, P. C. (2003). "Revisiting Software Protection". Information Security (PDF). Lecture Notes in Computer Science. 2851. pp. 1–13. doi:10.1007/10958513_1. ISBN 978-3-540-20176-2

Permissions

Index

A

Abac, 59-64, 75-76

Active Attack, 3, 22

Alert Protocol, 196-197

Amplification, 29, 32-33

Analysis, 2, 7, 10, 15, 35, 40, 46, 67, 83, 87-88, 103, 115, 120, 132-133, 138, 142-145, 147-148, 153, 208, 220, 229, 238, 256, 262, 265

Anti-keylogger, 264-265

Anti-subversion, 266

Anti-tamper, 267

Antivirus Software, 1, 141, 159, 205, 208, 212, 215, 218, 220, 222-224, 227, 235, 239, 251, 253, 255-261, 263

Application, 11, 13, 24-25, 27, 35, 59-60, 75-76, 80, 92-93, 101-103, 114, 128, 139-142, 155, 163, 180, 197, 203, 223, 231, 242, 258-259, 266-267

Attack Surface Analyzer, 7-11

Attacker, 4-7, 16, 18-19, 22, 26-33, 39, 41, 47-48, 79, 82, 104, 118-120, 122, 126, 138, 145-146, 150, 155, 160, 174, 188, 192, 209, 230-231, 267

Authorization, 3, 53-55, 58, 60-61, 63, 67, 72-73, 131, 137, 185, 203

Availability, 1-2, 4, 16, 29, 36, 75, 81, 84, 132, 229, 265

B

Baseline Scan, 10-11

Botnet, 26-28, 31, 154, 229, 233, 255, 268

Buffer Overflow, 6, 15, 27, 50, 78, 86, 134, 146, 186

C

Ciphers, 175, 178-179, 183-185, 194, 197, 199, 201, 268

Client Responds, 190-191

Clienthello, 179, 189, 191, 193, 195-196, 200, 203

Coding, 79, 88, 90, 133-134, 266

Computer Security, 1-2, 6, 43, 52-53, 64, 66, 68, 71, 76-77, 80, 83, 115, 149, 153, 162, 215, 223, 237, 255

Confidentiality, 1-2, 4, 116, 156-157, 269

Cybercriminals, 15, 114

D

Dac, 54, 56-57, 62, 64-65, 67, 69, 72, 74, 82

Data, 1-3, 6, 9-11, 15, 24, 30-31, 40, 48, 50-51, 64, 74-76, 90, 102-103, 112, 124-125, 131, 153-159, 162, 178-186, 199, 223-224, 252, 266-271

Data at Rest, 268-271

Data in Transit, 268-269

Data Signals, 117-118

Ddos, 22-29, 31-33, 35, 37-38, 40, 144, 154, 255

Decryption, 175, 190, 192-194, 220, 230-231, 236

Denial-of-service, 5, 12, 22-23, 25-29, 31, 33-36, 38-40, 48, 50, 154, 204, 206

Device, 2, 31, 49, 55, 66, 80, 111-112, 115, 120, 122-124, 127-129, 133, 141, 143, 156, 159, 162, 172, 210, 234, 237-238, 243, 263, 270

E

Ebac, 58-59

Electromagnetic Emanations, 115, 117-119

Encryption, 44, 66, 79, 82, 122, 125, 131-132, 153, 162, 164, 173-179, 181, 183, 190, 192, 196, 201-202, 219-220, 230-231, 233, 259, 267-271

F

Fin Scanning, 12, 14

Fingerprinting, 12, 208

Firewall, 1-2, 8, 10, 13, 18, 22, 37, 55, 62, 66, 101, 137-142, 144, 148, 158, 163, 198, 227, 251, 253, 262

Firmware, 31, 46, 128-129, 251, 261

Forward Secrecy, 174-175, 177, 188

H

Hardware, 2, 10, 31, 35, 81-82, 99, 105, 108, 112, 114-115, 119, 126-129, 131-132, 136, 138, 140, 148, 162, 208, 212, 239, 261-262, 264, 267

Harmonics, 115, 118

Host Address, 11, 17

Hping, 16, 20-21

I

Ibac, 58, 66, 76

Immune, 22, 148, 172, 182

Information Security, 1-2, 4, 7, 79, 136, 147, 254, 261, 271

Integrity, 1-4, 16, 62, 67, 69-70, 99-100, 108, 127-128, 155-158, 163, 173-174, 178-179, 219, 267, 269

Ip Header, 18, 28, 34, 50-51, 165-166, 170

M

Multi-factor Authentication, 108-109, 111, 113-114, 156

N

Network Firewall, 262

Network Security, 2, 9, 39-40, 66, 101, 137-138, 142, 144, 147, 153, 204

Nmap, 12-14, 16, 19, 21-22, 102, 104-105

O

Open Systems Interconnection, 24, 158

P

Passive Attack, 3-4, 11

Pdp, 61, 63

Phishing Scam, 222, 253

Ping of Death, 5, 30, 37, 50-51

Platform Module, 126-127, 129, 132, 136

Policies, 4, 11, 54, 60-64, 66-67, 70-72, 75, 82-83, 131, 137, 143, 162, 171, 236, 243, 269

Port Number, 11, 17, 158, 174

Port Scan, 5, 11, 15-16, 21

Processor, 115, 118, 125-126, 207

Product Scan, 10-11

Protocol, 11-14, 17-18, 30, 32-33, 37, 41, 45, 47-48, 50-52, 66, 102, 117, 139, 148, 155, 157-159, 165-170, 173-176, 180-181, 189-204, 230, 269

Proxy, 14-15, 21, 46-47, 140-141, 146, 158, 161, 172, 185, 229, 241

Public Key Certificates, 161, 177

R

Radiation, 115

Rbac, 56-60, 62, 69, 72-76

Responsibility, 60, 76, 100, 128

S

Safe, 1, 151, 160, 163, 212, 221, 224, 241, 244, 264

Scanner, 11-13, 16-17, 101-102, 211-212, 219-220, 224, 241, 257, 262-263

Scareware, 154, 205, 231, 251-253

Security, 1-7, 9, 11-12, 15-18, 24, 28, 39-40, 49, 63-72, 98-104, 126-128, 130-139, 146-150, 158-164, 171-182, 194, 233-239, 244, 251, 269, 271

Security Audit, 5, 103

Sms, 35, 110-112, 114

Software, 1-2, 5-11, 16, 27, 42, 49, 69, 79, 86-93, 96, 114, 124, 138, 148, 152-154, 161, 176, 185-186, 200, 205-225, 229-233, 242-243, 245-271

Starttls, 175, 200

Syn, 12-14, 18-21, 25, 29, 33, 37

Syn Scanning, 12

System, 2-5, 7-13, 16-18, 22, 26-28, 35, 37-38, 49-51, 72, 87-88, 96, 111, 126, 133, 154, 167, 204, 215-219, 230-231, 237-240, 244, 270-271

T

Tcp/ip, 11-12, 17, 34, 40, 50-51, 139-140, 146, 155, 165, 175, 200, 262

Teardrop Attack, 34, 170

Telephony Denial-of-service, 34-35

Temperature, 112, 115, 124, 132

Tls Handshake, 174-176, 186, 189, 191-192, 200, 202

Tools, 13, 19, 25-29, 35, 62, 64, 87-88, 90, 96, 103-104, 138, 146, 151, 153, 160-161, 208-209, 212-213, 215, 224, 236, 239-240, 263, 268, 270

Transmission, 12, 17-18, 33, 35, 45, 48, 50, 111, 118, 140, 157, 165, 174, 183, 269-270

Transmission Control Protocol, 12, 33, 45

U

Udp, 13-14, 17, 29, 32-33, 51, 67, 139, 202

User Name, 137, 265

Users, 1, 7, 22-23, 38-39, 41, 54, 77, 80, 90, 101, 114-116, 122, 137, 154-155, 173, 185-186, 205-207, 213, 221-225, 232-235, 257-258, 266, 268

V

Validation, 55, 107, 131, 161, 188

Virtual, 27, 114, 116, 126, 130, 133, 150, 157, 163-164, 179, 200, 243, 256, 262, 267

W

Web Server, 16-17, 33, 77, 101, 180-181, 185

Z

Zombie Candidate, 21-22

Printed in the USA
CPSIA information can be obtained
at www.ICGtesting.com
JSHW051409221024
72173JS00006B/1330

9 781682 857458